Popular Culture and Legal Pluralism

Drawing upon theories of critical legal pluralism and psychological theories of narrative identity, this book argues for an understanding of popular culture as legal authority, unmediated by translation into state law. In narrating our identities, we draw upon collective cultural narratives, and our narrative/nomos obligational selves become the nexus for law and popular culture as mutually constitutive discourse.

The author demonstrates the efficacy and desirability of applying a pluralist legal analysis to examine a much broader scope of subject matter than is possible through the restricted perspective of state law alone. The study considers whether presumptively illegal acts might actually be instances of a re-imagined, alternative legality, and the concomitant implications. As an illustrative example, works of critical dystopia and the beliefs and behaviours of eco/animal-terrorists can be understood as shared narrative and normative commitments that constitute law just as fully as does the state when it legislates and adjudicates.

This book will be of great interest to academics and scholars of law and popular culture, as well as those involved in interdisciplinary work in legal pluralism.

Wendy A. Adams is Associate Professor of Law, McGill University, Canada. Her research interests are in the areas of legal pluralism, law and popular culture, commodification, and human-animal studies. She has published on these and related topics.

"Studies in legal pluralism and in law and popular culture have kept a wary distance from each other – worried perhaps that, like matter and anti-matter, they could not survive the encounter. But Wendy Adams has blown them up, showing what happens if you take them both seriously. She unpacks the unspoken assumptions and necessary implications of a body of work led by Rod Macdonald, and behind him Robert Cover. Neither could be said to be shrinking violets, but Adams has expounded a theory of legal consciousness and identity far more uncompromising. While critics from these different fields will find much to argue with, all will now have to take account of Adams' ambitious argument and its radical and confronting conclusions."

Desmond Manderson, Australian National University

Popular Culture and Legal Pluralism

Narrative as law

Wendy A. Adams, Faculty of Law, McGill University

Routledge
Taylor & Francis Group
LONDON AND NEW YORK

First published 2017
by Routledge

2 Park Square, Milton Park, Abingdon, Oxfordshire OX14 4RN
52 Vanderbilt Avenue, New York, NY 10017

Routledge is an imprint of the Taylor & Francis Group, an informa business

First issued in paperback 2020

British Library Cataloguing in Publication Data
A catalogue record for this book is available from the British Library

Library of Congress Cataloging-in-Publication Data
Names: Adams, Wendy A., author.
Title: Popular culture and legal pluralism : narrative as law / By Wendy A. Adams.
Description: Burlington, VT : Ashgate, 2016. | Series: Law, justice and power | Includes bibliographical references and index.
Identifiers: LCCN 2015046646 | ISBN 9781409465454 (hardback : alk. paper) | ISBN 9781409465478 (epub)
Subjects: LCSH: Legal polycentricity. | Popular culture.
Classification: LCC K236 .A33 2016 | DDC 340.9—dc23
LC record available at http://lccn.loc.gov/2015046646

ISBN: 978-1-4094-6545-4 (hbk)
ISBN: 978-0-367-59639-2 (pbk)

Typeset in Times New Roman
by Apex CoVantage, LLC

To my wife, Nairne, and our family, Toby, Lucie, and Wilson

Contents

1 Introduction

Narrative/*nomos*

This project is based on my interest in a recurring question in scholarship, one that arises as well in my experience teaching law and popular culture. How might popular culture function as law, unmediated by translation into state law?[1] This is not an inconsequential inquiry, particularly for legal pluralists. The normative force of popular culture is an aspect of Cover's more general question, also unanswered, of the relationship between *nomos* and narrative.[2] Apart from instances noted below, I was unable to locate an answer. I found many different kinds of relationships articulated and defended but no specific response to the question asked.[3] I then inflicted this question on my research seminar students, in the hope that our collective ability might succeed where I had so far singly failed. We came full circle to our initial point of departure, which is an understanding of law and culture as an integrated knowledge domain of authoritative reference, but the law referenced by this understanding is still a monist conception of state law. In addition, an explanation of how this understanding might be operationalized remains illusive.

The difficulty in finding an answer may be a function of how the question is asked. If we presuppose an analytical distinction between narrative and *nomos*, we will ask how these two distinct domains are related to each other. What would be the implications for analyzing how popular culture might function as law if we abandoned this presupposition, while still insisting on a pluralist response? Why not analyze narrative and *nomos*, or more specifically, popular culture and law, from a pluralist perspective that denies relations altogether? The familiar conjunction of "law and" encourages us to think of law and culture as separate and autonomous domains, engaged in relations of reciprocal insight or influence.[4] By dispensing with this conjunction, we can examine unmediated the normative force of popular culture without reference to state law.

Accordingly, I do not examine that which is called popular culture and that which is called law as dependent and independent variables, looking for influences of law on popular culture or popular culture on law. I do not look for representations of law in popular culture, either to assess their validity from the perspective of law or to survey how law is understood from the perspective of popular culture. I do not look for popular cultural aspects of law to argue that legal interpretation should be informed by interpretive methods more generally applied to popular culture. I do not use popular culture as law's interlocutor, capable of explaining the broader social, political, and economic context in which law takes place. Nor do I use popular culture as law's conscience, appealing to the moral imagination of fiction to bring justice closer to law in circumstances where the latter is deemed deficient.

I do not mean to suggest that relational analysis by any of these methods is in any way invalid or inferior, only that my preference is otherwise. I am interested in joining an ongoing conversation that brings law and culture closer together than conjunction will allow. I argue not for law in popular culture, nor popular culture in law, but rather for popular culture as law. To use a concept increasingly gaining purchase, my claim is that popular culture and law are discursively integrated.[5] Even within the framework of a discursive approach, however, I have been unable to locate an explicit explanation of how popular culture might function as legal authority, without the necessity of translation into state law. The objective of this book is to answer this question by hypothesizing law and popular culture as mutually constitutive discourse, an inherently pluralist perspective, and by developing that which does not yet exist, being the necessary analytical framework pursuant to which inquiry can proceed. This involves an expansive approach to how we think of law, even taking into account the diversity of concepts recognized by theories of legal pluralism. The result is a radical re-imagination of law, but one based nonetheless on various points of departure found in scholarship in legal pluralism, law and culture, and law and the humanities.

Many forms of pluralist scholarship adopt a comprehensive approach to the concept of law but not necessarily in a way that rejects common assumptions, for example, that law is an exogenous force applied to legal subjects or that hierarchical distinctions exist between legal rules (superior) and other types of normativity (inferior). If we conceive of popular culture and law as discursively integrated, these unexamined assumptions regarding *a priori* distinctions between law and culture become difficult to sustain. We cannot simply assume to privilege legal rules relative to norms, consigning the latter to culture as distinct from law, if we no longer conceive of law and culture as inherently distinct domains of knowledge and experience.

As we engage in legal practice, teaching, and scholarship, we tend not to examine the assumption that law is distinct from culture because we are relying upon this assumption to carry out these activities. The distinction is at most an analytical habit, a matter of convenience rather than necessity. To demonstrate, assume a sufficient consensus regarding two points: (a) that law is not self-defining; and (b) that the process of defining law is purposive and not merely descriptive. The precise allocation between prescriptive and descriptive aspects of defining law makes for an interesting argument but is not relevant here. We need only acknowledge that if the bifurcation of normative authority between law and lesser forms of normativity is purposive to some extent, this purpose should be communicated and its legitimacy defended. We should be able to explain why we extract from culture anything that counts as law and consign to culture all the lesser norms.

I do not contest the logic of normative heterogeneity.[6] At a certain point we need to choose between the various claims proffered as legal obligations in our relations with others.[7] What we understand as justice is instantiated in the kinds of relational claims we affirm and deny and our commitments to act accordingly. My claim is that we need a reason (apart from self-reference) for why we cannot choose between claims, which are in every case reasons for action, until we have first applied definitional distinctions to separate legal rules from mere norms. Once we make this distinction, mere norms are irrelevant for legal analysis, regardless of their relevance to the people involved. Given that the distinction between law and norm is intentional, what do we gain by limiting the word law to certain types of norms, elevating these by definition (as opposed to relevance) over all others? Perhaps more importantly, what do we lose?

Quite apart from the implications for our agency as legal subjects, we reduce the scope and thus the efficacy of legal analysis. Jurists might readily acknowledge the various ways in which culture influences law.[8] For the most part, however, attention remains fixed on an established canon of legal rules, particularly those originating with the political state. Precisely because of their experience, however, jurists should hold no illusions regarding the influence of state law in everyday life. The relationship between the intended purpose of a legal rule and its actual effect on people's normative behavior can be tenuous and even inversely proportional. Why then should jurists participate in maintaining the reputation of state law as an authoritative, exclusive, and instrumental means of social control?

Why do we not simply dispense with the assumption that inherent and self-identified distinctions exist between law and culture? As jurists, why do we not encourage ourselves to apply our skills in ways that avoid the dubious analytical restrictions imposed by a canon of state law artefacts and institutional practices? Perhaps we are concerned that if law is culture and culture is law, jurists no longer have anything meaningful to say about law. This underestimates the distinctive nature of legal analysis while overestimating the distinctive nature of symbolic expressions of state law. Perhaps we are concerned not with a deficit of law but rather with its excess, in that law will colonize all aspects of culture. This concern conflates the manner of inquiry with its subject matter; a legal analysis does not transform people following rules into codes and precedents, no more than an economic analysis transforms consumers and suppliers into supply and demand curves.

Inherently pluralist and potentially emancipatory, an analysis of law and popular culture as mutually constitute discourse broadens our contemplation of normative aspiration and the many different ways we consider ourselves bound by law. We also return inevitably to Cover's unanswered question on the nature of the relationship between *nomos* and narrative. Cover provides a powerful metaphor of law as alternity, as a bridge of belief and committed behaviors that takes us from the world-that-is-to the world-that-ought-to-be.[9] To claim that popular culture narrative is *nomos*, unmediated by translation into state law or its analogues, may push associational logic to its limits. When we talk about law and popular culture, we talk about inference and influence. Our image of law is an exogenous entity of instrumental force controlled by the state.[10] A steady increase in "law and" scholarship (e.g. law and economics, law and literature, law and film) appears to reinforce rather than subvert this understanding. We benefit from insights provided by different perspectives, but scholarship tends to focus on law's relations with its other, either as reciprocal representations and influences or as nominally analogous in operation.[11]

Perhaps the persistence of scholarly and professional preoccupation with the exclusivity of state law is to be expected. Our professional commitments to clients provide limited scope to explore alternative perspectives. Our teaching commitments to students (and the accreditation of our faculties) may keep us focused on state law, even as we expand our curriculums to include a broader range of legal traditions and disciplinary perspectives. Our research reflects this statist fixation, even as we take up a more eclectic mix of theoretical and inter-disciplinary materials. Inevitably we end up reinforcing statism in cultural understandings of law. Law is the consequence of state action in constituting, legislating, administrating, and enforcing legal rules. Law is delivered through state modalities such as legislative assemblies, administrative officials, and the familiar (albeit seldom encountered) figure of the judiciary presiding over courts of law. Any attempt to argue for the legal force of popular culture from this perspective faces formidable opposition. Law is not a movie, a book, a popular song, a Super Bowl Sunday. Law is authoritative, definitive in its prohibitions, relentless in the event of breach. The advantage of legal orthodoxy is the clarity of purpose we find in a single voice of authority. The rule of law is an impartial force, protecting us from the whims of majesty and the tyranny of power. Law must remain forever faithful to this definition, for within this definition we find justice.[12]

Whatever the advantages of analyzing law in this manner, we need to keep in mind that symbolic expressions of law have no power or effect independent of the people who use these symbols in their everyday lives. Otherwise, we too easily progress from conceiving of law as an exogenous force, already a problematic concept, to an even more extreme process of reification. We come to understand law as an entity, one that can be examined in the abstract as distinct from human agency. Our habit of nominalizing law may facilitate productive communication.[13] The process nonetheless leads us to conflate symbolic expression with our actual normative beliefs and behaviors. Neglecting our agency and disclaiming our responsibility, we forget that symbolic expressions are at best static approximations, imperfectly capturing our commitments as we respond to normative heterogeneity. In other words, we begin to forget that law is more aptly considered as a verb rather than a noun, that law is something we do, not an entity that exists.[14] Law is what we do when we conceive of normative beliefs and then commit to the behaviors necessary for governing ourselves accordingly.

To say something meaningful about law, we do need to distinguish that which is law from that which is not law, but nominalization arguably obscures more than it clarifies. When we think of law as an exogenous entity, analysis involving different perspectives becomes a "law and" inquiry. We direct our attention to what we assume are *a priori* analytically distinct domains. We may search for the ideal manner of nexus, so that we might better reflect nuances of relations between these domains. We may strive for dynamic rather than static conceptions, so that we might better represent the complexity of human relations. But this habit of conjunction will limit always the scope of our exploration.

If we are to fully investigate the discursive and mutually constitutive nature of law and popular culture, we need to focus on dynamic constitution rather than the static boundaries implied by conjunction, however porous they may be.[15] Law is differentiated from other types of social activity, but to speak of "law and" simply reinforces an illusion of isolated entities.[16] We need to think of law unmodified,[17] an approach that does not depend on unexamined assumptions of distinctions between law and culture or between law and norms. Perhaps we could set aside our preoccupation with relational entities in favor of a *pensée métisse*, a reflection upon the ongoing process of encounter and exchange between different aspects of culture.[18] Differentiation and boundaries are not rendered obsolete but are viewed as more provisional in nature, negotiated in accordance with the purpose of analysis or the intentions of the participants.

Admittedly, the absence of a clear distinction between law and culture may be difficult to reconcile with foundational concepts such as the rule of law. To understand law as an aspect of social relations though is not a recent development.[19] Law without the rule of law is operationally meaningless, but to conceive of law as autonomous provides an image of order and certainty more illusory than real. Do we define what we see, or do we see what we define? In either case, perspective is everything. Just as there are "painters who transform the sun into a yellow spot," there are others who "transform a yellow spot into the sun."[20] The former conveys the simplicity of autonomous state law. The latter conveys the complexity of normative heterogeneity.

From the vantage point of legal orthodoxy,[21] simplicity is preferred. Legal orthodoxy acknowledges an infinite variety of human behavior guided by rules[22] but limits the definition of law to exclusive state legal authority. Legal rules are excised from extensive normative roots like so many cut flowers and then arranged in symbolic expression to create an illusion of autonomy. To do otherwise would be to lose the specificity of legal meaning in the general complexity of normative behavior. The difficulty with this perspective is assuming what must be decided. Concerns of generality and specificity arise because we presuppose that law is distinct from culture. Left unexamined are important questions of why and how this distinction is made. From the perspective of legal pluralism, complexity is preferred although perhaps not fully embraced. Legal pluralism need not reject the assumption of law as an exogenous force, as a power relation between authoritative addressors and compliant (or transgressive) addressees. A pluralist analysis may result in a multiplicity of autonomous legal domains, as distinct from culture as they are from each other. Complexity is also characteristic of law and culture analysis, but rejecting law's autonomy does not necessarily challenge the state's exclusive legal authority.[23]

As I discuss in more detail in Chapter 2, analyzing law and popular culture as mutually constitutive discourse requires some manner of reconciliation between trends of singularity and isolation that appear in existing theoretical approaches. A pluralist approach corrects for a tendency of singularity in law and culture analysis, thus expanding the scope of investigation beyond state law and its analogues. Law is an occurrence of bringing order to normative heterogeneity as we evaluate different claims of what we are obliged to do. While the extent to which these occurrences count as law depends upon the theory adopted, legal pluralism offers viable alternatives to an exclusive focus on state law.

In turn, law and culture analysis can correct for a tendency of isolation in legal pluralism, thus expanding the scope of investigation to include more than competing claims in contested jurisdictions. Theories of legal pluralism do not necessarily reject either positivism or an understanding of law as an exogenous instrumentality. The potential contribution of law and culture analysis is conceiving of law as part of culture rather than distinct from it. The difficulty is that analysis operates at a fairly high level of abstraction (e.g. metaphorical explanations of law and culture as a seamless web of authority).[24] This is not to dispute the validity of the metaphor nor the guidance conveyed but to hypothesize popular culture's legal authority requires greater specificity.

Taking all these points together, I can now outline the analysis that follows. The objective is to provide a specific hypothesis of how popular culture might function as legal authority, unmediated by translation or association with state law. I argue that this is possible if we conceive of popular culture and law as mutually constitutive discourse, and provide the necessary analytical framework for interrogating this hypothesis.

In Chapter 2, I address three preliminary issues. The first is the tension between law and justice in both legal theory and popular culture. The second is the definition of key terms such as popular culture and cultural analysis. Third, I explain in more detail why I must first develop that which does not yet exist, being an analytical framework capable of demonstrating with sufficient specificity how popular culture might function as legal authority. I canvas three modes of scholarship that offer relevant contributions, legal pluralism and law and culture as discussed above, as well as law and humanities. No one mode of thought provides a complete account, but taken together they offer insight and guidance. Tracing a trajectory that begins with Cover, progresses to postmodern legal pluralism, and includes law and culture and law and humanities, I propose an analytical framework in which discursive legal pluralism provides the necessary theoretical foundation.

In Chapter 3, I consider two apparently contradictory but equally compelling theories, Macdonald's critical legal pluralism and Melissaris's ubiquitous law, which I characterize as definitional contextualism. Avoiding the oversimplification of an abbreviated conclusion, I work through both of these theoretical accounts with particular attention paid to the issue of definition. In teaching law and popular culture, I have come to appreciate the necessity of addressing this issue. When I explain to students that our primary course objective is to consider whether and to what extent popular culture might function as law, many students want to proceed by comparing popular culture to law. If popular culture is sufficiently analogous to law, then popular culture can function as law. Placing these two theories alongside each other provides a productive encounter and exchange on the nature of law and legal pluralism more generally and has implications for how I conceive of a re-imagined narrative/*nomos* plural legality.

I conclude that critical legal pluralism is the more viable alternative based not only on threshold requirements of discourse, narrative, and alternity, but also on the distinction discussed above between law as a verb, oriented toward our capacity to create legal meaning, and law as a noun, oriented toward an outcome of normative heterogeneity. In Melissaris's theory of definitional contextualism – and this is my own conclusion on this point – legal pluralism resolves capacity in favor of result. Melissaris's stated objective is to reconcile emancipation, being the diversity of our jurisgenerative capacities, with regulation, being the implications of recognizing plural legalities. Hegemonic dominance is not an appropriate response to normative heterogeneity, but then neither is allowing plurality to lapse into endless conflict.[25] Accordingly, a theory of legal pluralism is successful only to the extent it fulfills its meta-jurisprudential potential.[26] This accounts for the necessity of a transcontextual definition of law; absent some metric of evaluation as to what constitutes law, problems of normative heterogeneity cannot be communicated or addressed in an appropriately interperspectival form.

For Macdonald, legal pluralism is a question of how legal subjects themselves understand law and how they acknowledge and respond to claims of legal authority in the context in which they arise. A successful hypothesis of legal pluralism is one that accounts for legal subjects' jurisgenerative capacity, in that people themselves conceive of the laws that constitute their legal subjectivity and guide their normative behavior. Contrary to Melissaris's approach, the conditions of inter-legality cannot be specified in advance, nor can we assume that normative heterogeneity will indeed manifest as inter-legality. Normative heterogeneity is a construct conceived by legal subjects as they acknowledge, affirm, and deny claims that arise in their relations with others.

A particularly relevant aspect of critical legal pluralism is the significance of narrative both as a means of communication and, albeit more in passing, as a means of constituting our identity. There is also an implicit sense of legal subjects as being inherently normative in nature.[27] Given the brevity of these and other passages, these attributes of legal subjectivity require further development. In Chapter 4, I elaborate upon critical legal pluralism's jurisgenerative legal subject, incorporating cognitive and psychological theories of narrative identity formation to develop the concept of a narrative/*nomos* obligational self. I refer to the work of Bruner and McAdams, both of whom argue that we constitute our identities through processes of self-narration. The narrative/*nomos* obligational self thus becomes the nexus of mutually constitutive discourse of popular culture and law. Narrative identity formation is an ongoing negotiation among social and psychic aspects of popular culture as we self-narrate our obligational identities with reference to collective cultural narratives.

The narrative/*nomos* obligational self instantiates Cover's understanding of law as alternity, as the bridge that takes us from worlds-that-are to worlds-that-ought-to-be. The obligational self integrates narrative and *nomos* in our ongoing narrations of our identities; the question of what kind of person I am cannot be disaggregated from the question of what I am obliged to do.[28] By integrating critical legal pluralism, psychological theories of narrative identity formation, and Cover's understanding of law as alternity, the narrative/*nomos* obligational self allows us to explore the specific operation and emancipatory potential of re-imagining popular culture and law as mutually constitutive discourse.

Having developed the necessary analytical framework and the construct of the narrative/*nomos* obligational self, I provide a proof of concept in Chapter 5 in the form of an illustrative case study. I examine resistance narrative in bio-punk critical dystopia and the beliefs and behaviors of eco/animal activists engaged in resistance movements. I use the term *activist* not to evaluate their legal status but to reflect the self-characterization of those involved and to highlight the emancipatory potential of re-imagining law in the manner I propose.[29] In the United States, acts involving property damage in the absence of personal injury have been prosecuted as terrorism offences. In re-imagining law with reference to narrative/*nomos* obligational selves, activists could, if they so desired, recast moral imperatives as legal claims.

This is more than a sustained discussion of the familiar aphorism that one man's terrorist is another man's freedom fighter. To even articulate normative heterogeneity in these terms is to privilege the singularity of state law. I do not claim that eco/animal activists should reconceive of resistance to law as a plural legality; my analysis is not programmatic. The intent is to examine but not prescribe the normative implications of popular culture as legal authority. The jurisgenerative capacity of narrative/*nomos* obligational selves reconciles what Cover describes as a regrettable bifurcation between law as meaning and law as social control.[30] Resistance has rules, and through our engagement with popular culture they are already familiar to us.

I emphasize this is proof of concept, not proof of result, with subsequent analysis providing more comprehensive coverage. I also emphasize the relationship is not one of cause and effect, which would be an overly simplistic explanation of narrative and *nomos* as mutually constitutive.[31] As a project of re-imagining law, I do not argue that eco/animal activists presently consider themselves as acting lawfully. We are unlikely to locate evidence of a re-imagined law that does not yet exist. The objective is to demonstrate the potential of an analysis that does not seek to define law (positivism), evaluate law (normativism), or critique law (critical legal studies).[32] The concept of the narrative/*nomos* obligational self re-imagines the legal authority of popular culture as a process of knowledge and commitment. We have a better understanding of how and why we consider ourselves obliged to act, and we govern ourselves accordingly.

In Chapter 6, I conclude by raising another question about the limits of our legal imagination. In this emancipatory project of re-imagining law, who precisely is being emancipated? A fundamental contribution of critical legal pluralism is an understanding of jurisgenerative legal subjects as both law-creators and law-followers. Narrative/*nomos* obligational selves are themselves responsible for the concept of law by which they constitute their legal subjectivity and pursuant to which they affirm their obligations to others. When eco/animal activists liberate animals from state law, should the law they re-imagine for themselves include a place for animals? How can we know whether animals want to be included in legal relations with humans and on what terms? To answer these questions, I consider whether the narrative/*nomos* obligational self is amenable to a posthumanist jurisprudence, one that challenges us to imagine legal relations from a perspective other than our own.

Notes

1 By "translation," I mean that we understand the normative significance of popular culture as a reciprocal relationship. Popular culture influences legal officials in their expression of state law, as well as participants' understanding of state law as expressed by legal officials, which in turn influences legal officials in their expression of state law, and so on.
2 Robert M. Cover, '*Nomos* and Narrative' (1983) 97 *Harvard Law Review* 4.
3 For taxonomies of scholarship in this area, see, for example: Christy Collis and Jason Bainbridge, 'Introduction – Popular Cultures and the Law' (2005) 19 *Continuum: Journal of Media & Cultural Studies* 159; Orit Kamir, 'Why "Law and Film" and What Does it Actually Mean? A Perspective' (2005) 19 *Continuum: Journal of Media & Cultural Studies* 255; Douglas J. Goodman, 'Approaches to Law and Popular Culture' (2006) 31 *Law & Social Inquiry* 757; Robin West, 'Literature, Culture, and Law at Duke University' in Austin Sarat, Catherine O. Frank, and Matthew Daniel Anderson (eds), *Teaching Law and Literature* (Modern Language Association of America 2011).
4 Note that the relationship between story and law is an explicit feature of some legal traditions, even as scholars begin to take up the challenge of examining the implicit nature of this relationship in common law and civilian legal traditions. See, for example: Government of Canada, *Report on the Royal Commission of Aboriginal Peoples* (1996) 33.
5 See, for example: Naomi Mezey, 'Law as Culture' (2001) 13 *Yale Journal of Law and the Humanities* 35.
6 I prefer the term "normative heterogeneity" as opposed to what might be a more familiar phrase, such as "inter-legality," which can be traced to de Sousa Santos: Boaventura de Sousa Santos, *Toward a New Legal Common Sense: Law, Science and Politics in the Paradigmatic Transition (After the Law)* (Routledge 1995). My intention is not to collapse law into a more general conception of normativity but rather to indicate, consistent with a fundamental premise of both Macdonald's and Melissaris's theories of legal pluralism, that what constitutes law cannot be determined without reference to the understandings of the participants themselves.
7 See, for example, Webber on this point: Jeremy Webber, 'Legal Pluralism and Human Agency' (2006) 44 *Osgoode Hall Law Journal* 167. Law requires a mechanism for bringing normative agreement to at least provisional closure, so that collective norms may prevail. I discuss this in Chapter Four.
8 See, for example: Mezey (2001) 35.
9 Cover (1983).
10 See, for example: Nicholas Kasirer, 'Larger Than Life' (1995) 10 *Canadian Journal of Law and Society* 185. Although Kasirer notes that visual symbols can constitute a *lex non scripta*, the law referred to is nonetheless state law.
11 A related concern in "law and" scholarship is the tendency to conceive of law and other fields in both causal and hierarchal terms. As Manderson notes, "The 'and' in 'law and literature' holds an implied claim about causal relevance (literature is relevant to law) and hierarchical position (literature is answerable to law)." See: Desmond Manderson,

'Modernism and the Critique of Law and Literature' (2011) 35 *Australian Feminist Law Journal* 107, 110, citing Shoshana Felman, 'To Open the Question' (1977) 55/56 *Yale French Studies* 5.

12 While I refer to this perspective as both "traditional" and "prevailing," our understanding of law as a unitary body of rules originating with the state is of relatively recent origin. Increasing consolidation of state power displaced the legal pluralism of the medieval period. See: Brian Z. Tamanaha, 'Understanding Legal Pluralism: Past to Present, Local to Global' (2007) 29 *Sydney Law Review* 375.

13 Bal refers to "nominalization" as a process of forming a noun from a verb. The advantage of nominalization is the ease with which a concept can be analyzed and discussed. The disadvantage is that when we discuss the concept as an entity, we tend to overlook the actors and processes involved. See: Mieke Bal, *Narratology: Introduction to the Theory of Narrative* (Third Edition, University of Toronto Press 2009).

14 I adopt Manderson's terminology here. Manderson argues that neither literature nor law should be objectified. Literature is an experience that transforms us, not a proposition that instructs us. Similarly, law is a means, not an end, a way of engaging with the complexity and uncertainty of questions. See: Manderson (2011) 125.

15 Coombe argued early on that the nexus between law and culture is not a bridge but rather a process of terms engaged in mutual disruption. See: Rosemary J. Coombe, 'Critical Cultural Legal Studies' (1998) 10 *Yale Journal of Law & the Humanities* 463, 472.

16 See, for example: Mezey (2001).

17 I have adapted this term, with no claim for scholastic equivalency, from MacKinnon's work, *Feminism Unmodified.* See: Catharine A. MacKinnon, *Feminism Unmodified: Discourses on Life and Law* (Harvard University Press 1987).

18 For a more complete explanation of *pensée métisse*, see: Nicholas Kasirer, 'Legal Education as Métissage' (2003) 78 *Tulane Law Review* 481.

19 See Geertz, for example, who argues that law is a form of social meaning: Clifford Geertz, *Local Knowledge: Further Essays in Interpretive Anthropology* (Basic Books 1983).

20 "There are painters who transform the sun into a yellow spot, but there are others who, thanks to their art and intelligence, transform a yellow spot into the sun." Pablo Picasso, 'There Are Painters Who Transform the Sun Into a Yellow Spot, But There Are Others Who, Thanks to Their Art and Intelligence, Transform a Yellow Spot Into the Sun' in James Beasley Simpson (ed.), *Simpson's Contemporary Quotations* (Houghton Mifflin Company 1988).

21 I adopt this admittedly rather imprecise phrase from Macdonald, who uses the term to describe the theoretical assumptions of State-based positive law. These assumptions include monism, centralism, positivism, prescriptivism, and chirographism, and are explained below. See: Roderick A. Macdonald, 'Pluralistic Human Rights? Universal Human Wrongs?' in René Provost and Colleen Sheppard (eds), *Dialogues on Human Rights and Legal Pluralism* (Springer Science & Business Media 2013) 23.

22 For those interested in and guided by the Star Trek canon, I would argue that Vulcans, the most logical of the represented species, would be legal pluralists, and furthermore would reject as rather quaint any notion of an innate distinction between laws and norms. Consider, for example, the phrase "infinite diversity in infinite combinations," which represents a fundamental precept in Vulcan philosophy that celebrates the infinite variability of possibility and outcome in the universe. See: the Star Trek Wiki Memory Alpha, 'Vulcan (Star Trek)' (*Memory Alpha, the Star Trek Wiki*) <http://en.memory-alpha.wikia.com/wiki/IDIC> accessed June 24, 2015.

23 Some scholarship in law and culture may be classified as cultural analysis of law, but not necessarily. See: Rosemary J. Coombe, 'Is There a Cultural Studies of Law?' in Toby Miller (ed), *A Companion to Cultural Studies* (Blackwell Reference Online Edition, Blackwell Publishing 2005) <http://www.blackwellreference.com/subscriber/tocnode.html?id=g9781405141758_chunk_g97814051417584> accessed April 12,

2016. West provides a typology of scholarship in law and literature and subsequently law and culture as literary, jurisprudential, and hermeneutic approaches. The jurisprudential approach, most relevant to this project, proposes that literature/culture might have the force of law, either historically or in present or future circumstances. See: West (2011).

24 West (2011).

25 Emmanuel Melissaris, *Ubiquitous Law: Legal Theory and the Space for Legal Pluralism* (Ashgate Publishing Company 2009) 3.

26 As Melissaris notes in discussing the necessity of inter-perspectival dialogue between plural legal orders, all legal theories should be pluralist, in the sense of being aware of the contextual circumstances in which any legal theory originates, and thus acknowledging the plurality of law as a subject matter. See: Melissaris (2009) 77.

27 Martha-Marie Kleinhans and Roderick A. Macdonald, 'What Is a Critical Legal Pluralism?' (1997) 12 *Canadian Journal of Law and Society* 25; Roderick A. Macdonald, 'Here, There and Everywhere: Theorizing Legal Pluralism; Theorizing Jacques Vanderlinden' in Nicholas Kasirer (ed), *Étudier Et Enseigner Le Droit: Hier, Aujourd'hui Et Demain – Études Offertes À Jacques Vanderlinden* (Éditions Yvon Blais 2006).

28 The concept of the obligational self is evocative of the significance of character in virtue ethics. Possible connections to and integration with virtue ethics would be a productive line of enquiry but is not explored here.

29 When presenting on this topic, I am often asked whether the ideas expressed could be used to justify well-known examples of terrorism. My refusal to answer either yes or no is not a matter of tact, avoidance, or obfuscation. I have not written this book to answer these questions from others but so that others might answer these questions for themselves.

30 Cover (1983) 18.

31 Cover (1983). Along with others, I note that Cover is ambiguous on the precise nature of the relationship between *nomos* and narrative, a point I address below.

32 I owe this insight to David Sandomierski, SJD Candidate, Faculty of Law, University of Toronto. His conversations clarified and guided my thoughts on this point in relation to legal pluralism.

2 A framework for re-imagining law

Between law and justice

My analysis begins with an observation that both legal theory and popular culture devote considerable attention to the question of whether law is commensurate with justice.[1] How this question is answered depends upon how it is asked. In traditional legal theory, the relationship between law and justice is addressed as a question of law's origins and works its way through an endless oscillation between positivism and normativism.[2] Legitimacy is assessed with reference to either procedurally valid enactment or moral imperative, and given the mutually exclusive nature of these arguments, ontological inquiry (what is law) becomes a conversation that never seems to end.[3] Critical legal theories provide an alternative wherein the relationship between law and justice is viewed more in the nature of law's operation rather than law's origin. Criticism is focused on how dominant groups frustrate the proper functioning of law to satisfy their interests at the expense of others. Thus the working assumption must be that in a better world, law can indeed be just, since the objective is reform rather than systemic exit.[4]

As positivism and normativism attend to the problem of reconciling incommensurables, and as critical legal theory attends to the problem of power, so too does popular culture reflect and refract the same preoccupations as legal theory, albeit in narrative form. That law does not necessarily result in justice (or that justice is not necessarily achieved through law) is a familiar trope.[5] We have so many different variations on the theme of a courageous hero (or occasionally a heroine) fighting "the system" to achieve justice. Vic Mackey pummels us through seven seasons of *The Shield*; our protection depends upon police breaking the rules, even if they personally benefit in the process.[6] William Munny confounds us in *Unforgiven*; has he righted a wrong or engaged in a senseless rampage of violence, and what does it matter anyway if "we all have it coming" and "deserve's got nothing to do with it."[7] Whatever Mitchell Stevens may be trying to achieve in *The Sweet Hereafter*, until Nicole Burnell abruptly ends the legal process with a lie, we have difficulty seeing a future beyond tragedy.[8] The tag line for *A Civil Action* warns us of the relationship between the objectives and outcomes of civil litigation: Justice has its price.[9]

Indeed, popular culture provides many different expressions across a wide variety of media of what Macdonald refers to as "the symbolic failure of law."[10] How should we account for the popularity of narratives exploring our disappointment with law? One could simply argue that these narratives are a reliable source of dramatic tension, that is to say, that the appeal is one of affect rather than a conscious enquiry into the relationship between law and justice. But we would then be faced with a logically prior question, which is why do such narratives produce dramatic tension to which we respond? As with legal theory, popular culture appears unable to provide a definitive account of the relationship between law and justice; we keep asking the question because no single answer ever satisfies. The theoretical enquiries of positivism, normativism, and critical legal theory are simply rewritten in narrative form.

Adopting the analytical frameworks of traditional legal theory, narratives of law and justice within popular culture produce a range of familiar protagonist dilemmas. Viewed through a positivist lens, we will see within popular culture instances of protagonists faced with a validly enacted but unjust law; what must be decided is whether to disobey law in order to achieve justice. Viewed from the perspective of normativism, we will see examples of protagonists coming to the realization that an unjust law is no law at all; the objective is to demonstrate this fact to others so that through collective disavowal, justice will prevail. Examining popular culture from the perspective of critical legal theory, we will see narrative patterns wherein protagonists face injustice at a systemic level; the objective is to convince others that justice is not possible so long as power subverts law.

Let us assume without deciding for now that popular culture narratives instantiate, in some manner and to some degree, law as described and defined in legal theory. If prevailing and predominant legal theories argue or assume that the political state is the exclusive legal authority, then popular culture narratives will necessarily portray an uneasy relationship between law and justice. As to whether this is desirable or discouraging, the result depends upon one's perception of the validity of the legal theories in question. I do not critique these theories, a challenge more ably taken up by others.[11] Instead my intention is to take note of how a legal pluralist perspective, specifically critical legal pluralism, reframes relationships between law and justice in a way that avoids repetitive cycling through countervailing claims of positivism, normativism, and critical legal theory.[12]

State law is unable to accommodate the multiplicity of legal meanings expressed by those seeking to meet the demands of justice[13] through legal means, recasting these claims as resistance or transgression. State law is amenable to a conflicts analysis, as for example in the logic and operation of private international law. This is not, however, a conflict between law and justice per se, but rather a conflict of competing claims of jurisdiction by two or more political states. But if we adopt a more expansive pluralist perspective, one in which law is not the exclusive purview of political states, the relationship between law and justice may be similarly reconfigured. As we shift our understanding from monist theories of law to legal pluralism, our familiar narratives may change accordingly. What we see as the failure of state law to achieve justice is only the logical limitation of any system that insists on exclusive control over legal meaning.[14] From a pluralist perspective, the situation would be reframed as an instance of normative heterogeneity.

If legal pluralism is narrow in scope, the idea of conflict between law and a "mere" norm may persist. This simply returns us to the familiar oscillation between law and justice. We see echoes of this in the written reasons of common law cases. Consider for example, the absence of a duty to rescue in common law, an obligation generally included in civil law jurisdictions. In reasons for decision, common law judges tend to express regret that law does not accord with a community's moral sensibilities.[15] As cold comfort indeed, they acknowledge the inherent imperfection of state law and refer claimants, rather incoherently, to the more perfect law of cultural norms.[16] If, however, legal pluralism is broad in scope, the likelihood increases that the situation reflects conflict between laws, one of which may indeed provide participants with a result that is both lawful and just.

The paradox of monist conceptions of legal authority is how they create the conditions whereby law fails to achieve justice. Consider for example the dilemma of civil disobedience, the moral obligation to disobey an unjust law.[17] This dramatic and familiar conflict between law and justice is a function of the way in which state legal authority is configured. If only one law exists, normative heterogeneity must be framed as a conflict between law and norms, although in these cases the normative authority of morality is, as noted above, considered superior to that of state law. From the perspective of legal pluralism, however, normative heterogeneity anticipates cooperation and conflict both across and within legalities. A moral obligation to obey an unjust law could just as readily be characterized as a legal commitment, albeit with reference to law that does not originate with the state. I do not presume to advocate for recourse to plural law over civil disobedience for those engaged in eco/animal activism; the choice is most certainly not mine to make. But the example demonstrates the emancipatory potential of re-imagining legality. Given the binary logic of state law, the concept of civil disobedience provides an escape clause, so to speak, from the limitations of state law when engaged in the pursuit of justice, but the language of transgression remains. A pluralist approach to normative heterogeneity would allow participants to speak of justice pursued through lawful means.

The implications are more than symbolic. Adopting a pluralist account of law may affect how we characterize and respond to transgressions of state law. How should we characterize any particular instance of non-compliance? Is it an act of civil disobedience or an act in compliance with a compelling alternative to what we typically understand as law?[18] The concerns of moral relativism that tend to arise demonstrate if nothing else the persistence of our cognitive habits; responding to moral relativism involves yet again the familiar oscillation between law and justice.

Consider the inevitable question of whether an expansive approach to legal pluralism, wherein we consider the *prima facie* validity of every claim of law, means we would countenance terrorism as a lawful act. I want to repeat here, for the sake of retention, that this project is not an extended conversation on reimagining terrorists as freedom fighters or freedom fighters as terrorists. This "flip side of the same coin" approach merely replicates the endless binary oscillation between law and justice that I wish to avoid. The question so framed anticipates and demands a definitional, positivist response or an evaluative, normative response. These alternatives are inconsistent with my intention to re-imagine law as verb rather than noun, to understand law as our capacity for normative aspiration realized through belief and behavior, and to demonstrate law as being more than the deceptive simplicity of the outcome of conflicting reified rules operating independently of culture (and each other) in bounded jurisdictional space. To restrict our understanding of law to a reified result, terrorist on one side, freedom fighter on the other, is a fatalistic approach that ignores the human potential inherent in the many ways we might consider ourselves bound by law.

This is also the appropriate place to clarify, in advance of any misapprehension, that recognizing the legitimacy of plural claims of legality in any instance of normative heterogeneity does not require acquiescence by any party to any particular claim. A *prima facie* valid legal claim does not presuppose universal legitimacy among plural legalities; claims will exist in varying patterns of conflict, complementarity, and neutrality. My argument in favor of the normative force of popular culture does not mean that political states (or other types of legal authorities) can no longer address non-compliant behavior. Indeed, the inevitable "terrorism" question above appears to ignore the extent to which state law is saturated with questions of choice of law, from quotidian transactions (all those governing law clauses in online purchase agreements) to fundamental questions of civic identity (such as the role of religious authority in family law).

We need not address or dispute choice of law decision rules for recognizing or rejecting competing legal claims. We need only acknowledge that which is already accepted even from the perspective of orthodox legal theory, that determinations of legal/illegal are judged from the internal perspective of a particular legal system. Are you in possession of cannabis at the moment? Whether you are engaged in unlawful behavior will depend upon your geographic location as characterized with reference to the concept of legal jurisdiction. Ideally, you are in an Amsterdam coffee shop. Ideally, you are not in any state that declares a "war" on drugs. Circumstances of normative heterogeneity are generally more detailed than this example, but the concept itself is not necessarily more complex.

To return to the dramatic tension between law and justice, perhaps our popular culture narratives do implicitly express our suspicion that there is more to see than what we have been led to believe.[19] The difficulty is that those who defy state law have no words to characterize their behavior other than those that affirm the legitimacy of the state's exclusive monopoly over the power of law. Civil disobedience, conscientious objection – these are comforting terms that provide transgressors with moral virtue but do nothing to counter the state's claim as the sole arbiter of law. Furthermore, the compensations of moral virtue might be seen as rather limited. Quite apart from the material harm of punishment is the corrosive effect of living in circumstances where the deficiency of law in achieving justice is given tacit approval. If we begin to develop alternative images of law, how might we begin to imagine differently the nature of our purported transgressions? The inevitability of punishment is unlikely to be affected, given the nature and extent of state power. Those who deny state law, however, can do so on terms that actively oppose rather than reinforce the state's claim to a monopoly over law. A pluralist legal perspective reframes the relationship between law and justice, providing people with an opportunity not just to claim moral virtue, but also to use the full signifying power of law.

This alternative image of law is an opportunity, not a prescription. In arguing the case for re-imagining law, I do not claim that we presently characterize our behavior in these terms.[20] People engaged in challenging what they perceive to be unjust state laws may well want to refer to their actions as resistance, as fighting the good fight, as standing up to powerful forces without regard for the personal cost. When justice is not likely to occur in one's lifetime, these sustaining narratives are necessary if people are not to lose hope, but the alternatives are not mutually exclusive. On the other hand, I am not claiming that belief in the exclusivity of state law is false consciousness.[21] The meta-theoretical nature of legal pluralism somewhat paradoxically accommodates understandings of law that contract legal pluralism, such as belief in centralized and singular state law. Arguably, however, the success of legal orthodoxy has indeed hobbled our normative imagination. We see what we have been told exists, being an exclusive state law that manifests in the form of constitutions and codes, judicial pronouncements, and administrative decisions.[22]

The emancipatory potential of examining popular culture and law as mutually constitutive discourse is that beliefs can change. Significantly, this means that emancipation exists in the acknowledgement of our constructive capacity, and not in any particular re-configuration of outcomes of normative heterogeneity. As already noted, this analysis is not meant to be programmatic. Certainly no one should expect any success in raising such arguments in state law courts any time in the near future. Still, this analysis is not mere whimsical foray, but rather a sustained enquiry into a plausible alternative image of law, one that extends beyond what is present into what may well be possible. The difficulty in imagining what has not yet been imagined is demonstrating the legitimacy of the exercise. What must be remembered is that while the destination may be so distant as to be imperceptible, the point of departure is well within reach. The objective of this project is to suggest how we might begin to move from here to there, how we might, if we are not satisfied with a yellow spot, choose instead to paint the sun.

Defining terms

An analysis of popular culture as law is necessarily interdisciplinary, and thus terms must be defined with clarity and precision in order to facilitate communication and avoid misunderstandings.[23] I begin by situating this analysis in relation to the larger context of cultural studies more generally and by developing a provisional definition of popular culture. In terms of the former, I describe different approaches as a matter of emphasis, not exclusion, with my own preference being to analyze text within context rather than the context of text. As Bal explains, cultural analysis does not study culture but mediates between the significance of cultural context and the significance of an object within culture on its own terms.[24] As for the definition of "popular" and "culture," both terms appear self-explanatory until explanations are actually required. Nor can we avoid the prescriptive nature of explanations for these terms. Nonetheless, I need to provide a workable definition of the concept being discussed so that evaluation and critique can address the merits of my claim without the distraction of disagreement based on different understandings of terminology. Aiming for a provisional and flexible approach, I define popular culture as consisting of signifying practices, wherein popularity is assessed in both qualitative and quantitative terms.

To begin, while I am interested in analyzing popular culture and law as mutually constitutive discourse, I am not engaged in what might understood as a project of cultural studies (a term that introduces further questions of definition). The necessity of a cultural study of law has been well established, and furtherance of the aims of this project is the subject of others' expertise.[25] But I do situate my claim within the scope of cultural analysis, and the distinction between these two modes of inquiry is subtle but significant. Both cultural studies and cultural analysis are interpretive practices. The distinction between them, as explained by Sarat and Simon, is that cultural analysis focuses on the "interpretation of symbolic processes and the analysis of beliefs and values," whereas cultural studies "embeds the interpretation of symbolic processes, beliefs and values in an examination of the material conditions that shape the production, presentation, circulation, and consumption of mediated images and information."[26] I adopt this approach with further reference to Bal, who provides a succinct account of the distinction in stating that unlike, for example, cultural anthropology, cultural analysis examines objects in culture rather than culture itself. This does not mean a return to practices whereby cultural objects are examined in abstract isolation. Rather, objects participate, so to speak, as interlocutors for the cultural context in which they are situated.[27]

If text exists in relation to context, so too does context exist in relation to text. As with figure and ground, neither can be perceived without reference to the other. Focus exclusively on text, and the conditions of production and reception are marginalized. On the other hand, focus exclusively on context, and the text becomes a symptom of the context being analyzed, its content overdetermined and underinterpreted. To better explain my own approach, I conceive of the distinction as more akin to focusing a camera lens. Depth of field – that is to say, what appears in sharpest focus within a frame – is a matter of emphasis, not exclusion.

The distinction could be further elaborated, but this account is sufficient for purposes of analytical distinction. First, I do not want to enter into longstanding debates in literary theory by polarizing these approaches as text versus context. The approaches are related, not mutually exclusive.[28] Second, the analytical framework I develop here for analyzing popular culture and law as mutually constitutive discourse is amenable to different disciplinary and methodological approaches, including those that adopt a preference for cultural studies over cultural analysis. My own application is not intended as a paradigmatic example.

Acknowledging a fluid relationship between text and context addresses a legitimate critique of analysis of law and popular culture, or law and culture more generally, which is the predominance of traditional legal analysis applied to paradigmatic legal texts. Apart from the limited range of materials, a tendency toward reification means that these symbolic expressions take on a strange form of self-animation. Law appears to act of its own volition in that law is said to apply, to govern, to regulate. While this may be at most disciplinary shorthand, what cannot be denied is that the focus is on what law means in the abstract. Law is an entity that possesses a meaning that can be discerned without reference to the people who actually create, maintain, and contest the rules that are symbolically expressed.[29] As Knox notes, "Sitting squarely on the indefinite article linking culture and law is the body."[30] While I have already rejected conjunction, I agree we must be aware that legal discourse is an embodied practice, so that we do not reject reification of law only to reify discourse in turn.

No doubt this tendency to give life to symbolic expression is a function of the positivist, statist assumptions that not only is law an identifiable entity, but it is one that originates with the exclusive authority of the political state. Scholars of cultural studies would no doubt understand literature as a concept produced by cultural practices that abstract a specific form of expression from more complex arrangements of human discursive activity.[31] The isolation of law as both an academic discipline and a practice is a similar abstraction, but not necessarily one that is as widely acknowledged by legal scholars. If one begins with statist assumptions, human actors who are not state officials are accorded less significance, and thus their function in the creation of legal meaning will remain unexplored.

Adopting a discursive approach arguably addresses the curious absence of human actors in legal analysis. As Kleinhans and Macdonald note, an appropriately pluralist legal analysis cannot address "the web of legal normativity without also addressing questions about who spins its filaments."[32] When we turn our attention to everyday actors, we need to consider the actual impact on anyone's life of symbolic expression of state legal rules. Legal texts originating with the state may well be of less significance in creating legal meaning in our lives than the representations of law in popular culture.[33] By this I do not mean that representations in popular culture are more likely to inform our understanding of a state legal system than are its official and highly inaccessible texts, although this is likely the case.[34] What I mean is that other forms of cultural expression, particularly those of popular culture in which we are so heavily immersed, are far more representative and informative of our understanding of the ways in which we are obliged to act in relations with others. That such understandings are not given the official imprimatur of state law does not render them less relevant from a legal pluralist perspective.

If one begins, however, with a statist rather than discursive perspective, then the potential for integrating analysis of law and culture will be similarly constrained. The full potential of analyzing law and popular culture is more likely to be realized when we not only acknowledge legal pluralism, but also adopt a more expansive approach as to the range of symbolic expression such legal pluralism entails. Reasoning by analogy, the favored methodology of common law, one might say that just as an interest in narrative reorients our understanding of literature, an interest in legal pluralism should reorient our understanding of law.

Analysis of narrativity, that is to say, the narrative properties that exist in common across a diverse range of expressive texts, arguably reflects a growing understanding that canonical texts are representative but not exhaustive of the processes through which significant cultural meanings are conveyed.[35] Similarly, aspects of law can also exist across a diverse range of beliefs and behaviors, of which the canon of state law is but a representative example, not of law's form but of the nature of law as commitment to normative obligation.

As for the definition of popular culture, this requires a more detailed explanation. As Mezey notes, culture is a word that is ". . . everywhere invoked and virtually nowhere explained,"[36] a claim that is supported by Williams's observation that culture is "one of the two or three most complicated words in the English language."[37] One solution would be to acknowledge that definitions of culture are inevitably guided by ideology[38] and thus proceed on the basis that any definition is necessarily provisional. Given that this project involves developing an open-source[39] analytical framework for exploring popular culture and law as mutually constitutive, then perhaps definitional components should be project-specific.

One possibility would be to bracket for now a more detailed description and assume that however popular culture is defined, the term necessarily includes texts such as movies, books, and music. Perhaps we could do the same for the threshold criteria of what constitutes "popular" and assume the term necessarily includes texts that are "best-selling." The difficulty is that even this presumptively straightforward description does not so much delay the process of description as render it invisible. Popular culture seems to somehow naturally and necessarily include that which has been specified. Should the definition include practices such as sports activities or shopping at the mall? Should the definition include what constitutes popular in specific markets, such as faith-based entertainment marketed to Evangelical Christians living in the United States?

Simply to refer to contemporary commercial culture is not sufficient. Popular culture is not limited to any particular society or historical period, nor can questions of definition be separated from explanatory theoretical perspectives. As Storey explains, any definition "will bring into play a complex combination of the different meanings of the term 'culture' with the different meanings of the term 'popular.'"[40] Williams, for example, suggests four different meanings of "popular culture," not all of which are complementary with each other: a work that is "well-liked by many people"; "inferior kinds of work"; "work deliberately setting out to win favour with the people"; and "culture actually made by the people for themselves."[41]

Storey provides a concise overview of the predominant ways in which popular culture is analyzed, not to articulate the term as having a fixed and stable meaning, but rather to demonstrate how various definitions inform analysis. An obvious starting point adopts a quantitative perspective, defining popular culture as "culture that is widely favoured or well liked by many people." The difficulty is that while the qualifier "popular" does indicate some quantitative aspect, fixing a line of demarcation to distinguish popular culture from culture more generally can be difficult. For example, the popularity of items typically viewed as "high culture" can often exceed that which is labelled "popular culture"; opera can have higher sales figures than popular music, depending upon the recordings in question.[42]

Perhaps this difficulty is what leads to defining popular culture in the negative as a residual category of "texts and practices that fail to meet the required standards to qualify as high culture."[43] Distinguishing between popular and high culture is a matter of making a value judgment based on qualities of the text. High culture entails a certain degree of difficulty and/or sophistication. In contrast to the mass-production of popular culture, high culture reflects individual creativity. Quite apart from the ideological function of using taste preferences to justify class distinctions,[44] the division is highly unstable. The classic refutation is the example of William Shakespeare, "[n]ow seen as the epitome of high culture, yet as late as the nineteenth century his work was very much part of popular theatre."[45] Nor is movement only one-way. Storey cites the example of Pavarotti; in 1990, his recording of "Nessun Dorma" ranked first on British music charts (that the aria was "The Official BBC Grandstand World Cup Theme" supports rather than detracts from this point), and on July 30, 1991, his free concert in London's Hyde Park attracted 100,000 people (250,000 were expected, but heavy rains resulted in decreased attendance).[46]

Similar to the distinction between popular and high culture is the association of popular culture with mass culture, a "formulaic, manipulative" culture, commercially produced for "non-discriminating" consumers. Popular culture in these terms is also specifically American, in the sense of being American in origin, and in the sense of the "homogenizing influence of American culture" following the global export of cultural products from the United States.[47] In contrast, a fourth definition of popular culture as folk culture sees culture as originating with an authentic community, a culture "of the people and for the people," rather than something which is imposed from above on passive consumers. Apart from a tendency to romanticize "the people" without fully providing an account of who "the people" might be, a difficulty with this definition is the extent to which the commercial nature of popular culture is de-emphasized. As Storey notes, however we define popular culture, ". . . the fact remains that people do not spontaneously produce culture from raw materials of their own making . . . its raw materials are those which are commercially provided."[48]

Another approach would be to reject static distinctions between popular culture and high culture. Working with Gramsci's concept of hegemony, popular culture could be analyzed as a site of struggle between the interests of dominant groups in incorporation and the interests of subordinate groups in resistance. Popular culture is neither imposed from above nor emergent from below but is rather a terrain of exchange and negotiation, what Gramsci refers to as a "compromise equilibrium." Storey uses film noir as an example; what originated as a form of popular cinema, more typically described as "melodramatic" at the time, is now studied as art cinema, celebrated for its sophisticated visual style. Central to this definition is a process of articulation and disarticulation, as dominant and subordinate groups contest cultural meanings.[49]

Finally, one could adopt an approach informed directly by postmodernism and deny altogether the existence of any distinction between popular culture and whatever may be defined as that which popular culture is not. Attempts to define popular culture as distinct from other forms of culture inevitably adopt to some degree an arbitrary distinction between authentic and commercial culture. Rather than seeking to establish distinctions that become definitions, postmodern analysis of popular culture focuses on the interpenetration of commerce and culture.[50] Again, Storey provides an illustrative example, this time using the relationship between popular music and television advertising. Storey cites a growing number of recording artists whose music appears in television commercials and poses the question, what is being sold in this case, the product or the song? Storey notes a "wonderful circularity" in the marketing of CDs of music used in television advertising: "Songs are used to sell products and the fact that they do this successfully is then used to sell the songs."[51] We can also take note of the Starbucks "Pick of the Week," advertised in stores and available on iTunes, and involving consumers in a micro eco-system of coffee and entertainment.

As Storey's examples indicate, those who study popular culture are well aware of the difficulties involved in seeking definitional closure. Popular culture is neither a "historically fixed set of popular texts and practices" nor a "historically fixed conceptual category." Satisfying as it may be to provide a circumscribed definition, to do so would be to ignore the many ways in which existing scholarship concerning popular culture has addressed the question of definition. But here a caveat is required. The object of my analysis is not first and foremost to contribute to ongoing conversations within existing theoretical accounts of popular culture but to advance a theory of popular culture and law as mutually constitutive discourse.

As Mezey notes, however, if we are to communicate meaningfully in our analysis of law and popular culture, some sort of definitional purchase is required, even if tentative and provisional.[52] Exploring the many ways in which culture has been described and defined, including arguments against definition itself,[53] Mezey adopts a working definition as follows: ". . . [I] will provisionally call culture any set of shared, signifying practices – practices by which meaning is produced, performed, contested, or transformed."[54]

The significance of this definition is the way in which it allows for Mezey to define the relationship between law and popular culture as mutually constitutive discourse. Note, however, that while Mezey adopts a discursive approach to law, rejecting claims that law exists as an autonomous and self-referential system, her conception of law is nonetheless primarily statist in perspective. The law that is being mutually constituted alongside popular culture originates with the state. Mezey cites the familiar example of the Miranda warning in criminal law as a demonstration of the ways in which "formal legal meaning-making" and "the signifying practices of culture" are inter-related. In the initial decision of the United States Supreme Court in *Miranda* v. *Arizona*,[55] the Court responded to the problem of compelled confessions with the legal requirement that the accused be notified of his or her legal rights. The Miranda warning is so prevalent in crime dramas and police procedurals that many of us, even those of us who do not live in the United States, can at least recite the beginning of the text that speaks specifically to the Fifth Amendment requirement, "You have the right to remain silent . . ." From its beginning as a legal rule in the United States, the Miranda warning subsequently found its way into global popular culture.

Mezey argues that the Court's reconsideration of the *Miranda* decision forty years later in *Dickerson* v. *United States*[56] demonstrates this influence works in both directions. In the years following the *Miranda* decision, some ambiguity remained as to whether the Constitution mandated the Miranda warning itself or whether alternative, legislated solutions could also satisfy constitutional requirements. Following the result in *Miranda*, Congress enacted legislation that negated the Miranda requirement; a confession is admissible pursuant to the Fifth Amendment so long as it is given voluntarily. In *Dickerson*, a majority of the Court upheld the *Miranda* decision on constitutional grounds, with respect owed to the principle of *stare decisis*. The Court did so, however, apparently without affirming that the Miranda warning is indeed a constitutional requirement for the admissibility of confessions. The *Miranda* decision actually left open the possibility of legislative experimentation, but the Court noted the extent to which the Miranda warning had become "embedded in routine police practice to the point where the warnings have become part of our natural culture."[57]

I cite this example not as proof of my own argument that popular culture and law are mutually constitutive discourse but to demonstrate that while Mezey articulates a new and promising way to analyze the relationship between law and popular culture, law remains defined as that which originates with the state, however porous may be its boundaries. Thus, while I adopt both Mezey's definition of culture as well as her characterization, also articulated by others, of law and popular culture as mutually constituted discourse, I argue in favor of a much broader understanding of law from the perspective of critical legal pluralism.

Keeping in mind, however, the caveats addressed by the different theoretical approaches discussed above, I also turn to Williams's account of the use of both "culture" and "popular" to more fully articulate what is meant by popular culture, as opposed to culture unmodified. Accordingly, while culture is defined, as per Mezey, with reference to shared, signifying practices, the types of signifying practices in which I am interested are of a particular sort – that is to say, they would come within some common understanding of what is meant by popular culture or culture modified with reference to both quantity and quality.

In quantitative terms, popularity indicates practices that are well liked by many people or intended to appeal to many people. A quantitative threshold, however, can only be defined in relative, not absolute, terms, and thus what counts as "many" will depend upon the specific media and circumstances being analyzed. In qualitative terms, as an evaluation of aesthetic value, popular culture may be defined as that which is designated as inferior in comparison with high culture. The point is not to indicate agreement with the designation, and certainly I would never put Ms Atwood's works, which I examine below, in this category. Instead, I refer to this distinction in order to stress the importance of asking by whom the designation is made and for what purposes. To ignore the operation of this distinction would leave power relations unexamined. Why, for example, are the graphics in comic books not generally considered as serious art works?[58]

Qualitatively, as an evaluation of origin, popular culture may also indicate culture made by people for themselves, although identifying where consumption ends and production begins is necessarily arbitrary to a certain extent. Social networks based on fandom, for example, do not exist apart from the commercial products that attracted such fans in the first place. The same applies to fan fiction, which in turn might become a commercial product of its own.[59] Finally, qualitatively as an indication of manner of circulation, popularity may indicate passive indoctrination, active resistance, or neither or both, depending upon the particular circumstances.

Choices we make, actions we take

Analysis of law and popular culture as mutually constitutive discourse requires a robust analytical framework built upon credible theoretical foundations if I am to proceed in a disciplined manner to examine the specific ways in which this might be conceived. If I move directly from the premise of law as discourse to an analysis of cultural artefacts, beliefs, and behaviors, I am leaving unaccounted the most significant (and often overlooked) part of the problem, being the existence of quite a number of intervening steps that require explanation. The complexity of the argument requires me to attend not only to higher levels of abstraction, but also to detailed explanations of processes involved. This will permit productive discussion and disagreement on the merits of my hypothesis without the distraction of miscommunication. Those who disagree will be able to distinguish readily between objections to the analytical framework, objections to the manner in which the framework is applied, and objections to proffered results and conclusions. Those who agree, admittedly perhaps not so numerous when radical re-imagining is the stated objective, will benefit in the same manner.

Different possibilities exist for carrying out this type of analysis, and I have tried to address constructive criticism of theory and method,[60] in particular those that derive as already discussed from perceiving law as distinct from culture. This has often led to a misconception of "law" and "popular culture" as distinct albeit reciprocal objects of inquiry.[61] Legal scholars may indeed be doing law rather than studying law as Kahn argues, although perhaps not so categorically as a distinction between doing and studying implies.[62] In any event, if law is thought to be distinct from culture, methodologies of legal analysis will erroneously exclude cultural considerations as beyond institutional competence. One need only consider complaints regarding references to public policy in common law legal judgments to recognize this effect. The concern is that while we may expand our subject matter, we retain interpretive methods designed for legal texts, not all of which fully account for differences in social context and consequences.[63] A second, related concern is the persistence of reification in legal analysis, even from those of us, myself included, who adopt constructivist approaches. As a result, "the law" appears to act of its own volition; the law speaks, the law rules, the law decides. Left unaccounted are the people who act with agency in creating, obeying, disobeying, and even ignoring legal rules.[64]

The challenge as I discussed in the introduction is that while different modes of scholarship offer relevant contributions, no one approach provides a complete account of how we might conceive of law and popular culture as mutually constitutive discourse. In Chapter 1, I argued this project of re-imagining law addresses tendencies of isolation and singularity that can at times arise in legal pluralism and analysis of law and culture. In returning to this point, I include related work in law and humanities. A compelling case exists for integrating these different approaches. Legal pluralism is well established, as is scholarship in law and humanities, and both are of increasing popularity and relevance. As Knox and Davies note, the foundations of legal pluralism and law and humanities can be found in legal anthropology, with Malinowski's consideration of the relationship between law and society.[65] Origins of legal pluralism in particular reflect an intention to understand law as social practices rather than symbolic expressions of state law.[66] Nonetheless, legal pluralism scholarship generally does not attend to the possibility of popular culture as plural law.

A pluralist account of law may serve to reinforce rather than disrupt traditional assumptions of what constitutes law.[67] Legal pluralism critiques singular conceptions of law but does not necessarily reject an understanding of law as an exogenous force applied to legal subjects.[68] For example, positivism is a fundamental characteristic of what Kleinhans and Macdonald refer to as social-scientific legal pluralism and[69] what Melissaris characterizes as empiricist-positivist theories.[70] Macdonald criticizes how these theories conceive of law as an empirically verifiable social fact. When the positivist image of state law is accepted as a default template, plural law is simply recognition (or analytical imposition) of the occurrence of this basic model in other contexts.[71] Legal pluralism of this nature arguably does not express the full scope of normative possibilities, nor for the purpose of this analysis does it overcome the limitations of the "law and" conjunction. Law simply expands to include plural legal orders, interacting along and within contested boundaries and competencies of jurisdiction. The fundamental assumption remains; that is to say, law is an instrumental and exogenous force distinct from the legal subjects it presumably governs.

Turning from legal pluralism to analysis of law and culture, Coombe calls into question whether a cultural study of law can, does, or should exist. Coombe explores relevant scholarship incorporating cultural perspectives on law, providing examples of those who study law culturally with reference to "legal discourse" but whose materials are confined to traditional state legal artefacts of codes, legislation, cases, and commentary. Comparative readings of literature and film are limited to brief explications of legal issues addressed in discrete texts, lacking any reference to social context or consequences. Accordingly, Coombe cautions that "a cultural studies of law will only emerge as a distinctive field of academic inquiry when scholars stop reifying law and start analyzing it as culture."[72] Otherwise, scholars in this field have produced foundational work advocating for a change in perspective and methodology so that we may better understand and analyze law as culture.[73] This mode of scholarship addresses the issue of isolation, but the difficulty for my project is that the issue of singularity remains. Law is still understood primarily if not exclusively with reference to the state, albeit no longer institutionally isolated from culture.

Difficulties exist as well with law and humanities scholarship, which might be expected to offer the most specific guidance for re-imagining law and popular culture as mutually constitutive discourse. Manderson calls attention to the problem that legal reification has a tendency to reify or objectify literature in turn. Literature becomes merely law's substitute, made to operate subject to the same (misguided) textual and interpretive assumptions of certainty and determinacy, thereby performing the same functions of law albeit by different means.[74] For example, literature may be mined for legal truth claims, as if content and plot produced verifiable propositions, ready to be deployed in legal argument and capable of mimicking the questionable determinacy of legal decision-making. From this perspective, the "and" in "law and literature" betrays an assumption of causal relevance that literature is both relevant and answerable to law.[75] Law and life are forever dichotomous, which means not only that interdisciplinary potential is limited, but furthermore that once again literature must prove useful to law on law's terms.[76]

This returns us to Cover's work on *nomos* and narrative, in which the significance of narrative (and thus culture) cannot be denied.[77] The precise relationship between *nomos* and narrative is difficult to determine in Cover's work; does narrative create or merely reveal law?[78] Similarly, one might argue that Cover is an interpretive pluralist rather than a legal pluralist, that is to say, that pluralism in his work refers to the range of possible interpretations of official law but not plural legalities in addition to state law. These ambiguities create the necessary space for arguments to the contrary.[79] In terms of *nomos*, Cover recognizes at the very least that legal orders are inherently plural, else there would be no need for a jurispathic state to counter the contradictory influences of plural jurisgenerative communities. For this reason, many legal pluralists have been inspired by Cover's work to focus their attention on the confrontation between jurisgenerative communities and the jurispathic consequences of their interaction with the state.[80]

As for the narrative aspect of *nomos* and narrative, the focus on narrative in law and humanities scholarship is arguably a function of Boyd's work rather than Cover's.[81] Nonetheless, the point remains that Cover's work provides foundational theoretical support for combining legal pluralism with a discursive approach to law that emphasizes the significance of narrative. One particularly relevant aspect for this analysis is the way in which Cover describes a radical dichotomy between law as social meaning and law as social control. The jurisgenerative meaning-making activities of different communities produce a multiplicity of law as social meaning, which is a threat to the efficacy of law as social control. Hence the need for the jurispathic action of state law as a solution to too much law,[82] The argument is not that multiple meanings are not legitimate in and of themselves; hence the maxim, as Cover notes, that courts of final jurisdiction are not final because they are infallible but rather infallible because they are final.[83] Arguably, in analyzing law and popular culture as mutually constitutive, we are able to avoid what Cover saw as an inevitable distinction between social meaning and social control; a pluralist, discursive approach merges both aspects, thus dispensing with the problem of either too much meaning or too much law.

Drawing upon these different modes of scholarship, I now have a point of departure for this project of re-imagining law. The theoretical basis necessarily begins with legal pluralism, albeit with an approach that rejects the assumption of autonomous law. The most promising alternative is what might be termed post-modern theories of legal pluralism, the defining characteristic being rejection of a reified understanding of legal orders clashing within the contested space of over-lapping jurisdictions.[84] Despite its pervasive presence in our lives, state law is neither the most exemplary nor most persuasive cultural resource for signifying obligational beliefs and behaviors.[85] This is not to deny the power of the state but simply to acknowledge its power is not monolithic. Postmodern legal pluralism adopts an understanding of law, including state law, as "complex relations of force and discourse."[86] In Chapter 3, I consider two alternatives, Macdonald's critical legal pluralism and Melissaris's definitional contextualism, although Melissaris would not include his work within the postmodern classification.

With respect to both analysis of law and culture and law and humanities, I incorporate insights from a range of materials rather than adopting any one theory as foundational to my analysis. Manderson's work is the most viable and well-established point of departure in this respect, although I do not mean to indicate here that law and culture and law and humanities are contemporaneous fields of study. Significantly, Manderson has argued that understanding the plurality and discursive openness of law is fundamental to analyzing law and culture.[87] He acknowledges the benefits of recent scholarship treating law and literature as mutually constitutive forces rather than suppletive and opposite entities.[88] Finally, he also rejects reification by arguing in favor of both law and literature as verbs rather than nouns,[89] a theme I adopt and develop throughout this project.

Manderson argues that literature is agency, a way of thinking that does not tell us some "thing" but rather makes us some "one."[90] Similarly, if we begin to think of legal judgment as a verb rather than a noun, we begin to understand "how law and literature are already connected to each other, already speaking not about the same thing but in the same mode as it were."[91] We err to the extent that we take our prevailing conception of law as propositional outcome, that is to say a noun, and seek to identify similar characteristics and functions within literature. The direction should be reversed; we should begin with how literature functions as a verb, as a transformative experience, and conceive of law in these terms, as a way to approach questions and engage with their complexity.[92] Justice becomes a means rather than an end, an experiential pursuit rather than a definitive outcome, and a way of discussing and dealing with the full range and diversity of normative complexity. Both law and literature are never ending quests for justification and cannot be reduced to mere instrumentalities as problem-solving tools.[93]

West's metaphorical reference to discursively integrated webs of cultural authority provides additional insight.[94] West constructs a typology of scholarship that began in law and literature and subsequently continued in law and culture as literary, jurisprudential, and hermeneutic approaches. The jurisprudential approach, which is the most relevant to this project, proposes that literature and culture might have the force of law, either historically or in present or future circumstances. This is not to say that literature or culture is analogous to state law in either form or function. West provides historical evidence, however, to indicate that the line between law and literature has not always been so strictly demarcated. Lawyers, being educated people drawn from the culturally elite, viewed law and literature on more equivalent terms as part of a "seamless web of cultural authority."[95] Culture is part of law, and thus law can only be understood when analyzed as part of this cultural context. Mutual constitution is by way of reciprocation, in that law incorporates culture and in turn influences the culture it incorporates.[96] Turning from past practices to present day, Mezey argues this web of authority should not be limited to cultural works characterized as intellectually elite.[97]

Building upon these contributions, I hope to bring a greater degree of specificity to the analysis first by hypothesizing law and popular culture as mutually constitutive discourse and second by developing the necessary analytical framework pursuant to which inquiry can proceed. The analytical framework should negate to the extent possible an understanding of legal pluralism as a noun, in the sense that a theory of plural law should provide a means for resolving competing claims among plural legal orders. Instead, analysis should affirm to the extent possible an understanding of legal pluralism as a verb, in the sense that plural law should provide a means for understanding how legal subjects comprehend and negotiate their experiences of normative heterogeneity.

Situating my analysis in a familiar context, the legal authority of popular culture follows logically from Geertz's characterization of law as meaning, widely circulated and cited as "a distinctive manner of imagining the real."[98] Law is an explanation, not an artefact,[99] an explanation of human behavior from a legal perspective.[100] This is a logical progression as well from Cover's characterization of law as a bridge between reality and alternity. Cover adopts the latter term from Steiner, who refers to alternities as the creation through language of what is not and what is not yet.[101] More than a mere reference to alternative options, an alternity is an explicit counter-factual imagination of the other than the case, of the world as other than it is.[102] Law is, in Cover's terms, a normative bridge that connects our understanding of the world-that-is with our aspirations toward the worlds-that-might-be instead: "Law connects 'reality' to 'alternity', constituting a new reality with a bridge built out of committed social behaviour."[103] Cover does not intend this statement as a definition of law but rather as an argument for extending the use of the term to "all collective behavior entailing systematic understandings of our commitments to future worlds."[104] To understand law with reference to alternity is to understand that what takes us from our present real to imagined ideal, from normative heterogeneity to legal claim, is our jurisgenerative capacity.[105] Law is belief and behavior in pursuit of normative aspiration in the hope of moving from worlds-that-are to worlds-as-we-think-they-ought-to-be.[106]

When the focus of legal analysis moves from artifacts of reification to the social construction of legal meaning as normative aspiration, the normative force of popular culture as well as the necessity of a pluralist approach become apparent. Understood in these terms, no compelling reason exists for excluding any type of discourse, *ab initio*, from consideration as law. This is not to say we will find law in every type of discourse, but rather that every type of discourse merits at least preliminary consideration. If no compelling reason exists for excluding any particular discourse from consideration, then popular culture not only can but also should be analyzed as potentially constitutive of law.[107] Rest assured I am not suggesting we replace the *Criminal Code*[108] with a screening of *Kill Bill*.[109] The intent is to pluralize popular culture, not negate state law, and for this reason I do not discount the significance of how popular culture both illustrates and influences state law. From a legal pluralist perspective, popular culture narratives may constitute and communicate implicit and inferential alternative legalities.[110]

Before proceeding to Chapter 3, I note two additional points. First, in arguing that popular culture and law are mutually constitutive discourse I am indeed claiming that all normative behavior, however conceived, however instantiated, has at least a *prima facie* claim of legal validity,[111] by which I mean the nature of the claim and not the merits of its substantive content. I do not claim that all norms are law, and both Macdonald and Melissaris are explicit on this point albeit for different reasons. I do claim, as I argued in Chapter 1, that a distinction between law and norm should be explicit and defended, not implicit and assumed. Assuming that popular culture has a pervasive influence in our lives, I am often asked why I am not content to acknowledge this as a system of normative ordering. Why do I insist on the possibility of law? My response is to inquire in return, why do others insist that only state law and its analogues should be recognized as law? Reversing a question may appear as empty rhetoric, a technique used to avoid the necessity of providing a well-reasoned response. But consider how this line of argument demonstrates that when we impose on others the burden of a qualifying objective,[112] in reference to any definition not just law, we are imposing our own internalized and thus invisible (to us) prescriptive standards.

The most traditional definitions can be the ones most vehemently defended, and yet by nature these are definitions in which the greatest reliance is placed on unexamined assumptions. We derive dominance from difference, perhaps even more so when differences are of our own design.[113] The distinction between state law and other qualified forms of law facilitates hierarchal relationships between what would otherwise be perceived as differentiated but not necessarily subordinated normative systems. As a result, state law has greater authority than other forms of law, which in turn have greater authority than mere norms. This arrangement, however, is neither inherent nor inevitable. Given the historical evidence of legal pluralism in medieval Europe, perhaps the burden of the qualifying adjective should be placed on those who argue for the exclusivity of state and analogous systems of law.[114]

The second related point involves a logical consequence of re-imagining law. People do not characterize their beliefs and behaviors in a manner consistent with a concept of law that has yet to be communicated and accepted (or rejected). If our prevailing understanding of law distinguishes between state law and cultural norms, we will not refer to our behavior as legal in nature. In Chapter 5, I discuss how eco/animal activists characterize their actions as moral imperatives that take precedence over unjust laws. Moral reasoning in support of direct action tracks the familiar distinction in legal theory between positivism and normativism and is consistent with the premise of civil disobedience that one need not obey unjust laws. This does not negate the importance of looking for the possibility of law in popular culture. The emancipatory potential of re-imagining law is to provide people with an opportunity if they so choose to advance moral imperatives as legal claims. If the ability to claim the word law were irrelevant, then arguably limits on its use would not be so vehemently defended.

Notes

1 As Melissaris notes: ". . . [T]he internalism/externalism, law/morality, ideal/real antinomies have dominated legal philosophical debate to the point of even stifling or misdirecting any attempts at critically re-theorizing the legal." See: Emmanuel Melissaris, *Ubiquitous Law: Legal Theory and the Space for Legal Pluralism* (Ashgate Publishing Company 2009) 18. In reflecting upon the law/justice antimony in legal theory with respect to positivism, normativism, and critical legal theory, I am guided in part by Melissaris's account of the methodological deficiencies of each approach. See: Melissaris (2009) 7.

2 Melissaris describes this as the "all too familiar distinction between conventional positivism . . . and normativism," in reference to H.L.A. Hart (positivism) and Ronald Dworkin (normativism). He identifies a similar problem with critical legal theory, which focused on the deficiencies of orthodox legal theories in pursuit of demonstrating false claims of objectivity and justice. See: Melissaris (2009) 3.

3 Solum identifies two recurring antimonies in contemporary legal theory, the first between rights and consequences, the second between realism and formalism, which give rise to fulsome debate but are never resolved. This is one of the reasons Solum presents virtue ethics, and more specifically, virtue jurisprudence, as an alternative to prevailing legal theories. See: Lawrence B. Solum, 'Virtue Jurisprudence: Towards an Aretaic Theory of Law' in Liesbeth Huppes-Cluysenaer and Nuno M.M.S. Coelho (eds), *Aristotle and the Philosophy of Law: Theory, Practice and Justice* (Springer 2013).

4 Emmanuel Melissaris, 'Perspective, Critique, and Pluralism in Legal Theory' (2006) 57 *Northern Ireland Legal Quarterly* 597, 607.

5 See, for example, the different variations and examples of "Vigilante Man" at the TV Tropes website: TV Tropes, 'Vigilante Man' <http://tvtropes.org/pmwiki/pmwiki.php/Main/VigilanteMan> accessed June 22, 2015.

6 *The Shield* (Shawn Ryan 2002–2008).

7 *Unforgiven* (Clint Eastwood 1992).

8 *The Sweet Hereafter* (Atom Egoyan 1997).

9 *A Civil Action* (Steven Zaillian 1998).

10 Roderick A. Macdonald, 'Critical Legal Pluralism as a Construction of Normativity and the Emergence of Law' in Andrée Lajoie, Roderick A. Macdonald, Richard Janda, and Guy Rocher (eds), *Théories Et Émergence Du Droit: Pluralisme, Surdétermination, Effectivité* (Éditions Thémis 1998) 12.

11 Melissaris (2009) 7.

12 I do not discuss Derrida's "aporia" between law and justice. See: Jacques Derrida, 'Force de Loi: le fondement mystique de l'autorité' (1989) 11 *Cardozo Law Review* 920. I share Melissaris's assessment that this understanding of incommensurability between law and justice is "frustratingly eschatological." See: Melissaris (2009) 93.

13 For the legitimacy of equivalent interpretive authority among plural interpretive communities, see Cover: Robert M. Cover, '*Nomos* and Narrative' (1983) 97 *Harvard Law Review* 4.

14 As Macdonald argues, "Whatever the instrumental leverage of State legal regulation, it has little purchase on the symbolic construction of most social life." See: Macdonald (1998) 11; Macdonald and Sandomierski ascribe increasing disengagement from governance processes such as elections to a "felt distance between law and norm." See: Roderick A. Macdonald and David Sandomierski, 'Against Nomopolies' (2006) 57 *Northern Ireland Legal Quarterly* 610, 612.

15 This type of language is typical, for example, in common law cases upholding the absence of a duty to rescue, notwithstanding broad acceptance of such a duty in civil law systems. See, for example: *Union Pac. Ry. Co. v. Cappier* 66 Kan 649.

16 "For withholding relief from the suffering, for failure to respond to the calls of worthy charity, or for faltering in the bestowment of brotherly love on the unfortunate, penalties are found not in the laws of men, but in that higher law, the violation of which is condemned by the voice of conscience, whose sentence of punishment for the recreant act is swift and sure." *Union Pac. Ry. Co. v. Cappier* 658.

17 See, for example: Martin Luther King Jr, 'Letter from Birmingham Jail' (1992–1993) 26 *UC Davis Law Review* 835.

18 Roderick A. Macdonald, 'Metaphors of Multiplicity: Civil Society, Regimes, and Legal Pluralism' (1998) 15 *Arizona Journal of International and Comparative Law* 69, 79.

19 Mieke Bal, *Travelling Concepts in the Humanities: A Rough Guide* (University of Toronto Press 2002) 99.

20 Although note that as Macdonald and Sandomierski argue, actors may not perceive their actions at the time as normative, but this does not preclude the characterization as such. Often we do not think about the normative basis of our actions unless we are called upon to explain or justify what we have done. See: Macdonald and Sandomierski (2006) 619.

21 Our consciousness, however, has not been constant in this respect. As Tamanaha notes, legal pluralism is an established part of the legal heritage of medieval Europe. See: Brian Z. Tamanaha, 'Understanding Legal Pluralism: Past to Present, Local to Global' (2007) 29 *Sydney Law Review* 375, 376.

22 As Macdonald and Sandomierski argue, when we come to recognize legitimacy not in law's normative foundations but in its origin with the political state, we erase our own agency. Our normative options become severely constrained. See: Macdonald and Sandomierski (2006) 620.

23 On the importance of defining (or not defining) terms in this area of scholarship, see: Rosemary J. Coombe, 'Contingent Articulations: A Critical Cultural Studies of Law' in Austin Sarat and Thomas R. Kearns (eds), *Law in the Domains of Culture* (University of Michigan Press 2000); Naomi Mezey, 'Law as Culture' (2001) 13 *Yale Journal of Law and the Humanities* 35.

24 Bal fully acknowledges the significance of polyphony, the inherent ambiguity of meaning, and the role of context-specific readers in producing these meanings. See: Bal (2002) 6.

25 For a cultural studies approach to law as culture, see: Mezey (2001); Lieve Gies, 'Law as Popular Culture: Cross-Disciplinary Encounters' (2005) 19 *Continuum: Journal of Media & Cultural Studies* 165. On the related question of whether there is a cultural

studies of law, see: Rosemary J. Coombe, 'Is there a Cultural Studies of Law?' in Toby Miller (ed), *A Companion to Cultural Studies* (Blackwell Reference Online Edition, Blackwell Publishing 2005) <http://www.blackwellreference.com/subscriber/tocnode.html?id=g9781405141758_chunk_g97814051417584> accessed April 12, 2016.

26 Austin Sarat and Jonathan Simon, 'Beyond Legal Realism?: Cultural Analysis, Cultural Studies, and the Situation of Legal Scholarship' (2001) 13 *Yale Journal of Law and the Humanities* 3, 9.

27 Bal (2002) 9.

28 Urpo Kovala, 'Cultural Studies and Cultural Text Analysis' (2002) 4 *CLC Web: Comparative Literature and Culture* 2. See Phelan on this point as well in comparing rhetorical poetics to cultural thematics: James Phelan, *Experiencing Fiction: Judgments, Progressions, and the Rhetorical Theory of Narrative* (Ohio State University Press 2007) 89.

29 Coombe (2005), citing Austin D. Sarat, 'Redirecting Legal Scholarship in Law Schools' (2000) 12 *Yale Journal of Law & the Humanities* 129, 139.

30 Sara L. Knox and Cristyn Davies, 'The Force of Meaning' (2013) 27 *Cultural Studies* 1, 7.

31 Coombe (2005).

32 Martha-Marie Kleinhans and Roderick A. Macdonald, 'What Is a Critical Legal Pluralism?' (1997) 12 *Canadian Journal of Law and Society* 25, 36.

33 Roderick A. Macdonald, 'Pluralistic Human Rights? Universal Human Wrongs?' in René Provost and Colleen Sheppard (eds), *Dialogues on Human Rights and Legal Pluralism* (Springer Science & Business Media 2013) 30.

34 See, for example: Richard K. Sherwin, *When Law Goes Pop: The Vanishing Line Between Law and Popular Culture* (University of Chicago Press 2002).

35 See, for example: Mieke Bal, *Narratology: Introduction to the Theory of Narrative* (Third Edition, University of Toronto Press 2009) 4.

36 Mezey (2001) 35.

37 Mezey (2001) 37.

38 Bal (2002) 9.

39 I adopt the term "open-source" as it is used to refer to software wherein source code is distributed for adaptation and modification, either to improve functionality or to meet specific requirements. See, for example: Bruce Kogut and Anca Metiu, 'Open-Source Software Development and Distributed Innovation' (2001) 17 *Oxford Review of Economic Policy* 248.

40 John Storey, *Cultural Theory and Popular Culture: An Introduction* (Fifth Edition, Pearson Education Limited 2009) 5.

41 Storey (2009) 1.

42 Storey (2009) 5.

43 Storey (2009) 6.

44 Pierre Bourdieu, *Distinction: A Social Critique of the Judgment of Taste* (Richard Nice tr, Reprint Edition, Harvard University Press 1984).

45 Storey (2009) 6.

46 Storey (2009) 6.

47 Storey (2009) 8.

48 Storey (2009) 9.

49 Storey (2009) 10.

50 Storey (2009) 12.

51 Storey (2009) 12.

52 Mezey (2001) 38.

53 Coombe (2000).

54 Mezey (2001) 37.

55 384 U.S. 436 (1966).

56 530 U.S. 428 (2000).

57 530 U.S. 428 (2000).

58 In *Unbreakable*, a comic book collector and expert, Elijah Price, is the owner of an art gallery specializing in comic book art. He is showing various works in his collection to a buyer when the buyer reveals that the work he is purchasing is for his young son. Mr. Price calls him out on his ignorance of comic book art as follows: "Do you see any Teletubbies in here? Do you see a slender plastic tag clipped to my shirt with my name printed on it? Do you see a little Asian child with a blank expression on his face sitting outside on a mechanical helicopter that shakes when you put quarters in it? No? Well, that's what you see at a toy store. And you must think you're in a toy store, because you're here shopping for an infant named Jeb." *Unbreakable* (M. Night Shyamain 2000).

59 See, for example, the success of the *Fifty Shades of Grey* trilogy, which began with author E.L. James posting her fan fiction online: E.L. James, *Fifty Shades Trilogy Bundle: Fifty Shades of Grey; Fifty Shades Darker; Fifty Shades Freed* (Random House LLC 2012).

60 Coombe (2000); Jessica M. Silbey, 'What We Do When We Do Law and Popular Culture' (2002) 27 *Law & Social Inquiry* 139; Gies (2005).

61 As Coombe notes, the question of whether a cultural study of law exists depends on the degree to which this conjunction persists: "I suggest that a cultural studies of law will only emerge as a distinctive field of academic inquiry when scholars stop reifying law and start analyzing it as culture." See: Coombe (2005). Knox and Davies refer to this statement as a "prescient warning," to which I have indeed attempted to respond. See: Knox and Davies (2013) 3.

62 Paul W. Kahn, *The Cultural Study of Law: Reconstructing Legal Scholarship* (University of Chicago Press 2000) 27.

63 Coombe (2005).

64 Sarat (2000) 139.

65 Knox and Davies (2013) 1, citing Bronislaw Malinowski, *Crime and Custom in Savage Society* (Harcourt Brace 1926).

66 Derek McKee, 'Review Essay: Emmanual Melissaris' Ubiquitous Law: Legal Theory and the Space for Legal Pluralism' (2010) 11 *German Law Journal* 573, 573.

67 See, for example, Kleinhans and Macdonald, who argue that social-scientific legal pluralism multiplies rather than disputes essentialist and positivist images of law: Kleinhans and Macdonald (1997) 34 But see also Tamanaha, who argues against attempts to label all normative social ordering as law based on essentialist understandings of how this term is defined: Brian Z. Tamanaha, 'The Folly of the "Social Scientific" Concept of Legal Pluralism' (1993) 20 *Journal of Law and Society* 192. Tamanaha advocates for a non-essentialist approach to law and legal pluralism, one that does not require an essential definition of law, is more productive. If legal theory in general has failed to achieve consensus in defining law, a search for definition within legal pluralism is misguided. See: Brian Z. Tamanaha, 'A Non-Essentialist Version of Legal Pluralism' (2000) 27 *Journal of Law and Society* 296.

68 For recent reviews of the history and classification of types of legal pluralism, see, for example: Tamanaha (2007); William Twining, 'Normative and Legal Pluralism: A Global Perspective' (2009) 20 *Duke Journal of Comparative & International Law* 473; McKee (2010); Victor M. Muñiz-Fraticelli, *The Structure of Pluralism* (Oxford University Press 2014).

69 Kleinhans and Macdonald (1997); Roderick A. Macdonald, 'Here, There and Everywhere: Theorizing Legal Pluralism; Theorizing Jacques Vanderlinden' in Nicholas Kasirer (ed), *Étudier Et Enseigner Le Droit: Hier, Aujourd'hui Et Demain – Études Offertes À Jacques Vanderlinden* (Éditions Yvon Blais 2006).

70 Melissaris (2009).

71 Macdonald (2006) 405; Kleinhans and Macdonald (1997). For Melissaris, the problem with these theories is that they rely on context-specific understandings of law. See: Melissaris (2009) 33.

72 Coombe (2005).

73 See, for example: Sarat and Simon (2001); Mezey (2001); Coombe (2005); Jessica Silbey, 'Truth Tales and Trial Films' (2007) 40 *Loyola of Los Angeles Law Review* 551.
74 Desmond Manderson, 'Modernism and the Critique of Law and Literature' (2011) 35 *Australian Feminist Law Journal* 107, 125.
75 Manderson (2011) 109.
76 Manderson (2011) 118.
77 Cover (1983); Robert M. Cover, 'Violence and the Word' (1986) 95 *The Yale Law Journal* 1601.
78 Melissaris (2009) 53.
79 For a discussion of whether Cover is an interpretive or legal pluralist, see, for example: Macdonald and Sandomierski (2006) 614. For an argument that Cover is a legal pluralist, see: Melissaris (2009) 55.
80 Muñiz-Fraticelli 'Law as Intelligibility' (2014).
81 See, for example, Manderson's argument on this point: Manderson (2011) 108.
82 Cover (1983) 18.
83 Cover (1983) 42.
84 See, for example: Desmond Manderson, 'Beyond the Provincial: Space, Aethetics, and Modernist Legal Theory' (1995) 20 *Melbourne University Law Review* 1048; Margaret Davies, 'The Ethos of Pluralism' (2005) 27 *Sydney Law Review* 87; Kleinhans and Macdonald (1997). Melissaris describes these as postmodern theories of legal pluralism, in contrast to earlier, empiricist-positivist theories. See: Melissaris (2009) 35.
85 For the influential power of forms of popular culture, see, for example: Rosemary J. Coombe, 'Objects of Property and Subjects of Politics: Intellectual Property Laws and Democratic Dialogue' (1990) 69 *Texas Law Review* 1853, 864.
86 Desmond Manderson, 'Trust Us Justice: 24, Popular Culture, and the Law' in Austin Sarat (ed), *Imagining Legality: Where Law Meets Popular Culture* (The University of Alabama Press 2011).
87 Desmond Manderson, 'Memory and Echo: Pop Cult, Hi Tech and the Irony of Tradition' (2013) 27 *Cultural Studies* 11. See also: Desmond Manderson, 'From Hunger to Love: Myths of the Source, Interpretation, and Constitution of Law in Children's Literature' (2003) 15 *Law and Literature* 87; Manderson (2011); Manderson (2013).
88 Manderson (2011) 120.
89 Manderson (2011) 121.
90 Manderson (2011) 125.
91 Manderson (2011) 125.
92 Manderson (2011) 125. See also: Desmond Manderson, 'Mikhail Bakhtin and the Field of Law and Literature' (2012) 8 *Law, Culture, and the Humanities* 1; Desmond Manderson, 'Modernism, Polarity, and the Rule of Law' (2013) 24 *Yale Journal of Law & the Humanities* 475; Desmond Manderson, 'Judgment in Law and the Humanities' (2013) 1 *Revista Forumul Judecatorilor* 43.
93 Manderson (2011) 125.
94 Robin West, 'Literature, Culture, and Law at Duke University' in Austin Sarat, Catherine O. Frank, and Matthew Daniel Anderson (eds), *Teaching Law and Literature* (Modern Language Association of America 2011).
95 West (2011) 6.
96 West (2011) 15.
97 Mezey (2001).
98 Clifford Geertz, *Local Knowledge: Further Essays in Interpretive Anthropology* (Basic Books 1983) 184.
99 I adopt the language of artefact and explanation from both Kleinhans and Macdonald and Macdonald and Sandomierski. See: Kleinhans and Macdonald (1997); Macdonald and Sandomierski (2006).
100 As I discuss below, Macdonald argues that we are engaged in thinking about law when we direct our attention to "the endeavour of symbolizing human conduct and interaction as governed by rules." Macdonald (2006) 393.

101 Phil Goodwin, 'Ethical Problems in Translation: Why We Might Need Steiner After All' (2010) 16 *The Translator* 19, 28.
102 See, for example, Ronald A. Sharp, 'Interrogation at the Borders: George Steiner and the Trope of Translation' (1989) 21 *New Literary History* 133, 141, citing George Steiner, *After Babel* (Oxford University Press 1975) 222: "The main function of language, then, is to create alternities," by which he means "the 'other than the case,' the counter-factual propositions, images, shapes of will and evasion with which we charge our mental being and by means of which we build the changing, largely fictive milieu of our somatic and social existence."
103 Robert M. Cover, 'The Folktales of Justice: Tales of Jurisdiction' (1984) 14 *Capital University Law Review* 179, 181.
104 Cover (1984) 181.
105 Cover (1983). Whether Cover's work involves legal pluralism is an open question. As Melissaris notes, Cover's work is often characterized as interpretive rather than legal pluralism. Melissaris disagrees with this characterization, relying on Cover's work to initiate and support his argument that legal pluralism necessarily includes a transcontextual definition of law, as discussed below. See: Melissaris (2009) 51. See also Macdonald and Sandomierski on this point: Macdonald and Sandomierski (2006) 614.
106 As discussed below, re-imagining law in these terms adopts Cover's characterization of law as alternity. "Law may be viewed as a system of tension or a bridge linking a concept of a reality to an imagined alternative . . .". See: Cover (1983) 9, citing Steiner (1975) 222.
107 Wendy A. Adams, '"I Made a Promise to a Lady": Critical Legal Pluralism as Improvised Law in *Buffy the Vampire Slayer*' *Critical Studies in Improvisation* <https://journal.lib.uoguelph.ca/index.php/csieci/article/viewArticle/1083>.
108 Criminal Code (R.S.C., 1985, c. C-46).
109 *Kill Bill: Vol. 1* (Quentin Tarantino 2003).
110 For the significance and primacy of implicit and inferential normativity, see: Roderick A. Macdonald, 'Custom Made – For a Non-Chirographic Critical Legal Pluralism' (2011) 26 *Canadian Journal of Law and Society* 301.
111 See, for example: Kleinhans and Macdonald (1997).
112 For a discussion of the "burden of the qualifying objective," see: Macdonald (1998) 72.
113 For example, Mackinnon provides a foundational and influential contribution to feminist and legal theory in her explication of a dominance approach to inequality. Gender is not an explanation of difference between men and women but rather socialized power relations of dominance and subordination: "Gender might not even code as difference, might not mean distinction epistemologically, were it not for its consequences for social power." See: Catharine A. MacKinnon, *Feminism Unmodified: Discourses on Life and Law* (Harvard University Press 1987) 40. Mackinnon has also approached the issue of legal rights for animals from this perspective, noting instructive similarities in socialized hierarchies of dominance between men and women, humans and animals. See: Catharine A. MacKinnon, 'Of Mice and Men: A Feminist Fragment on Animal Rights' in Cass R. Sunstein and Martha C. Nussbaum (eds), *Animal Rights: Current Debates and New Directions* (Oxford University Press 2004) 263.
114 See, for example, Tamanaha's discussion of the history of legal pluralism from the medieval period to the present: Tamanaha (2007).

3 Legal pluralism as capacity and result

Introduction

As discussed in Chapter 1, in the process of re-imagining law I must first develop the necessary analytical framework, one that facilitates discussion and allows me to provide a specific account of how we can conceive of popular culture and law as mutually constitutive discourse. I also discussed the necessity of legal pluralism as the theoretical foundation. The task here is to consider which theory of legal pluralism is appropriate, keeping in mind the need to address mistaken assumptions of both singularity and isolation. Recall that theories of legal pluralism address the issue of singularity but do not necessarily negate the assumption of law as an autonomous entity, separate and distinct from culture. Accordingly, a discursive theory of legal pluralism is required, one which has sufficient scope to conceptualize law, with reference to Geertz's work, as meaning[1] and interaction rather than entity and artefacts. A discursive theory of legal pluralism acknowledges that law is crowd-sourced knowledge, so to speak, rather than a unidirectional relationship whereby authoritative addressors impose obligations on subjected addressees.

A discursive approach, however, is necessary but not sufficient. An inquiry into the legal force of popular culture can be characterized as an inquiry into the legal force of narrative, given that narrative is the means by which we find meaning across a broad range of works of popular culture. This returns us to Cover's analysis of *nomos* and narrative, although[2] Cover was somewhat ambiguous as to the nature of this relationship.[3] As noted in Chapter 2, whether approached with reference to Cover, as a legal pluralist analysis, as an analysis of law and culture, or as an analysis of law and humanities, the ambiguity of this relationship is never fully resolved. This may be the reason we have difficulty understanding specifically (as opposed to metaphorically) how popular culture might function as law. So in addition to addressing the issues of singularity and isolation, we need to account as well for the normative force of narrative, unmediated by translation into state law.[4] A functional role for narrative is essential not only because narrative is a predominant way in which we make sense of what is happening around us,[5] but also because popular culture does not provide traditional legal texts or practices for interpretation. Not all aspects of popular culture are narrative, but my initial focus is on works rather than practices of popular culture, to the extent this can be treated as distinct, and narrative is pervasive across a wide variety of these texts. If we are to understand popular culture and law as mutually constitutive discourse, we need to begin not with symbolized legal rules but with narrative.

I have indicated as well my preference for re-orienting our understanding of legality toward law as a verb, meaning our capacity to create legal knowledge, and away from law as a noun, meaning the outcome produced when we resolve issues of interpretation or inter-legality. This explains my emphasis on another aspect of Cover's work, being his characterization of law as alternity, as a normative bridge that takes us from worlds-that-are to worlds-as-we-think-they-ought-to-be.[6] The ability to accommodate an understanding of law as alternity is a logical implication of developing an analytical framework predicated upon a discursive theory of legal pluralism. If law is explanation rather than artefact, then legal obligation involves legal subjects exercising agency in pursuit of normative aspirations, however constrained we might conceive of this agency as a function of our preferred position on the relationship between structure and agency. Law is not the outcome achieved by the application of an instrumental and exogenous force but our capacity for normative commitment whereby we instantiate our beliefs through rule-governed behavior. In summary, a discursive approach to legal pluralism must incorporate not only a significant function for narrative, but also a means to understand and express law as alternity.

With these requirements in mind, I identify and analyze two discursive theories of legal pluralism.[7] The first is Macdonald's theory of critical legal pluralism, developed over the course of several years and a number of articles.[8] The second theoretical approach was developed by Melissaris, first in a series of articles[9] and then more fully elaborated in his book, *Ubiquitous Law*,[10] followed by additional specification regarding some of the procedural requirements of interperspectival dialogue.[11] I refer to his approach as definitional contextualism, with apologies for the inexactitude of this label. Neither author has addressed the efficacy of his theories for analyzing relations, or lack thereof, between law and popular culture, although Macdonald has applied critical legal pluralism to a number of specific factual contexts.[12] Avoiding the oversimplification of presenting a conclusory result, I work through both of these theoretical accounts with particular attention paid to the issue of definition.

The significant distinction between the two theories is the question of definition in legal pluralism: is definition a threshold requirement for acknowledging the legitimacy of plural legal claims?[13] For Melissaris, the question of definition is the foundation of his approach. Melissaris argues that the fundamental error of critical legal pluralism is the failure to provide a definition of law. When we collapse law into all kinds of normativity and social control, we become incapable of saying anything meaningful about law as distinguished from that which is not law.[14] Macdonald, on the other hand, explicitly rejects definitional approaches to legal pluralism as misguided. Stipulated definitions are at best unexamined assumptions and are prescriptive rather than descriptive in nature. Definitions of law contradict that which they seek to define, since they are political acts directed toward political purposes.[15] Instead, Macdonald argues for differentiation based on the mode of analysis rather than the subject matter being analyzed. Law is a way of making sense of human behavior from a normative perspective by attending to how we negotiate our relationships with others.[16]

In examining these theories in relation to each other, I came to appreciate the implications of this distinction between what are otherwise fairly complementary approaches to the emancipatory potential of jurisgenerative legal subjects.[17] The question of definition has both informed and confirmed my characterization of a re-imagined plural legality of narrative/*nomos* as an orientation away from law as noun and toward law as a verb. Emphasizing legal subjects' capacity for knowledge and meaning resists a pluralist tendency to focus on the correct and/or possible outcomes of normative heterogeneity. Relational analysis also confirmed what I had intuited from teaching experience, that the significance of definition couldn't be overstated. For many students, the question of whether popular culture can function as law cannot proceed until first resolving a logically prior question of what is (and what is not) law. Their need for definition persists even after reviewing the extent to which prevailing legal theories have extensively addressed this question without yet producing a definitive consensus.[18]

I also came to realize that despite this irreconcilable difference, adopting Macdonald's non-definitional theory of critical legal pluralism does not necessarily contradict Melissaris's theory of plural law as definitional contextualism. This apparent paradox is resolved with reference to a point made by both Macdonald and Melissaris, that the meta-theoretical potential of legal pluralism includes the ability to recognize as legitimate concepts of law that are contradictory with the premises of the theory itself.[19] While a more complete discussion is pursued below, suffice to note for now that pursuant to Macdonald's theory of critical legal pluralism, definition is not necessary, but neither is it prohibited. Accordingly, critical legal pluralism can acknowledge the legitimacy of concepts of law that are plural contextualizations of Melissaris's threshold requirement of a transcontextual definition. The reverse, however, is not the case.

Amid the increasing prevalence of scholarship addressing questions of theory, methodology, and subject matter relative to legal pluralism, critical legal pluralism nonetheless stands out as a more radical approach.[20] Muñiz-Fraticelli states that the origins of critical legal pluralism can be traced to both anthropological legal pluralism and Fuller and Cover's critique of legal positivism.[21] Indeed, positivism is a common concern of what Melissaris describes as postmodern legal pluralism, a subset of which is critical legal pluralism. In addition to Kleinhans and Macdonald, Melissaris places Manderson and Davies in this category as well.[22] Manderson argues in favor of a "legal chaotics" approach, which involves, *inter alia*, rejecting law as reified rules operating in jurisdictions demarcated by spatial boundaries.[23] He is also one of the few scholars to apply legal pluralism to the relationship between law and literature, for example in analyzing an instance of children's literature as a constitutional document inaugurating legal subjectivity. Legal pluralism is an essential aspect of progressing beyond the limitations of law *and* literature toward law *as* literature and literature *as* law.[24]

Critical legal pluralism, however, stands out as the most sustained postmodern theory of legal pluralism, first articulated in a seminal article by Kleinhans and Macdonald[25] and then developed by Macdonald over a number of years[26] to provide both significant theoretical refinements and applications to new areas.[27] Briefly stated, critical legal pluralism may be viewed as a response to perceived deficiencies in social-scientific/empiricist-positivist theories of legal pluralism, particularly positivism as already noted, as well as prescriptivism. The "critical" aspect of the theory is the rejection of prevailing assumptions regarding the concept of law, for example, that law can be empirically identified as a social fact. Theorists have attempted to move beyond descriptions of competing entities in jurisdictional space, however defined, and turn their attention instead to legal subjectivity.

As required for this analysis, critical legal pluralism adopts a discursive approach that emphasizes the role of narrative in creating law. Macdonald reconceptualizes law, shifting our focus from privileged texts to intra-subjective and intersubjective creation of legal knowledge. We come to understand law as "meaning, not machinery; as aspiration, not structure; as narrative, not norm; as agency, not subjectivity."[28] The most significant insights are related to the ways in which legal subjects themselves are jurisgenerative, in that they both make law and apply law that is made.[29] Legal subjects hypothesize concepts of law to which they in turn refer to constitute their legal subjectivity. They are participants, as both subject and object, in dynamic processes of creating legal meaning by acknowledging and responding to circumstances of normative heterogeneity. Jurisgenerative capacity inverts prevailing understandings of legal subjectivity, wherein people are passive legal subjects governed by exogenous legal rules. The baseline for legal legitimacy is not an *a priori* transcontextual definition but rather an individual's consensual adherence, although[30] such consent is of course a function of the context in which the individual is situated.

I should note at this point that while I wish to remain consistent in using the phrase "normative heterogeneity," this introduces a minor complication when discussing Macdonald's critical legal pluralism and Melissaris's theory of legal pluralism as definitional contextualism. The issue is perhaps more acute when referencing Melissaris, who rejects the argument that no *a priori* distinction exists between institutionalized legal discourse and other types of normative discourse, as well as the argument that our intuitive distinction between legal and non-legal normative utterances reflects limitations of language.[31] Accordingly, references to normative heterogeneity when discussing Melissaris should be interpreted as involving legal claims only, as distinguished from other types of norms. As for Macdonald and critical legal pluralism, the argument is not that no distinction exists between laws and norms but rather that law does not exist prior to its recognition as law by legal subjects themselves. On the other hand, this does not mean that whatever we consider to be law is actually law. While critical legal pluralism eschews a definitional approach, Macdonald does agree that law as a human endeavor is characterized by reference to "assumptions, modalities, procedures, and aspirations." Hypothesizing law is thus conceived as "the endeavour of symbolizing human interaction as governed by rules."[32] Accordingly, references to normative heterogeneity when discussing Macdonald should be interpreted as involving legal claims as identified by legal subjects. I draw attention to this point here in order to avoid misrepresentation or misunderstanding in regard to either Macdonald's or Melissaris's work.

In contrast to Macdonald's hermeneutic approach, for Melissaris, the objective of a theory of legal pluralism, and the test of its validity, is to provide a transcontextual definition of law that reconciles both the emancipatory potential and the regulatory necessity of normative heterogeneity. The emancipatory potential of pluralism requires a definition sufficiently open so as not to exclude plural legal communities that look and operate quite differently from paradigmatic state law. Managing normative heterogeneity, on the other hand, requires some minimal definitional criteria so that we may meaningfully distinguish between law and other forms of normativity. Without this distinction, we are unable to provide the conditions by which interperspectival communication between members of legal communities[33] can take place. Without such communication, we cannot engage in the kind of productive mutual appraisal that must take place before we attempt to reconcile competing legal claims.

What is required, in other words, is a happy medium, an agreed-upon definition of law that is transcontextual, in the sense of being able to identify plural conceptions of law as they appear in different contexts, and yet is not so devoid of objective content that we lose the ability to engage in mutual critique.[34] The result is a thin, universal definition of law that neither overdetermines nor underprescribes that which constitutes law.[35] According to Melissaris, we can define law, and thus recognize plural legal communities, as a discourse uniquely capable of both evaluating and authorizing action. This mediation between the real and the ideal is made possible by the shared normative experiences of the participants, which Melissaris defines as the common characteristic of any concept of law.[36] Inherent in this description is a procedural (but not substantive) requirement of public justification; law proceeds by way of commitment, not coercion, but in order to commit, participants must be provided with a process for assessing the legitimacy of proffered reasons for legal rules.[37]

As to the choice of critical legal pluralism over definitional contextualism, both are compelling theories that demonstrate different aspects of the three threshold requirements of discourse, narrative function, and law as alternity. Both see the emancipatory potential of a constitutive approach, which rejects an understanding of law as a unidirectional flow of authority from governing law to governed legal subjects.[38] Both analyze legal discourse in a way that provides scope for analyzing law and popular culture as mutually constitutive discourse, particularly in terms of the jurisgenerative potential of legal subjects. Macdonald's theory, however, is more promising on this point. Given the way in which Macdonald rejects definition as a means of differentiation, sufficient scope exists within critical legal pluralism to hypothesize a concept of law as narrative/*nomos*. On the other hand, given Melissaris's insistence upon definition, my conclusions are more tentative in this regard. While I discuss this more fully below, I note that Melissaris not only differentiates law from other normative orders, but also conceptualizes law as an institutionalized legal discourse.[39] This may negate the possibility of mutual constitution between discourses of law and popular culture and consign popular culture once more to the role of influence rather than authority. On the other hand, given his understandable reluctance to specify in advance how shared normative experiences, which are the foundation of law, account specifically for law's institutionalization and autonomy,[40] this is not necessarily fatal.

As for the requirement of narrative, the notable advantage of critical legal pluralism is that narrative is a functional component of the theory. Macdonald provides a succinct characterization of how we might understand law from the perspective of critical legal pluralism: law is a function of self-narration and interaction.[41] Again, while I discuss this more fully in Chapter 4 in developing the concept of the narrative/*nomos* obligational self, narrative is foregrounded as an indispensable process for creating legal knowledge, and thus how we conceive of law, our own legal subjectivity, and the nature and extent of our obligations in relations with others. Surprisingly, while Melissaris relies upon Cover as support for both contextualism and shared normative experience as a form of alternity, narrative is explicitly excluded. In responding to the ambiguity in Cover's work regarding the nature of the relationship between narrative and *nomos*, Melissaris states that the question has no relevance for his theory.[42] The manner in which Melissaris leaves open the definition of shared normative experiences does not exclude the possibility that narrative may be constitutive, but this mere possibility is not sufficient to counter critical legal pluralism's explicit reliance on narrative.

As for the requirement of alternity, Melissaris is explicit on this point, whereas Macdonald is implicit. Melissaris adopts Cover's concept of law as alternity as an important aspect of definitional contextualism. Alternity is incorporated into his explanation of shared normative experiences as involving necessary presuppositions of our ability to transform our worlds through our normative commitments. The relevance of alternity is less readily apparent in Macdonald's theory of critical legal pluralism, and I admit I may be reading creatively on this point. I locate alternity as implicit in the relationship between concepts Macdonald uses to explain the jurisgenerative process, including references to self-narration and normative evaluation.[43] I render alternity explicit by adopting a theory of narrative identity formation[44] to elaborate upon critical legal pluralism's understanding of legal subjectivity, the result being my concept of the narrative/*nomos* obligational self, described in detail in Chapter 4.

Having addressed the three requirements of discourse, narrative, and alternity, I want to return now to my comments above regarding the ability of critical legal pluralism to acknowledge the legitimacy of plural legal communities that contradict its theoretical premises. An interesting challenge would be whether a theory of legal pluralism is capable of incorporating not only plural theories of law, but also plural theories of legal pluralism. Both theories provide the necessary meta-theoretical reconciliation whereby a theory of legal pluralism must account for not only different concepts of law, but also different theories of what constitutes law. Melissaris argues that legal theory itself should be pluralistic.[45]

Macdonald provides a useful example of how a theory of critical legal pluralism would acknowledge the legitimacy of statist conceptions of law.[46] Macdonald, however, extends meta-theoretical potential to theories of legal pluralism as well. Critical legal pluralism is a hypothesis of competing legalities but also a hypothesis of competing understandings of competing legalities.[47] Ideally, legal pluralism should be capable of this type of recursive reference, that is to say, capable of acknowledging a plurality of approaches to imaging how plurality is imagined. The way critical legal pluralism resolves this additional paradox provides an interesting comment on not only the way we might conceive of law and popular culture as mutually constitutive discourse, but also our understandings of law more generally.

For Melissaris, the emancipatory potential of legal pluralism is achieved by integrating theoretical, jurisprudential, meta-theoretical, and meta-jurisprudential aspects.[48] Legal pluralism is a theory of law, but being a pluralist theory, it must also be meta-theoretical in that it must account for plural theories of law, including monist theories that would contradict the premises of legal pluralism at the meta-theoretical level. In other words, a theory of legal pluralism must provide coherent theoretical support for the validity of legal theories that potentially discredit the validity of the meta-theory of legal pluralism that seeks to validate them.[49] As discussed, Melissaris and Macdonald agree on this point.[50]

Disagreement exists, however, with respect to the significance of legal pluralism's meta-jurisprudential aspect. According to Melissaris, in providing criteria for recognizing what constitutes a plural legality, legal pluralism also implicitly or explicitly provides criteria for hierarchical relations between plural legal communities, leading to its meta-jurisprudential potential in deciding which legal order ought to prevail.[51] Melissaris is careful to indicate, however, that the ways in which this theoretical requirement can be realized is an issue that can only be worked through in the context of specific instances of conflict between plural legal communities. The task of legal theory is to provide an appropriate (and indeed the only possible) forum for the necessary interperspectival dialogue involving claims of legitimacy raised by members of plural legal communities. Macdonald, however, addresses the meta-jurisprudential aspects in the way legal subjectivity is conceived from a critical legal pluralist perspective. As Macdonald succinctly states, both law and normative heterogeneity are noumenal, not phenomenal.[52]

This is a subtle but important distinction, one that explains the differences between these two theorists in their approach to what might be called legal pluralism's end game. For Melissaris, the end game is the management of normative heterogeneity, which is the reason he adopts a definitional approach.[53] In order to resolve conflicting claims between different legal communities, we must first agree that we are indeed dealing with legitimate legal claims, which means we need to have some minimal agreement as to what constitutes law. Note this is an inquiry into the concept of law and not its substantive content. Melissaris is adamant that a transcontextual understanding of law is limited to the question of what is law and not to questions of normative validity. Claims regarding what constitutes law as a concept do involve normative aspects to the extent that law is a claim of rightness.[54] Nonetheless, normativity arises as a function of participants' beliefs and commitments, that is to say, their context-specific shared normative experiences, and thus cannot be defined in advance of their participation or without their perspective.[55] In subsequent work, he identifies as an important next step whether his theory of legal pluralism can also account for the possibility of normative coordination between diverse plural *nomoi*.[56] For now, however, his theory provides a transcontextual definition of law that enables communication sufficient to engage in mutual critique of our concepts of law but not their normative content.

For Macdonald, there is no end game other than to reconceive of both law and legal pluralism in a way that more fully accounts for the beliefs and behaviors of legal subjects themselves. Macdonald acknowledges the uncontroversial point that we do need to distinguish law from that which is not law. Otherwise, we will be unable to say anything useful that is particular to law. The reason why I refer to this as uncontroversial is because the same holds true for any topic of discussion, no matter the degree of specificity or the level of abstraction. Information is difference after all,[57] in that I need to distinguish zero from one in order to discuss either zero or one. Where Macdonald departs from Melissaris is in his argument that we can differentiate by means other than by definition.[58] As noted above, we reflect upon law when we consider "the endeavour of symbolizing human conduct and interaction as governed by rules."[59]

Thus we have progressed from a meta-theoretical potential of theories of legal pluralism that accommodate plural theories of law, including those that disavow pluralism (which is arguably implicit in the function of pluralism itself), to a meta-theoretical potential of a theory of legal pluralism that accommodates plural theories of pluralism that disavow this theory of legal pluralism. Critical legal pluralism is able to resolve this paradox by identifying our capacity to create legal meaning, rather than the legal meaning created per se, as the more relevant unit of analysis. Focusing on creation of legal meaning is the common thread that joins critical legal pluralism to hermeneutic accounts of law more generally. Indeed, Macdonald explicitly refers to Geertz' succinct and familiar characterization of law as meaning, not machinery.[60]

An element of instrumentalism is present in Melissaris's approach to law's emancipatory potential, in that a transcontextual definition of law is designed with reference to both emancipation and regulation. Arguably, emancipation is placed in the service of regulation, given that the end game is not to emancipate for its own sake but to provide conditions for managing the normative heterogeneity that is a consequence of acknowledging pluralism. In Macdonald's non-definitional approach, emancipatory potential stands on its own, at least at the theoretical level. Legal subjects do need to respond to normative heterogeneity, but emancipation extends to the manner in which they conceive not only of law but of inter-legality as well.

Appearances to the contrary, my discussion of critical legal pluralism's capacity for recursive reference is relevant for this analysis. Recursion is an important metaphor for understanding the complexity of normativity from a critical legal pluralist perspective. We hypothesize the concept of law that creates our legal subjectivity, which we have conceived in order to hypothesize a concept of law. We externalize our conceptions of legal rules so that we might refer to them and guide our behavior accordingly, which we internalize as an important aspect of our normative identity, being the normative identity we used in externalizing our conceptions of legal rules.

In re-imagining law, the movement from singularity to pluralism is a given. A more demanding challenge is to re-orient the way we think of law by setting aside a preoccupation with outcome in favor of an inquiry into our constructive capacity. When law is not distinct from culture, we no longer have a pre-legal history. We are always already situated in normative relation to each other, even as we conceive of how to explain and justify how we live in normative relation to each other. We exercise our jurisgenerative capacity when we engage in the ongoing recursive process of conception, symbolization, commitment, and behavior, always already situated in normative relations that we may or may not hypothesize as law.

The following analysis demonstrates many productive similarities between these two theoretical accounts and identifies the ways in which each could contribute a theoretical foundation for the analytical framework necessary for examining law and popular culture as mutually constitutive discourse. But the encounter and exchange between these two theories produces the additional insight that the scope of the project can include a more ambitious re-imagining of law. My objective[61] is not to define law (positivism), evaluate law (normativism), or even critique law (critical legal theory). The objective and potential of this analytical framework is to affirm an understanding of law as an ongoing process of knowledge, meaning, and commitment. I want to consider the emancipatory potential of re-imagining law in a way that focuses on our capacity for making sense of normative heterogeneity but does not prescribe either the means for resolving normative heterogeneity or the necessary outcome. If legal subjects have both the opportunity and the responsibility to conceive of law, we cannot disaggregate specific concepts of law from concepts of normative heterogeneity more generally. This is after all why Macdonald refers to both law and inter-legality as noumenal rather than phenomenal in nature.

Note that while I adopt critical legal pluralism rather than definitional contextualism as the appropriate theoretical foundation, this alone is not sufficient for developing the necessary analytical framework. In particular, the narrative aspects of the theory require further elaboration. Macdonald refers to narrative in two ways, both as a method of communicating legal meaning and as a means of constituting self-identity, although the second reference is decidedly embryonic. Also implicated in these narrative functions is an understanding of legal subjects as inherently normative, but again the discussion is not extensive.[62] Given the brevity of these and other passages, greater specificity on this topic is required. Accordingly, in Chapter 4, I elaborate upon the legal subject of critical legal pluralism with reference to cognitive and psychological theories of narrative identity formation, which produces the concept of the narrative/*nomos* obligational self. This allows me to more specifically articulate how the mutually constitutive discourse of narrative and popular culture might function to provide popular culture with legal authority.

An additional point to note is that in developing the necessary analytical framework, I do not claim that my hypothesis is either true or not true. I am following Macdonald's insistent guidance on this point, wherein he stated that the objective of his work was "to understand legal pluralism as hypotheses rather than as a claim about the true 'nature of things legal'."[63] Consider, for example, how Macdonald and Kleinhans dismiss as counterproductive attempts to ascribe to others the "burden of the qualifying adjective" when discussing law. Protagonists of exclusivity place the burden on legal pluralists to adopt qualifying adjectives, such as non-state or informal law. Legal pluralists argue that their opponents should adopt adjectives such as state law or official law in turn.[64] The verifiable truth of a definition is of less significance than identifying and understanding the ideology and objectives involved in its production.[65]

Consistent with Macdonald's guidance, my interest in developing an analytical framework is exploratory rather than programmatic. I do not dismiss the normative nature of my argument against the presumptive monopoly of state law and its analogues over the practical and signifying power of law. But the purpose of what follows is to identify explicitly my own assumptions and objectives. I am seeking to expand upon and rigorously defend my intuition that there is more to law and popular culture than reciprocal influence, and I rely upon the theoretical foundation of critical legal pluralism, elaborated with reference to the narrative/*nomos* obligational self, to support this claim.

Macdonald: knowledge and narrative

As discussed above, if I am to analyze the legal force of popular culture without rejecting the legitimacy of state law per se (as opposed to its claims of exclusivity), a discursive theory of legal pluralism is necessary, albeit not sufficient. Nonetheless, legal pluralism does provide the theoretical foundation of the analytical framework I develop in this project. In the following section, I evaluate the potential of critical legal pluralism to perform this function. Note that my intention is not to critique the efficacy of critical legal pluralism (or in the next section, definitional contextualism) in the abstract, that is to say, whether the theory provides a rigorous and defensible account of legal pluralism, with sufficient explanatory and predictive potential. Instead, I am interested in the explanatory potential of the theory relative to my own hypothesis of the mutually constitutive nature of law and popular culture discourse.

For the purposes of this project, the significance of critical legal pluralism is the manner in which legal subjectivity is hypothesized with reference to knowledge and narrative. Eschewing any concept of law as having an essence that can be defined, a critical legal pluralist hypothesis[66] directs our attention to "the endeavour of symbolizing human interaction as governed by rules."[67] Macdonald provides the explicit implications of these terms for understanding law, thus immunizing against claims of void for vagueness, at least in reference to the formulation itself.

"Endeavor" means that law is purposive and intentional; it does not happen to us but through us as we commit to its achievement. The significance of "symbolizing" is that law is a function of perception and reflection by legal subjects of that which is symbolized, as opposed to locating law in the symbols themselves. "Conduct" indicates that law requires action as well as thought, a point so significant to Cover that it forms the basis of his conception of law as alternity; the bridge from here to there is crossed not simply by belief, but also by committed behavior.[68] The implication of "interaction" is that people, not conceptual entities, create law. Law is constituted in and through our bi- and multi-lateral relationships, not by the social fields with which we might identify when engaged in these relationships. "Governance" implies that we align our intentions and actions with an external point of reference, even though the reference point is of our own creation. Finally, "rules" implies generalized norms or prescriptions that predate the human behavior being symbolized, whether these are prohibitive, permissive, or facilitative in nature.

The significance of this formulation is how it provides a non-definitional way to look for law in human belief and behavior. Law is not an object to be identified but rather a form of knowledge created and maintained by the inter- and intra-subjective narrations of legal subjects (as is explained more fully below). Not simply law abiding but also law inventing, jurisgenerative legal subjects hypothesize the law that constitutes their legal subjectivity.[69] Another aspect particularly relevant for this analysis is that Macdonald does not view legal pluralism as a claim of truth but rather as a hypothesis of how legal subjects themselves conceive of law and their own jurisgenerative potential. There is no end game, so to speak, in terms of relying upon legal pluralism as a means for reconciling normative heterogeneity. What is offered is a hypothesis of law, a viable perspective for analyzing beliefs and behaviors of people who appear to be acting from a sense of obligation.

Critical legal pluralism shifts the focus of law away from the artefacts of reified legal rules and toward the agency of legal subjects' jurisgenerative capacity.[70] This is a theme of movement from verb to noun, analogous to how Manderson uses these terms to characterize legal judgment, and justice more generally, as being experience rather than outcome.[71] Accordingly, critical legal pluralism is amenable to a project of re-imagining law as verb rather than a noun, as our capacity for creating and maintaining legal knowledge rather than the outcome to be achieved in circumstances of normative heterogeneity. Critical legal pluralism is an interpretive choice not only for legal analysts who wish to know more about law, but also for legal agents who wish to know more about their own constructive capacity.[72] Indeed, the emancipatory potential of critical legal pluralism is not a simplistic liberation from unidirectional authority but a more complex assumption of responsibility for normative choices and inevitable normative failures.

Contrast this with Melissaris, for whom the full potential of legal pluralism is realized only when a theory is able to account for, *inter alia*, pluralism's jurisprudential and meta-jurisprudential aspects.[73] This is why Melissaris focuses on the problem and requirement of definition; a fully realized theory of legal pluralism will enable mutual communication and critique between legal communities as a necessary part of reconciling emancipation and regulation. A shared, transcontextual definition of law allows participants from different *nomoi* to engage in a self-reflexive and dialogic process. An interperspectival, critical method thus provides the necessary conditions for understanding and cooperation.[74] Admittedly, this aspect reflects a dynamic process amenable to being characterized as more verb than noun in this limited and specific sense. More significant, however, is that the requirement of a transcontextual definition is in service of the outcome of legal pluralism's meta-jurisprudential potential, and thus definitional contextualism is more aptly characterized as noun rather than verb.

From the perspective of critical legal pluralism, not only is law an activity rather than an entity, but also the nature of the activity is particularly relevant. The two thematic concepts that particularly illustrate the radical nature of critical legal pluralism are knowledge and narrative. As for knowledge, legal subjects are jurisgenerative in the sense that law is not an independent social fact, an exogenous force applied to legal subjects, but rather a form of knowledge maintained by legal subjects themselves. Law, however conceived, exists as a result of our faith in its hypothesis and our participation in creating and maintaining the reality of beliefs and committed behaviors through which this hypothesis is instantiated. As noted above, the trajectory of law as meaning rather than reified rules can be traced back to Geertz,[75] particularly with reference to his characterization of law as "a distinctive manner of imagining the real."[76]

A preliminary point to note regarding narrative and meaning is that legal meaning is necessarily intra- and inter-subjective. As legal subjects, we reflect and refract the hypotheses of law in which we are currently situated, and narrative is a means by which meaning is created and communicated. The extent to which our agency is constrained is always a matter for debate,[77] but nonetheless we readily acknowledge that we do not begin with a blank slate, so to speak.[78] In addition, in order to function as law rather than simply an assertion of power, not only must one person claim that an action is justified by law, but another person must acknowledge the legitimacy of this claim, not necessarily as to substance but as to its character as law.[79] Simply stated, we can only create law in relation to others.

Within critical legal pluralism, the significance of narrative is as a means by which legal meaning is conveyed and identity is created. Recall Cover's work on the relationship between *nomos* and narrative and his argument that law does not exist apart from the narratives that instantiate a *nomos* and give meaning to legal rules.[80] Critical legal pluralism expands upon this concept by incorporating both inter- and intra-subjective communication in the constitution of legal meaning. Macdonald refers to life as a "continuing narrative of meaning,"[81] in which the stories we tell of who we are and how we came to be are infused with the normative choices we have made among the many possibilities offered to us. Thus does Macdonald describe law as a "consequence of personal narration and interaction."[82] As I discuss below, this aspect of legal subjectivity is only minimally referenced and requires further elaboration, for which I refer to cognitive and personality theories of psychology addressing narrative identity formation. Nonetheless, for now this account of narrative meaning will suffice.

As an aside, amid all this discussion of narrative and meaning, I should respond to what might be emerging as a potential objection or perhaps a hint of impatience. To understand law as knowledge/meaning does not mean that legal analysis can wander at will in the realm of abstracted belief, unbounded by the messy necessity of behavior. Normative thought is by nature aspirational, but law is also intentional in the sense that we commit ourselves to an indicated course of action. I would also be remiss if I did not include here an important caveat from Kleinhans and Macdonald, which is that they characterize their work as "a" critical legal pluralism, with the indefinite article meant to convey diverse possibilities for theorization in this area. Their own approach is predicated upon hermeneutic and narrative analysis, but they do not claim that the scope of critical legal pluralism is necessarily restricted to these aspects.[83]

Having outlined these key concepts of meaning and narrative, the following sections investigate the relevant foundational premises of critical legal pluralism. I have taken the liberty of organizing the concepts and premises in a way that makes sense for the purpose of developing an analytical framework. I am not presenting a theory of critical legal pluralism in precisely the same manner as articulated, developed, and applied by Macdonald. Nonetheless, I have taken care not to distort the meaning, thematic coherence, or significance of the theory in the process. I organize the discussion as follows: (a) Macdonald's development of critical legal pluralism as a response to problems identified with social-scientific legal pluralism and legal orthodoxy more generally; (b) rejecting a reified understanding of law as an exogenous entity; (c) inverting legal subjectivity so that the focus is on the jurisgenerative[84] capacity of legal subjects as law-creating, not simply law-obeying; and (d) locating jurisgenerative capacity in the self-narration of legal subjects.

Responding to legal orthodoxy

Macdonald developed a theory of critical legal pluralism in a manner consistent with the premises of the theory itself, in the sense of being a reflexive evaluation of the dialogic nature of law's authority.[85] Macdonald's objective was to understand legal pluralism not as an argument about the true nature of law, but rather as a hypothesis of how legal subjects themselves might conceive of law.[86] In particular, critical legal pluralism was his response to the assumption common to social-scientific theories of legal pluralism that law could be identified as a social fact. Taking note of how features of orthodox legal theory influence theories of legal pluralism, Macdonald developed critical legal pluralism in opposition to five tenets of what he referred to as orthodox, analytical legal theory,[87] or legal orthodoxy. These features were monism, centralism, positivism, prescriptivism,[88] and, more recently, chirographism.[89]

Recall the discussion in Chapter 2 regarding the persistent and unexamined assumption that a distinction necessarily exists between law and mere norms. Recall as well that I posed the question of what we might gain (and lose) by enforcing this distinction. According to Macdonald, the five tenets of legal orthodoxy represent an "exclusionary ambition"[90] to distinguish law from that which is not law, with the result being a nomopoly, or *nomos* monopoly.[91] Law's hierarchy over other norms depends not on reasoned deliberation but upon the fact of the distinction itself.

In legal analysis, this would be an unacceptable definitional defense, in that you cannot use a challenged definition to argue against challenges to the definition. For example, if your argument against same-sex marriage is that marriage is defined as a man and a woman, this would be a definitional defense. The definition of marriage as a man and a woman is precisely what is being challenged. What is required is a justification for why marriage is defined as a man and a woman. Similarly, with the distinction between law and mere norms, what is required is a justification other than simply, if we call all norms law, how we will be able to say anything meaningful about law. If the definition of law, however, includes all norms, then we would be able to say something meaningful about law.

To return to Macdonald's five tenets of legal orthodoxy and his argument regarding exclusionary ambition, law is distinguished from other types of normativity along five dimensions: (a) numerically through monism, on the basis that only one legal order can exist in a claimed jurisdictional space; (b) institutionally through centralism, on the basis that law is exclusively a result of a political state's institutional processes; (c) analytically through positivism,[92] being the belief that an *ex ante* criterion (such as the sources thesis) can be used to distinguish law from other norms; (d) ontologically through prescriptivism, on the basis that law consists of exogenous rules applied to govern the behavior of recipient legal subjects; and (e) semiotically, on the basis that legal norms can be fully expressed through words.[93]

The radical[94] nature of critical legal pluralism is in rejecting all of these assumptions of the nature of law. Compare this with social-scientific theories, which need only reject monism and are otherwise compatible with the rest of the list. Macdonald and Kleinhans have argued that the error of social-scientific legal pluralism is the persistence of state law as the paradigmatic example of what constitutes legality and thus the template for recognizing claims of legal plurality. The result is that the scope of legal pluralism is confined to state law and its analogues, with analysis directed toward identifying which of these plural legal orders can claim to govern a particular legal subject in a particular place at a particular time. In a misguided search for reified legal orders conflicting in jurisdictional space, we lose sight of the agency of legal subjects in creating and affirming the multiplicity of both their identity and their normative references.[95]

As Kleinhans and Macdonald note, we cannot understand webs of normative identity without first considering the nature and activities of those who spin the filaments.[96] Critical legal pluralism accomplishes this task by hypothesizing a different understanding of legality, which, as explained below, rejects a reified understanding of law, inverts legal subjectivity to focus on the jurisgenerative capacity of legal subjects themselves, and considers law as a function of interaction and narration, particularly self-narration. Whereas with Cover, the precise nature of the relationship between *nomos* and narrative is ambiguous, with Macdonald's critical legal pluralism, the precise nature of the operation and potential is not specified. Accordingly, I elaborate upon the narrative components of jurisgenerative capacity in Chapter 4. Suffice it to say for now that resolving the narrative/*nomos* relationship allows us to imagine law in a way that merges what Cover identified as a tragic divide between law as social meaning and law as social control.[97] We accomplish this by recognizing how jurisgenerative legal subjects do not obey law but rather commit to law. We hypothesize the concepts of law that establish our legal subjectivity when we devise the legal rules that serve as external reference points for our behavior, and when we confront circumstances of normative heterogeneity, it is our own understandings of what we are obliged to do that leads us to govern ourselves accordingly.

Rejecting reification

Law is perceived in terms of how it is conceptualized by those for whom law is a meaningful concept for understanding human behavior. Traditional understandings of law, however much they may differ in terms of theoretical perspective, nonetheless share a (perhaps unintended) conceptual commitment to reification, that is to say, an understanding of an intellectual concept as an external object. Law is understood as an externally verifiable social fact. When we are asked to identify that which we understand to be law, we refer to legal artefacts, typically those created by the state, such as constitutions, codes, legislation, and judicial decisions. By identifying law in this manner, however, we have arguably conflated symbolic expression with that which is capable of being expressed. We regard articulated legal rules, particularly those seen as originating with a political state, as constituting what is meant by law, that is to say, the normative aspects of human behavior.

Reification as a habit of speech is perhaps understandable. Bal refers to this process of creating a noun from a verb as nominalization, and notes its advantages in facilitating discussion of complex concepts. In writing this manuscript, for example, I tried to avoid nominalizing the various theoretical approaches under discussion, but could not reconcile this with a clear and concise writing style. Similarly, in my experience of teaching law I've found that nominalization facilitates learning, particularly at earlier stages in the process. The disadvantage is that over time we tend to neglect the subject of the action to which the verb initially referred. When we do not identify actions as having subjects, we do not assign responsibility for choices and consequences.[98] Instead, actions come to be seen as existing in and of themselves. This is how we come to see state law as naturalized, exogenous, and – most importantly – inevitable. If the political state is the source of law, we are confined by prescription to live under its command. But we are also relieved of responsibility for the normative failures involved. At best we may appreciate that we are in some sense indirectly responsible, given that legislators are accountable to voters, but this sense of responsibility will be tempered by whatever democratic deficits may apply.

Critical legal pluralism rejects reification, an understanding of law as a thing, in favor of understanding law as knowledge. Law is an explanation, not an artefact, a way in which we understand our beliefs, actions, and interactions as guided by rules. Our sense of obligation does not originate with the form or content of a reified legal system, the deus ex machina of a rulebook in the sky, applied to govern passive legal subjects. Obligation begins instead with the social construction of legal meaning as a form of knowledge created and maintained by legal subjects themselves. The objective is not to analyze how reified law (in either textual or institutional form) applies to abstracted legal subjects, but rather to analyze how legal subjects themselves conceive of law, and, in the process, constitute their own legal subjectivities.

Reification is a function of conceptualizing law as a social fact existing independently of legal subjects. As discussed above, Macdonald sees legal orthodoxy as mistakenly preoccupied with "delineating the legal from the non-legal – whether numerically (monism), spatially (centralism), analytically (positivism), ontologically (prescriptivism) or semiotically (chirographism)."[99] This is not to deny that human beings create law, but our legal imagination is far too circumscribed when we conceive of law as the end product of specialized methods of production. The ostensible result, at least analytically, is a form of legal purity, a clean abstraction of manifest legal rules distilled from the untidy clamor of undifferentiated human behavior. The actual result, most certainly empirically, is the instantiation of a powerful nomopoly, or *nomos* monopoly,[100] that denies the agency of legal subjects by conceiving of law strictly in prescriptivist terms.[101]

Reification excises human agency from our conception of law. Once we have created the necessary legal machinery – laws, procedures, institutions, and a cadre of specialized experts – our role as legal subjects is to submit to this machinery's operation. Legal machinery is not necessarily devoid of human presence. We do affect state law, such as by initiating law reform, but this reduces our constructive capacity to nothing more than an occasional manner of influencing law constructed by the state. Our normative aspirations are recognized as law only when mediated by institutional processes designed to identify and interpret legitimate sources of law. All other instances of normative behavior are deemed extra-legal and thus excluded from legal analysis. We assume that the entirety of our legal existence in relation to others can be expressed through a set of comprehensive, coherent rules identified by experts and based on their interpretation of artefacts originating with official sources. The legal aspect of our lives is determined not by our own understanding of interactional obligations, but in more limited terms as the application of reified rules.

Critical legal pluralism rejects a reified understanding of law as an external object, originating with the state or otherwise, the presence of which can be empirically verified. Law is not a social fact, independent of legal subjects.[102] Since law is not conceived as external to legal subjects, enquiry begins not with reified rules, but with the everyday lives of legal subjects themselves. Everyday life is a process of understanding, interpreting, and applying standards to our behavior, and of reconstituting those standards in response to interactions with others.[103] Abstract interpretation of symbolic expression cannot substitute for contextual analysis of the intersubjective experience of creating, understanding, and reacting to rules.

We may more readily acknowledge the authority of state law on its own terms, but this is a function of the resources devoted to maintaining belief in its hypothesized existence.[104] An expert opinion of what state law requires tells us very little; we can predict compliance due to the presence of enforcement mechanisms, but the meaning and significance of any rule is a function of lived experience, not a pedigree of sources of law in the abstract.[105]

When law is conceived as transactional, as a way of using norms in our interactions with others, we are more likely to understand that law cannot be equated with its artefacts, whatever their manner of expression. Symbolic notation, no matter how expertly drafted or interpreted, represents but does not displace the dynamic process of human agency in creating and reacting to rules.[106] Rejecting reification inverts legal orthodoxy's order of operations. We do not begin with identification of the rules that apply to govern a particular set of circumstances, the factual relevance of which is a function of the rules (or the sources of the rules) rather than the lived experience of legal subjects. We begin instead with an inquiry into the understandings of legal subjects themselves as they interpret and respond to a sense of obligation in their interactions with others.

We are also more likely to understand the implications of human agency with respect to the arguments made on behalf of state law, that is to say, not only its legitimacy but also its claim that only state law is law property so called. No law can compel acceptance from those who do not acknowledge its legitimacy; law can be enforced, but only power is imposed. Legitimacy is a claim that is either accepted or rejected in the course of relations between someone who claims to act as authorized by law and someone who is the recipient of such action. That a majority may accept a claim that I reject does not negate my rejection; it merely consigns me to a minority position in relation to others. If I accept the legitimacy of state law, even as I breach its provisions, then enforcement mechanisms directed toward me are indeed enforcing law. If, on the other hand, I do not accept the legitimacy of state law, then enforcement mechanisms directed toward me are enforcing, in relation to me, not law but power, even though they may at the same time be enforcing law in relation to others who accept the claim of legitimacy. State law can coerce my behavior but cannot command me to believe that which I do not believe, no more than O'Brien can command Winston to see five fingers instead of four.[107]

Inverting legal subjectivity

In a scene from *Oryx and Crake*,[108] Jimmy, the protagonist, recalls playing chess as a teenager with his friend, Glenn. At one point, Jimmy asks why they don't use a real set, meaning a chess board with actual chess pieces, instead of playing the game on a computer. Glenn agrees that the computer game is not a real set, but then neither is a plastic chess set. The real set, Glenn tells Jimmy, is in your head.

This brief conversational exchange is an apt and illustrative metaphor for the significance of the manner in which critical legal pluralism inverts a traditional understanding of legal subjectivity, wherein law is the addressor and legal subjects are mere addressees.[109] The board is not the game, nor are the chess pieces, nor even the rules of play, which would be the most familiar analogy with law. The written rules are merely a symbolic expression of the normative commitments of the players as to how they will conduct themselves when they move their chess pieces across the board. The real game is in your head, as your knowledge of the rules, and in your actions, as you commit to playing in a manner consistent with these rules. As is the case for Jimmy and Glenn playing chess, so too is the case with our experience of legal rules. They have no meaning apart from the way in which they are conceived and instantiated by legal subjects themselves.

Critical legal pluralism is a heuristic device for analyzing normativity, which means it is no different from any other legal theory in this respect. Where critical legal pluralism departs from legal orthodoxy is in its reversal of the traditional focus of inquiry. Law is not an object external to legal subjects (in textual or institutional form) but rather a form of knowledge, the result of "perception and reflection" by people in the process of acknowledging normative claims.[110] Accordingly, the objective is not to identify law and how it applies to legal subjects, but rather to analyze how human beings conceive of law, and how they use these concepts of law to constitute their legal subjectivity.[111] Our legal imagination may be focused primarily on legal rules created by the political state, but we should keep in mind that what we understand as governing us is what we conceived to govern us. Our hypothesis of the political state as a desirable and legitimate form of social organization and control explains the fact of its existence. The relationship is recursive in that law does not simply encode preexisting identity, nor does it subsequently erase resistance from those it identifies. The relationship is also social in that we reflect and refract the understandings of legality expressed by and through relations with others in what Macdonald refers to as a "collective normative field."[112]

As Kleinhans and Macdonald acknowledge, the inversion of legal subjectivity may be a radical claim, but searching for the subject of law, that person to whom all this law presumptively applies, is not confined to a theory of critical legal pluralism.[113] Schlag, for instance, argues that American legal theory is both conceptually and socially constructed so as to avoid the question of the subject in law. Law is a discourse onto itself, such that the question of who (or what) is producing law is never explicitly asked.[114] Critical legal pluralism simply locates the subject as logically prior to law, although as a matter of social relations, the relationship is reciprocal rather than linear.

If we reject reified legal rules as illusory, as a fiction derived from a habit of nominalization, then as a matter of logic, the inversion of legal subjectivity at the core of the critical legal pluralist hypothesis necessarily follows. If we accept law as meaning rather than object, where else would meaning be located other than in the beliefs and behaviors of legal subjects as they respond to circumstances of normative heterogeneity? This is not to argue that legal subjects are possessed of unrestricted agency,[115] nor is this to assume the opposite, that jurisgenerative ability eventually spirals into idiosyncratic anarchy. As I have argued elsewhere, the possibility of truly idiosyncratic behavior is incompatible with critical legal pluralism's conception of law as a function of both inter- and intra-subjective communication. Idiosyncratic anarchy is, however, compatible with the possessive individualism of a type of legal subjectivity that critical legal pluralism rejects.[116]

From Cover to Macdonald, we can follow parallel themes of both agency and obligation in the constructive abilities of legal subjects. Cover's explanation of jurisgenerative capacity is certainly less contentious; he privileges the jurispathic political state over the proliferation of law created by jurisgenerative legal subjects.[117] Recall that Cover is concerned with an undesirable bifurcation of law's function as social meaning and law's function as social control, neither of which is inconsistent with Macdonald's approach to legal subjectivity. Where Cover and Macdonald differ is not so much on jurisgenerative capacity but in Macdonald's response to the problem, so to speak, of too much law.

For Cover, the social control aspect of law cannot function in the absence of jurispathic courts. Both Cover and Melissaris, as discussed below, begin their analysis with the end game of law, that is to say, of law as the outcome of either interpretive pluralism or legal pluralism. Notwithstanding attention paid to jurisgenerative ability, when the focus is on law as an outcome, the objective of analysis is to provide a means by which this outcome can be achieved. For Cover, jurispathic state courts achieve the outcome, while for Melissaris, this is achieved in part with a transcontextual definition of law. In contrast, Macdonald begins his analysis with the subjects of law, which places the focus on the nature and capacity of legal subjectivity. The objective is not to provide a means for an outcome but a means for understanding how we make sense of our capacity for normative belief and behavior. Macdonald takes quite seriously the implications of jurisgenerative legal subjectivity. The question is not how to respond to too much law but how do legal subjects themselves understand normative heterogeneity. They may understand heterogeneity as too much law, but this is not the only alternative.

While not an argument advanced by Macdonald, critical legal pluralism arguably merges what Cover has identified as bifurcated functions of social meaning and social control. From a critical legal pluralist perspective, jurisgenerative capacity is not simply norm-making that precedes state recognition but the capacity to create state law and non-state law alike. To understand how this merges social meaning and social control, consider the following. Assume without deciding that law is indeed an exogenous entity; the fundamental insight of critical legal pluralism is that the fact of law as an exogenous entity is derived not from empirical observation, however this may be conceived, but from the creative capacity of legal subjects. Legal subjects hypothesize law's existence, and as those who commit to its belief confirm the hypothesis of law, its continued existence as a means of social ordering is assured. As Scarry reminds us, everything is first made up before it is made real.[118] Legal rules are imagined, expressed, affirmed, and denied in the beliefs and behaviors of legal subjects. Accordingly, belief in the obligational nature of legal rules by legal subjects precedes and provides their obligational force.[119] Even if we hypothesize the converse of this order of operations, that is to say, if we hypothesize law as the addressor and ourselves as the addressees, this order of operations (belief precedes obligation) allows for this apparently contradictory hypothesis to be affirmed.

If we reject the premise that law exists outside and apart from legal subjects, other than in the illustrative exercise above, we can understand the apparent paradox whereby critical legal pluralism conceives of legal subjects as both subjects and objects of legal knowledge, as both creators of legal rules and followers of legal rules created. As legal subjects, understood always as plural rather than singular selves, we are situated simultaneously within a multiplicity of discourse, projecting our own understandings of law while simultaneously reflecting and refracting the projected understandings of other plural selves.[120] Through this inter- and intra-subjective communication, we hypothesize concepts of law, including those that inaugurate our legal subjectivity and our relationship to legal rules. Our acts of obligation do not originate with the form or content of a reified legal system, the *deus ex machina* of a rulebook in the sky, but with the psychic and social construction of legal meaning. Critical legal pluralism is thus able to acknowledge and pluralize Cover's function of law as social meaning without contradicting his function of law as social control.

The emancipatory potential of inverting legal subjectivity is evident in the implications for how we understand agency in making and being made by the legal rules to which we refer to govern our behavior.[121] The arguably prevailing view is that our legal subjectivity is conferred upon us by a particular legal order. Privileged as we are by our *de jure* status as legal subjects, we are *de facto* objects to which law applies. We are the recipients, passive or otherwise, of the application of law; quite literally, we are subject to law[122] Critical legal pluralism reverses this order of operations by hypothesizing law as legal knowledge rather than external object. As Macdonald argues, law does not create legal subjects; legal subjectivity is instead a creation of legal subjects themselves. If law is understood not as an object but as the knowledge we have of what legality means, then human beings as "believers and behavers" of law are both *de jure* and *de facto* legal subjects.

The operation is reciprocal rather than linear, in that we are always already in a normative universe that conditions how we conceive of law. But legal subjectivity does not self-identify any more than does gender, nationality, or any other number of identities we conceive to make sense of ourselves and relations with others. Relations of discourse produce the intra- and inter-subjective creation of meaning that is legal knowledge, and through this knowledge we constitute ourselves as legal subjects. This is not to remark upon the characteristics of the discourse or to say that the nature of the identity is not contested. Nor is this to assert that either intra- or inter-subjective communication is necessarily egalitarian.[123] This is only to say that when we hypothesize legal knowledge, we hypothesize as part of that knowledge our own status as legal subjects, and as legal subjects, we hypothesize our obligations as part of legal knowledge.

By inverting traditional understandings of legal subjectivity, critical legal pluralism reinvests legal subjects with agency. Within legal orthodoxy, the normative force of a legal rule is a function of its pedigree, not the significance given to the rule by the subjects to whom the rule purportedly applies. In contrast, critical legal pluralism rejects the premise that the normative force of rules can be analyzed in the abstract, without reference to the relevance these rules are accorded by legal subjects in specific contexts. Recall the analogy above regarding where the game of chess exists; Macdonald and Sandomierski use the analogy of technical measurements to illustrate this point. Kilograms, meters, and liters are symbolic expressions of measurement, but they also function as norms. We judge weight, distance, and volume with reference to these standards, but what gives these standards normative force is not their articulation by standards organizations, but the extent to which they are actually used in the act of measuring.[124]

In other words, simply classifying a norm as an official source of law provides no definitive information as to how or indeed whether this norm actually guides human behavior. Relevance cannot be determined in the abstract but only as a function of the lived experience of legal subjectivity. Law is instantiated in actions, not official sources, as acts of commitment or rejection by legal subjects in response to a range and variety of explicit and implicit claims of authority.[125] Legal inquiry thus begins not with taxonomy of official sources but with an open-ended inquiry into the way in which legal subjects use various standards as reference points for their behavior.[126]

Reconceiving legal subjectivity examines law from the perspective of the legal subject "looking out" so to speak, rather than from the perspective of an external law "looking in" at human behavior in order to apply the appropriate rule. Although these spatial metaphors are troublesome in that they appear to refer to a unitary and essential self, metaphors are nonetheless helpful as a means of associational knowledge, and in this case for communicating that which can be difficult to express. At any given time, our normative framework is composed not of reified legal rules but by interaction and communication involving multiple claims, each claim advancing an argument that one or more particular rules should govern our behavior. We construct our own legal subjectivity, as well as our understanding of law, as we evaluate claims of legal relevance and choose those that apply to bind ourselves by law.

Law may at times be expressed in unilateral terms, as in the situation where a legal expert interprets texts to determine how state law should apply to legal subjects. But despite how we conceive of the interpretive exercise, law actually cannot (and does not) operate unilaterally. Law cannot emerge from a claim of law alone, no matter how powerful the source may be. The claim must be accepted in order to constitute law.[127] From this perspective, we can more readily appreciate the agency of legal subjects as something more than a limited decision to obey or disobey expert pronouncements of law based on a concept of official sources. Arguably, we are indeed more likely to accord significance to claims advanced by the state and may readily identify state law as the only "real" law. What this indicates, however, is not the definitive monopoly of state law but rather the success achieved by advocates of this concept in advancing their claims of exclusivity.[128]

We may organize our expectations accordingly when we accept claims that official sources of state law are applicable, but state law is not a voice of legal conscience sitting on our shoulder, whispering in our ears as we go about our lives. In some cases, we may take part in normative interactions to which state law purports to apply, but its significance is unknown to us. For example, disagreements in interpersonal relationships may only become a problem of state law when one of the parties decides to contact a lawyer for advice concerning its resolution. If we consult instead our friends and family for advice, the problem may well be resolved without reference to state legal rules. In other cases, we may be involved in normative circumstances where state law makes no claim yet mistakenly assume its application. For example, we may be living in conjugal circumstances we think are legally binding only to find out they are not recognized by state law in the event of relationship breakdown. In either case, we act in accordance with our assessment in particular circumstances of the relevance of normative claims of which we have taken note.

This is not to say that a critical legal pluralist account of law is an invitation to chaos in the sense that legal subjects will use their creative capacity to authorize their own behaviors in ways that make them unaccountable to others. Law understood with reference to jurisgenerative legal subjectivity actually involves far more responsibility than command-and-control models of normative authority such as the prevailing concept of state law.[129] Legal[130] subjects cannot avoid responsibility for creating legal meaning by delegating this task to a reified legal order, thus absolving themselves of the consequences. Instead, legal subjects must assume for themselves the task of normative evaluation, in effect an endless process of evaluating their own behavior. As legal subjects, our conceptions and understandings are necessarily affected by the hypotheses of law we inherit, but we shape and reformulate these hypotheses in turn, communicating them to others as part of the circulation of legal meaning.[131]

Understanding the jurisgenerative capacity of legal subjectivity is an important aspect of critical legal pluralism. But we leave the task unfinished if we leave off here. The next step is to ask ourselves, what are our normative reference points, and where do they originate? Unlike a more traditional legal analysis, we are not confined to codes, legislation, cases, and commentary, authored and interpreted by a limited number of experts, with reference to a narrow band of acceptable terminologies and methodologies. Instead, we are able to contemplate and investigate any and all cultural materials that may constitute (and be constituted by) our normative beliefs and behaviors. In doing so, we may come to the conclusion that the most influential normative reference points are unlikely to be those symbolized in official legal artefacts.[132] And in turn, we would then ask ourselves, how might other aspects of cultural legal authority be imagined and expressed? While Macdonald's theory of critical legal pluralism requires further elaboration on this point, as discussed below, legal meaning from this perspective is a function of, *inter alia*, cultural narratives. When this function is more fully articulated, the result is to make explicit what Cover left ambiguous, being the relationship between narrative and *nomos*.

Narration, interaction, and nomos

As noted in the introduction to this section, a particularly relevant aspect of critical legal pluralism is the use of narrative as a functional component of jurisgenerative ability,[133] although more specific elaboration on this point as required is provided in Chapter 4. As jurisgenerative legal subjects, we participate in normative communities created by our own narratives. Constituting the circumstances of law is not a process whereby abstract legal rules are identified and then applied by legal officials to legal subjects. Instead, we begin to constitute law when we evaluate the many possible normative alternatives for the ways in which we might live in this world. This is a world we seek to understand, as we seek to understand ourselves, through the operation of narrative.

Stated in its most succinct form, Macdonald describes law as a "consequence of personal narration and interaction."[134] In rejecting a reified understanding of law in favor of a hypothesis of law as legal knowledge created and maintained by legal subjects themselves, we can begin to understand the potential of critical legal pluralism for radically re-imagining law and popular culture. Narrative is integral to jurisgenerative capacity in two ways. The first is as a means for communicating legal meaning.[135] The second, albeit only briefly referenced, is as a means of constituting a legal subject's self-identity.[136] Taken together, these two aspects of narrative explain how legal subjects, multiply identified, engage in creating legal knowledge, and thus the reality that is law, through inter- and intra-subjective narrative communication. Relations with others, including our other selves, are inherently normative in nature, presenting as they do different possibilities and choices for how we want to live in this world in relation to others.[137]

With its emphasis on narrative as a means for communicating legal meaning, and thus constituting legal reality, and to a lesser extent as a means for constituting an inherently normative self-identity, critical legal pluralism in some respects could be seen as continuing the conversation begun by Cover regarding the relationship between *nomos* and narrative. Cover argued that law and narrative are inseparable; law does not exist apart from the narratives that provide meaning and justification. Furthermore, law is aspirational, an alternity that links the shortcomings of our present reality to the preferences of our imagined alternatives. These two states of affairs attain normative significance through the operation of narrative.[138]

According to Macdonald, narrative is the means by which we communicate and commit to legal knowledge.[139] We inherit communal hypotheses of institutions such as the political state, law, and society, which we reflect and refract in our communications with others. Over time, we are able to shape the hypothesis of institutions that have shaped us. While changes might be imperceptible in the moment, they become evident over time. Legal reality is thus created through narrative communication, as we circulate various claims of legal meaning, and through narrative identity, in the way we narrate our own, inherently normative, self-understandings.

Critical legal pluralism, while emphasizing the significance of narrative, is nonetheless distinct from Cover's understanding of diverse *nomoi* that are eventually and inevitably incorporated into state law.[140] Macdonald argues against prescriptivist legal theories as failing to attend to the jurisgenerative capacity of legal subjects, whether toward state law or other plural legal communities. The legitimacy of law is located in reciprocal narrations between legal subjects and the concepts of legality they narrate, and by which legal subjects are narrated in turn. Law is a reciprocal construction by and among legal subjects, acting through "the momentary configuration and momentary narration of imposed, inherited and chosen institutions."[141]

Admittedly, Macdonald does not provide extensive argument to support these two conceptions of *nomos* and narrative, being narrative as a means of communication and narrative as a means of identity. In particular, while Kleinhans and Macdonald do refer in passing to the concept of self-narration,[142] Kleinhans is perhaps more explicit in arguing that "[legal] subjectivity is best understood through the lens of narrative."[143] Accordingly, I take the liberty of more fully developing this aspect of critical legal pluralism with reference to cognitive and psychological theories of narrative identity formation. Briefly stated, we constitute our subjective identities through a process of telling stories to explain "who and what we are, what's happened, and why we're doing what we're doing."[144] In Chapter 4, I draw upon the work of Bruner and McAdams to elaborate upon the jurisgenerative legal subject of critical legal pluralism with reference to what I refer to as the narrative/*nomos* obligational self. Our identity, the way we conceive of ourselves as selves (understood always as multiply identifying rather than essential and unitary), is a function of narrative communication and narrative identity formation. Not only do we make sense of our experiences based on the ways in which we narrate the stories of our lives, but also we are always in the process of becoming the person in the stories we narrate.[145]

If we conceive of legal subjectivity as a function of a psychological process of self-narration, then the selves that we narrate are inherently and necessarily normative. Questions of obligation cannot be disaggregated from questions of identity; when I ask myself, what kind of person am I, I am also asking myself, what am I obliged to do? With the concept of the narrative/*nomos* obligational self, I am able to provide a specific hypothesis of popular culture as legal authority, one that does not rely on processes of reciprocal influence or an unspecified operation of a web of cultural/legal authority. When we understand legal subjectivity as a function of a psychological process of narrative identity formation, taking place in a social context where meaning is also communicated by narrative, we understand the significance of narrative/normative legal subjectivity rather than reified rules as the origin of normative authority.[146] Our capacity to create legal meaning is a function of our ability, in narrating our inherently normative selves, to commit to a narrative communication of legal meaning we find persuasive.

As a concluding point, I would like to emphasize that hypothesizing jurisgenerative capacity with respect to the agency of legal subjects in creating and maintaining legal knowledge is not an exercise in misguided utopian thinking. Theoretical projects of reconceiving legal subjectivity, by focusing on emancipatory potential, do not as a result ignore relations of dominance and subjugation, differing capacities for jurisgenerative ability, constraints on imagination, or other factors. Macdonald recognizes this when he acknowledges that agency exists within relations of power and dominance and that legal subjects do not hypothesize legal relations independently of the social structures in which they are embedded.[147] The emancipatory potential of critical legal pluralism confers a corresponding burden of responsibility upon legal subjects in relations with others, one that has previously been assigned for better and worse to the political state. To impose legal rules on those not involved in the process of reciprocal construction, whether through obedience or transgression, is an exercise in power, not law.[148]

Melissaris: shared normative experience

Recall that for the purposes of this project, the most significant relevance of critical legal pluralism is the manner in which legal subjectivity is hypothesized with reference to knowledge and narrative. As I explain in this section, the most significant relevance of definitional contextualism is Melissaris's conception of shared normative experience.[149] Melissaris argues that the unique nature of legal discourse is the ability to mediate between the real and ideal by evaluating and authorizing action. In Cover's terms, this is law as alternity, acting as a bridge between our present reality and our imagined future. Participants in legal discourse presuppose the ability to merge fact and norm as required to transform word into deed and deed into word. The intelligibility of this process relies upon the participants' often tacit normative understandings of their world and their relations to others.

This is in contrast to the mistaken assumption, typically operational in state law, that facts and norms are distinct and self-contained categories. A closer examination of the pragmatics of legal discourse reveals that legal norms are always already infused with the factual content of participants' shared relational experiences of transforming their world through their normative commitments. This is why the concept of shared normative experience provides such a compelling entry point for analyzing the mutually constitutive nature of law and popular culture discourse. Law does not develop in isolation from participants' normative experiences of the world. Rather, law is actually constituted by these shared normative experiences, which are inescapably an aspect of culture.[150]

As noted in Chapter 2, the potential of either theory cannot be assessed adequately in the abstract. Only by examining these theories in relation to each other can we appreciate the implications of definition as a fundamental distinction between what are otherwise fairly complementary approaches to the emancipatory potential of jurisgenerative legal subjects. Significantly, the question of definition has both informed and confirmed my characterization of a re-imagined plural legality of popular culture as an orientation away from law as noun and toward law as verb. I want to emphasize legal subjects' capacity for knowledge and meaning, and resist a pluralist tendency to focus on the correct and/or possible outcomes of normative heterogeneity.

Melissaris is explicit in stating that his objective is not only to understand legality, which necessarily entails legal pluralism, but also to establish conditions under which meaningful and non-hegemonic communication between plural legal communities can take place.[151] In other words, his theory of legal pluralism (and legal theory more generally, given that all legal theory should be plural)[152] has an end game. Note that Melissaris does not offer a universal definition of law as a blueprint for managing conflict from the internal perspective of legal communities. This would reduce our concept of law to nothing more than the application of force, a negative understanding of law that Melissaris rejects. As Melissaris notes, with reference to Cover, a predominantly closed institutional legal order such as state law incorporates the specific normative commitments of its participants, and thus cannot avoid the jurispathic effect that follows when considering external legal claims. In cases of conflict, state law will characterize these external legal claims as either permitted exceptions or prohibited transgressions.[153] By focusing on how state law responds to external legal claims, we lose sense of a more emancipatory sense of law as a medium for confirming agreement and cooperation among plural legal communities. Even though disagreement is often present, inter-legality is not limited to conflict, and conflict is not inevitable.[154]

Instead, the meta-jurisprudential potential of legal pluralism is more fully realized by attempting to transcend the limitations of externalist and internist perspectives. Accordingly, Melissaris provides a definition of law not as a realist description, nor even a strong claim of truth,[155] but rather as a universalist claim raised in the process of an inquiry into what constitutes law.[156] Agreement on a universal definition of law, however plural its contextualizations, is what allows for meaningful communication between diverse legal communities. We cannot talk about anything, including law, without some common understanding of what constitutes the subject matter of our discussion. Nor can we substitute expert legal culture for accounts of law as experienced and communicated by the participants themselves.[157]

A certain conceptual similarity exists between Melissaris's rejection of experts in favor of participation by members of legal communities and Manderson's characterization of justice as correction. According to Manderson, the inherent imperfection of justice creates a requirement that reasons be communicated to non-expert members of society. Circulation and critique of reasons for decision involves community, law, and legal experts in a participatory social discourse, the democracy of which provides legitimacy to law.[158] Melissaris similarly argues that law's legitimacy is not a function of the authority of legal officials but rather the experienced normative world of participants in a *nomos*. This is why Melissaris seeks to displace the usual privileged position of legal experts for articulating and critiquing plural law. Instead, Melissaris advocates a process whereby participants engage in open, interperspectival dialogue that allows for mutual understanding and critique, albeit in a political rather than legal forum.

For Melissaris, the exceptional value of legal pluralism is its multifaceted nature composed of a legal theory of what is law, a jurisprudence dealing with normative claims, a meta-theory of plural understandings of law, and a meta-jurisprudence that addresses which plural legal order should prevail.[159] Prevailing theories of legal pluralism, which do not merge these aspects, fail to achieve legal pluralism's potential for reconciling diversity with order.[160] This is why Melissaris emphasizes the significance of interperspectival dialogue, the possibility of which is predicated upon a transcontextual concept of law, which is contextualized in plural legal communities. This is also why I conclude that definitional contextualism, being focused on outcome more than capacity, is more aptly characterized as an orientation toward plural law as noun rather than verb.

I acknowledge that a transcontextual concept of law is developed precisely so that members of plural legal communities can engage in processes of interperspectival dialogue. This does appear to indicate that definitional contextualism, being concerned with process, is oriented more toward law as verb than law as noun. Nonetheless, both the transcontextual definition of law and the recommendation of interperspectival dialogue are developed in service of outcome, which is law as noun, not verb. The objective is to realize the full, meta-jurisprudential potential of legal pluralism, even though the implications of dialogue between legal communities cannot be determined in advance.[161] This is evidenced by the way Melissaris begins *Ubiquitous Law* with a paradigmatic pluralist conflict of concerns that Sharia law is threatening the exclusive and appropriate authority of England's state law.[162] As Melissaris notes, once we reject the monist assumption that the political state is the only valid legal authority (if it is indeed valid),[163] we will need to address the problem of how to manage interaction between plural legal communities.

And thus from the first introduction, the focus is on outcome as the end game of law. Theoretical approaches to legal pluralism are limited precisely because problems of perspective negate the possibility of meaningful and productive communication between legal communities. Empiricist-positivist theories err to the extent that context-specific understandings of what constitutes law are adopted as criteria for acknowledging the legitimacy of claims of legal pluralism. Postmodern theories, on the other hand, err by rejecting the necessity of definitional criteria and thus cannot distinguish law from other types of normative orders. This lack of specificity undermines the purpose of pluralist legal theory. We cannot evaluate legal claims in the midst of normative heterogeneity, as distinguished from mere normative claims, unless we agree on at least some minimum requirements for what constitutes law. The solution to these problems of too much and too little perspective, and the path to legal pluralism's meta-jurisprudential potential, is to develop a transcontextual definition of law, one that does not overdetermine what constitutes law, yet at the same time does not underdetermine questions of conceptual legitimacy.[164]

Melissaris locates the theoretical basis for a transcontextual definition of law in Cover's work on *nomos* and narrative.[165] While Melissaris adopts Cover's concept of alternity,[166] he does not incorporate narrative in any way with respect to the jurisgenerative capacity of legal subjects. The significance of this will be discussed at the end of this section. Cover provides support for conceiving of legal pluralism as contextualization of a thin, universal sense of law, based on the normative commitments and experiences of the participants, as well as the concept of alternity, wherein law is understood as the bridge between the present real and future ideal. The imagined ideal future is achieved by mediating among the normative commitments of the participants and in turn by participants acting upon these commitments.[167] Each diverse *nomoi* is a contextualized instantiation of this bedrock concept of legality, being the participants' belief in their ability to transform their world through their normative commitments.

Having relied on Cover's political liberalism to hypothesize legal pluralism as contextualizations of a thin, universal concept of law, Melissaris then turns to discourse and speech act theory to more specifically define this concept of law as institutionalized legal discourse, unique and distinct from other forms of discourse, as well as law's normative and factual aspects. He starts with the pragmatics of state law, since any attempt to develop a transcontextual definition necessarily begins by offering our own experience as an invitation to interperspectival dialogue with members of other legal communities. The unique claim of legal discourse is its ability to mediate, with reference to Cover's alternity, between the real and ideal by evaluating and authorizing action. Participants necessarily presuppose, with reference to their shared normative commitments, the relationships between norms and facts that make this mediation possible.

Specifying the conditions for applying norms establishes the boundaries of institutional legal discourse; it is what makes law recognizable as law in plural contexts. Accordingly, Melissaris identifies these shared normative experiences as the basis of a universal concept of law. The result is an appropriately transcontextual definition of law. With reference to alternity, legal discourse is unique in its ability to mediate between the real and ideal by linking norm and fact, a relationship of mutual constitution based on the shared normative experiences of the participants. As a result, legal discourse is able to function as alternity, mediating between real and ideal by both evaluating and authorizing action.[168] In subsequent analysis, Melissaris expands upon this definition to argue for an inherent procedural requirement of public justification; law is not legitimate unless participants in a legal community recognize and acknowledge the binding nature of a legal rule, and accept the reasons given that justify the rule. Thus, public procedures are required pursuant to which participants can exchange views and reach agreement.[169]

Note that the transcontextual definition of law is *prima facie* rather than final, as Melissaris acknowledges that all concepts are subject to revision during the process of application.[170] A *prima facie* definition, however, is both necessary and sufficient to provide the conditions for what Melissaris refers to as interperspectival dialogue and mutual critique (including self-critique) between participants (rather than experts) in plural legal communities. Since shared normative experiences are the definitive criterion of a universal concept of law, only participants themselves can communicate these. Meaningful and productive interperspectival dialogue thus overcomes the persistent problems of trying to address inter-legality through internal perspectives. Legal experts can no longer assume a privileged position as objective interlocutors.[171]

As with my analysis of Macdonald's work, I am guided by my own requirements in selecting and arranging the relevant premises of Melissaris's theory of definitional contextualism, once again taking care not to distort the meaning of the work. I have organized the discussion as follows: (a) Melissaris's development of pluralism as contextualism, with reference to Cover, alternity, and the committed beliefs of participants in a *nomos*; (b) shared normative experience as the common basis of plural concepts of law, which accounts for the institutionalization and differentiation of legal discourse; (c) the necessity of interperspectival legal theory as a political rather than legal forum capable of accommodating dialogue and critique between participants of plural legal communities; and (d) the inescapable nature of legality, not as a relationship of power imposed upon legal subjects, but as an acknowledgment that rule-following is a central aspect of human nature.

Pluralism as definitional contextualism

Melissaris is motivated to develop a transcontextual definition of law not only as a necessary aspect of a pluralist account of law, but also in response to persistent methodological deficiencies he identifies in both conventional legal theory as well as theories of legal pluralism. Thus his objections apply not only to Hart's positivism, Dworkin's interpretivism, and critical legal theory, but also to empiricist-positivist theories of legal pluralism. All provide context-specific perspectives that cannot account for the diversity of plural law.[172] Postmodern theories of legal pluralism avoid the limitations of an internal perspective on law by attempting to define law in a-contextual terms. This results, however, in vague overgeneralization that subsumes all types of normativity under the label of law. In every case, the meta-jurisprudential potential of legal pluralism, which is to provide the conditions for meaningful dialogue between members of diverse legal communities, is precluded by deficiencies of definition.

Since my analysis begins with the assumption that legal pluralism is the necessary theoretical perspective for this project, I do not address Melissaris's arguments with respect to methodological shortcomings of positivism, normativism, or critical legal theory. Nor do I address Melissaris's objections to empiricist-positivist theories of legal pluralism, wherein he argues that despite claims of plurality, such theories nonetheless depend on context-specific criteria for identifying legal systems. Kleinhans and Macdonald provide similar arguments in rejecting what they refer to as social-scientific legal pluralism.[173] I do address at the end of this section, however, Melissaris's rejection of postmodern theories of legal pluralism, including Macdonald's critical legal pluralism, on the grounds that these theories presumably abandon the possibility of differentiating law from other normative orders. For now, I would simply bracket the question, since I do not disagree with the need for differentiation. I do disagree with the claim that the only way we can differentiate is by definition, specifically a definition that not only distinguishes normative from non-normative social practices, but also draws distinctions between normative practices themselves. This approach first assumes what must be decided, which is that a distinction does exist between law and other norms, and then further assumes that differentiation between law and norms must proceed by way of definition.

Nonetheless, for Melissaris the lack of differentiation by definition is a fatal deficiency. The validity of legal pluralism depends on whether "it is possible to formulate . . . a trans-contextual, trans-epochal sense of law . . ."[174] Whereas we might describe the entry points into Macdonald's critical legal pluralism as knowledge and narrative, the entry points for Melissaris's theory of ubiquitous law are failures of perspective and definition in current legal theory, including legal pluralism, which preclude the possibility of answering the significant and ontological question of what is law. A theory of legal pluralism will succeed only to the extent that it can provide a universal definition accounting for both the factual and normative aspects of law.[175] An appropriate definition is therefore a question of balance between description and normative critique. We need to be able to describe the fact of law so that it can be recognized in diverse legal communities. We also need, however, to be able to engage in critique, including self-critique, among members of plural legal communities. Absent this evaluative aspect, normative heterogeneity collapses into "perpetual conflict and normative meaninglessness."[176]

The challenge of producing a transcontextual definition of law is to provide sufficient specificity so that we are able to engage in mutual critique regarding plural claims of law, and yet not so specific that one particular conception of law overdetermines what constitutes law, and thus fails to acknowledge the diversity that constitutes legal pluralism. Thus critical legal pluralism, for example, by failing to differentiate law from other normative orders, cannot provide the necessary conditions for fostering communication and understanding between diverse plural legal communities.[177] As I argue below, I believe Melissaris is mistaken in his claim that critical legal pluralism is not properly pluralistic because it lacks an *a priori* definition of law. For now, I focus on how Melissaris establishes the necessity and nature of a transcontextual definition of law.

Melissaris begins with theoretical support from Cover's work on the relationship between *nomos* and narrative, and how this relates to the possibility of reconciling diversity with universality. First, Melissaris acknowledges (but does not accept) that Cover could be understood as adopting interpretive as opposed to legal pluralism, since the role of jurispathic state courts is to maintain law as a means of social control. Cover identifies law as a consequence of how narrative, normative belief, interpretation, and normative commitment (behavior) operate in a particular community. Given the significance of narrative context and social commitment, what constitutes law can only be determined with reference to the shared experiences of a particular community. As such, the concept of law would be context-specific, tied to a particular normative community, and thus would have much in common with the postmodern theories of legal pluralism that Melissaris discredits.[178]

As Melissaris argues, however, if Cover were simply an interpretive pluralist, he would not characterize jurispathic state courts as responding to a problem of too much law.[179] And indeed the idea of jurispathic state courts responding to legal excess is something we can identify in Cover's conclusion regarding an unfortunate bifurcation between law as social meaning and law as social control.[180] What distinguishes Cover from interpretive pluralists is his conclusion that interpretive conflicts cannot be resolved from within a *nomos*, whether this is the state or any other normative community. The particularity of how communities conceive of law means that various legal systems are incommensurable at a maximalist level, that is to say, the thick account of law as determined by the experiences of participants in a normative community. This thick concept of law means that the state is inevitably jurispathic, although a sense of failure with respect to law's potential accompanies this realization.[181]

As to the possibility of meaningful communication and cooperation between jurisgenerative legal communities, Melissaris admits his reading on Cover is somewhat creative on this point. Cover is committed to constitutionalism as a process that legitimizes not only state law, but also other social movements and communities, albeit not within the context of an established legal system. As Melissaris notes, plural legal claims in this context can be accommodated as exceptions or prohibited as transgressions, but they cannot thrive as the jurisgenerative origins of a new *nomos* within an existing legal order. Cover's account of the jurispathic tendencies of state courts does indicate that we need to reject institutionalized contexts as a potential site for pluralities of jurisgenerative activity. But he can also be read as acknowledging the potential for meaningful communication between diverse *nomoi*. His support of constitutionalism can be read as support for universal values that animate a constitution, as opposed to the way these values are contextually instantiated in any particular legal communities. Meaningful communication between members of plural legal communities is possible, albeit in a political rather than legal context.[182]

Cover's political liberalism is thus the point of departure for Melissaris's account of diverse *nomoi* as contextualizations of a universal concept of law, instantiated by participants' specific normative commitments. The advantage of this approach is the ability to deal with incommensurable legal systems on their own terms while still maintaining the possibility of developing a universal concept of law with both ontological and normative aspects.[183] Providing a thin, universal concept of law is a necessary precondition for engaging in legal analysis. Cover's argument that law can only be determined with reference to the normative background and commitment of a particular legal community suggests a contextual instantiation of this universal concept.[184] What participants of diverse *nomoi* have in common is an understanding of law, based on the concept of alternity, as their ability to shape their world through mediation of their shared normative commitments and their decisions to act on these commitments. Each diverse *nomoi* is a contextualized instantiation of this common understanding. Accordingly, Melissaris interprets Cover as offering a qualified contextualism, in which plural legal communities are "contextualizations of a universal sense of law in light of the participants' real commitments and normative experiences."[185] Outside the coercive power of the state, encounter between participants of plural *nomoi* can be cooperative rather than antagonistic.[186]

Note that while Melissaris elaborates upon aspects of Cover's work to develop law as definitional contextualism, he assigns a constitutive function to alternity but not to narrative. Cover is somewhat ambiguous in setting out the relationship between *nomos* and narrative, at times indicating that *nomos* constitutes narrative, while at others times indicating a less constitutive relationship wherein narrative merely reveal *nomos*. Melissaris takes note of this ambiguity but brackets the question as irrelevant to his theoretical objective of developing a transcontextual definition of law. He is not adamant on the point but does state he is inclined toward the view that narratives embody and reveal but do not create *nomos*.[187] I discuss the implications of this at the end of this section when evaluating the scope of definitional contextualism for conceiving of law and popular culture as mutually constitutive discourse.

Differentiated legal discourse

Melissaris locates in Cover's political liberalism an understanding of legal pluralism as contextualization of a universal concept of law. Participants in diverse legal communities share at the very least a common understanding of law as alternity, as a bridge from the real to the ideal. When law is understood as a bridge from present circumstances to a preferred and imagined future, participants can rely upon law to shape their world as they mediate among their normative commitments and act upon them accordingly. Where legal communities differ is in how these shared normative commitments are applied. To provide more specific content for this universal concept, Melissaris necessarily begins with our own experience of state law not to raise false claims of universality but rather as a first move toward interperspectival enquiry, communication, and critique.[188] According to Melissaris, with reference to Cover, legal discourse is predicated on participants' shared normative understanding of the world. These are the fundamental assumptions necessary to make communication within the discourse intelligible. They are also the means by which the discourse is institutionalized, given that deviations from these assumptions would not be acknowledged as part of legal discourse.[189]

To explain in more detail (although only to the extent necessary for this analysis), Melissaris argues that in legal discourse, constative and performative utterances are merged. Performative utterances, such as "I promise" or "You are at fault" are meaningful only in the context of implicit constative utterances about extra-discursive facts. These so-called first-order assumptions in turn depend upon second-order assumptions about the appropriate way to link facts and norms. In other words, participants must be able to assume the felicity of the normative significance of general statements about the world. Taken together, this creates the merging of performative and constative utterances that give rise to law. The necessary assumptions do not concern the subject matter under consideration but rather incorporate participants' shared perceptions of what is taking place when engaged in legal discourse.[190]

From this analysis of legal discourse in terms of speech acts, and building further upon Cover's work, an understanding of institutionalized legal discourse emerges. The unique nature of legal discourse is its claim to be able to operate, with reference to Cover, as alternity, to mediate between our present real and future ideal by evaluating and authorizing action. The possibility of this mediation, however, presupposes our ability to merge facts and norms in a meaningful way. Linking norms with material facts is not a logical process of induction or deduction. We are able to bridge the gaps between fact and norm, between word and deed, because we can rely among ourselves on common understandings based on our shared normative experiences. "Shared normative experience" is the phrase Melissaris uses to refer to the way we normatively understand ourselves in our environment in relation to others. The necessary assumptions upon which legal discourse is predicated reference the way we experience with others our ability to consider ourselves bound by law and to transform the world accordingly. Our shared normative experiences define the boundaries of institutionalized legal discourse, in the sense of demarcating limits for intelligible communication. The utterances within institutionalized legal discourse can always be traced back to these fundamental presuppositions.[191]

To explain this in more detail, participant's shared normative experiences refer to the possibility of transforming word into deed, and deed into word, in specific circumstances. In terms of word to deed, Melissaris uses the example of criminal law sentencing to illustrate this point. In moving from word to deed, what is implied in a performative statement such as "You are sentenced to ten years" is that an appropriate method exists for converting the norm into action. Moving from the opposite direction, implicit in the transformation of deed into word is the existence of an appropriate method for translating action into a norm. Again to take the case of a criminal sentence, what is implied is not only that a connection exists between the facts of the defendant's actions and the norm applied to these actions, but also that the connection proceeds from a process whereby we first reconstruct the historical truth independently of relevant norms, and only subsequently proceed to classify facts with reference to these norms.

Sentencing provides an illustrative example of how law transitions from general propositions to specific propositions that legitimate certain actions. At issue is what makes this transition possible. How can participants in a legal community determine, for example, that the appropriate punishment for the defendant's conduct is ten years? As Melissaris argues, the coherence of connections made in the process of criminal sentencing cannot be explained by reference to the content of the norm or to logical means such as deduction or induction. Coherence is rather a tacit function of our shared normative experiences.[192] Discussions of proportionality in sentencing presuppose our ability to link facts and norms in a way that is meaningful within the particular community. Members of the legal community share common experiences of their world and their ability to transform from real to ideal on the basis of their normative commitments.[193]

Law is embedded in our shared normative commitments, as is evidenced in the transition not only from word to deed, but also from deed to word, wherein we ascribe normative significance to facts in order to translate them into action. Melissaris demonstrates this with reference to the process of fact-finding in legal procedures. Various critiques of this process share a common understanding that the ascertainment of truth in a trial is inevitably subjective and biased. This may be a case of not enough information being available or a result of the fallibility of judges and juries. Given these inherent limitations, judgment is a leap of faith. The critique is valid to a point, in that the deficiency applies to state law as a self-inflicted wound. State law imagines the law and the world as separate, portions of which correspond on a one-to-one basis between law and fact. Since this image fails to capture the complexity of legal discourse, attempts to apply the model to lived circumstances will always be frustrating. What the model fails to recognize is that performative and constative, facts and norms, are always already merged in legal discourse.[194] In other words, the distinction in state law between norm and fact is artificial and arbitrary. Coherently describing and individuating events, to which we then ascribe legal meaning, is not possible. Instead, we need to be attentive to our lived and shared experiences of normativity.

To conclude this explanation, as simply as possible for this complex account of discourse and speech act theory, the necessary presuppositions that provide for conversion of word into deed and deed into word are formed by the experiences of participants in a particular *nomos*. Melissaris terms these presuppositions "shared normative experiences" in order to reflect Cover's idea of law as alternity, as the bridge from real to ideal.[195] They form the common bedrock of legality across diverse and plural *nomoi*. What traditional legal theory fails to recognize is that contextualization of this nature is nonetheless consistent with a universal sense of law. As Melissaris notes, state law is particularly concerned with confining the concept of law to its own internal perspective as a way of confirming the legitimacy of its function as a guarantor of stability through the rule of law. Thus the state will deny plural legal communities except as they might exist on its own terms. Left to its own devices, state law will simply ignore plurality, and normative heterogeneity will be more likely to lead to conflict rather than cooperation.

While Macdonald's inversion of legal subjectivity is perhaps a more explicit articulation and advocacy of the agency and constructive capacities of legal subjects, I think that Melissaris locates an equivalent sense of the emancipatory potential of law. The significance of shared normative experience as the common foundation of law, however contextually instantiated, is the predominance of the beliefs and committed behaviors of participants themselves for constituting law. Law is no longer a relationship of power between addressors and addressees who are presumed incapable of bringing normative order to their social relations in the absence of this imposition. As Melissaris notes, this is a rather sad commentary on the state of human nature.[196] The ubiquitous nature of law demonstrates the opposite, which is that rule-following is fundamental to human existence.[197] Law as shared normative experience is ubiquitous in this sense because sources of law may potentially be found in any instance of interpersonal interaction.

This is why shared normative experiences should not be overdetermined at this point in Melissaris's enquiry into the legal. Even with a *prima facie* concept of law that is both sufficiently universal and appropriately contextual, we cannot know in advance the various instantiations of law we will encounter.[198] Instead, this is a matter for examination in the context of interperspectival dialogue.[199] While the unavoidable vagueness of this concept has been questioned,[200] I think this intentional indeterminacy is essential for acknowledging the agency and jurisgenerative capacity of legal subjects arguably implicit in any discursive theory of law. I agree with Melissaris that expert legal theorizing is not a substitute for the voices of participants in a legal community, as only those engaged in shared normative experiences can explain meaning and significance based on their own self-understandings. This is not to argue that power is absent from legal discourse, which would be an astonishing claim. People do not exist independent of the political, social, and economic factors that constitute the context in which they live. As Melissaris notes, however, power no longer functions merely as a way to structurally separate the authority of addressors relative to the subjection of addressees.[201]

Interperspectival communication and critique

Recall that Melissaris is explicit in describing his transcontextual definition of law as a *prima facie* account, subject to revision during the process of application.[202] Nonetheless, this *prima facie* definition is sufficient to meet the end game of law as outcome, previewed in the introduction to *Ubiquitous Law*. Recall the discussion that claims of Sharia law might threaten the supremacy of England's state law and that a necessary consequence of acknowledging legal pluralism will be determining how to manage the resulting normative heterogeneity. Recall as well that the full potential of legal pluralism involves its theoretical, jurisprudential, meta-theoretical, and meta-jurisprudential aspects.[203] As for the latter, the potential of meta-jurisprudence is deciding which legal order ought to prevail. Melissaris does not operationalize this process, which would be contrary to the fundamental premises of his theory, being that communication and coordination between legal communities can only take place in an interperspectival dialogue that involves the participants themselves.[204]

The point of a *prima facie*, transcontextual concept of law is to provide the conditions under which this communication between members of plural legal communities can take place. Once we have agreement on a transcontextual definition, sufficiently thin to be universal yet not so thin as to negate evaluation, we can take the first steps toward coordinating our plural legal communities in a way that fosters cooperation and avoids conflict. Melissaris acknowledges that dialogue between members of plural legal orders cannot take place from within the internal perspective of a legal system. The utility of a transcontextual definition is to provide a starting point within legal theory to engage in inter-perspectival enquiry. Through self-reflection and mutual critique, we will be able to develop commonalities between our legal orders, which in turn will provide a basis for mutual understanding and cooperation.[205] We can facilitate this process by adopting shared normative experiences as the common denominator, so to speak, of any legitimate concept of law. Shared normative experience thus functions both contextually and transcontextually.[206]

The specifics of shared normative experience, however, can only be communicated by the participants of plural legal communities. This is a prerequisite for meaningful and productive interperspectival dialogue and critique. Legal experts cannot assume their usual privileged position as objective explainers of a legal community's normative understandings. Expert legal culture simply cannot provide the necessary participatory and democratic aspects of an intersubjective thematization of law.[207] The appropriate forum is political rather than legal, which is why Melissaris recommends academic legal theory as the place to initiate this dialogue. Academic legal theory, however, neither displaces participants nor assumes the position formerly held by expert legal culture. Academic theory is necessary because foundational beliefs concerning legality cannot be critiqued from within the legality they constitute. These beliefs necessarily limit the range of acceptable propositions and responses to those that do not threaten or contradict the existence of the legality.[208] Nonetheless, legal theory can be both pluralized and democratized by engaging participants and theorists on an equal footing; participants' normative commitments are the source of legality, and their perspective is required if we are to engage in mutual understanding and critique.[209]

On this point Macdonald and Melissaris agree, to the extent that enquiry into what is law must begin with the experiences of participants themselves.[210] Where Macdonald would disagree is that even a minimalist transcontextual definition of law would not include, for consideration at least, all *prima facie* claims raised by participants. Given that Macdonald agrees that not everything people say is law should be recognized as such,[211] one might be tempted to frame the disagreement as a question of timing. Do we exclude claims of legality prior to admission to interperspectival dialogue between legal communities, or do we disqualify participants during the dialogue itself? The disagreement is more fundamental, however, given that Macdonald conceives of normative heterogeneity as noumenal rather than phenomenal in nature.[212] The end-game of interperspectival dialogue and critique, for which a transcontextual definition of law is a prerequisite, cannot be transposed onto the nature of critical legal pluralism as a heuristic device for analyzing contingent and fluctuating patterns of normative interaction.[213]

The difference between Melissaris and Macdonald on this point is that definitional contextualism's presupposition of a separation of plural legal communities and specification of the conditions for their potential cooperation is incompatible with critical legal pluralism's insistence that legal subjects themselves are responsible for hypothesizing the law pursuant to which they constitute their legal subjectivity.[214] Taking first the approach of critical legal pluralism, normative heterogeneity is indeed pervasive, but how this heterogeneity is understood cannot be hypothesized in the absence of legal subjects, just as the question of law is one that can only be answered with reference to legal subjects themselves.[215] If we accept the premises of critical legal pluralism with respect to legal subjectivity and jurisgenerative capacity, Macdonald's argument on this point is logically consistent. We cannot acknowledge pluralism with reference to a legal subject's context-specific hypothesis of law but in turn assume the validity of an *a priori* universal conception of the experience of pluralism in the absence of inquiring how participants themselves hypothesize plurality. Multiplicity is one possible conception of normative heterogeneity; participants in a legal community will conceive of normative heterogeneity as the existence of plural legal communities that are not co-extant with their own. But if the experience of living in a hypothesized legal community is also the experience by which this community is hypothesized, then the way in which we recognize plural legal communities is also context-specific and contingent.[216]

Turning now to the approach of definitional contextualism, a preliminary issue to address is the unspecified nature of shared normative experience. How can we evaluate the efficacy of this concept in the absence of more detailed information regarding its content?[217] If, however, we accept the premises of definitional contextualism with respect to issues of perspective, and the necessity of deferring to the understandings of participants themselves, Melissaris's argument on this point is also logically consistent. Melissaris is adamant that the trajectory of his theory necessarily ends at the point of interperspectival dialogue involving mutual understanding and critique. Operationalizing this theory by specifying how to transition from dialogue to specifying the means of coordination and communication among legal communities contradicts the very premises of contextualism.[218] Given that communication and coordination between participants of plural legal communities must be worked out in the context in which it takes place, no specific method for addressing normative heterogeneity can be provided.

With the emancipation of shared normative experiences as foundational to the concept of law, and the necessity of involving participants in interperspectival dialogue, Melissaris may appear to be reimagining law, as does Macdonald, with reference to capacity rather than outcome, and thus as more consistent with law as verb than law as noun. On the other hand, the centrality of definition cannot be overlooked. The inquiry begins with and is framed by the problem (and opportunity) of how to manage normative heterogeneity. A transcontextual definition of law has been developed precisely for the purpose of addressing the challenges of normative heterogeneity as an outcome. In the balance between emancipation and regulation, emancipation is arguably placed in service of regulation. Accordingly, I conclude that definitional contextualism is directed more toward outcome, notwithstanding the substantial attention devoted to the question of capacity.

Inescapable legality

When the defining characteristic of law is conceived as participants' shared normative experiences, in the sense of a shared commitment to alternity, to the transformation of their world from real to ideal by mediating and acting upon their normative commitments, we come to understand why Melissaris titled his book *Ubiquitous Law*. We may potentially find law in any instance of associational activity that involves participants engaged in legal discourse.[219] A more expansive conception of law necessarily raises the potential for a more ubiquitous sense of law.

Legal communities are not analogous to political states or even the types of social fields identified by social-scientific legal pluralism, such as the workplace, schools, or social groups. Institutional legal discourse is not analogous to state law, with its plethora of authoritative officials, collections of organized artefacts, and widespread infrastructure for operationalizing a command-and-control model of organizing (ostensibly) the normative behavior of legal subjects. Legal communities are necessarily fragmented, in the sense that participants multiply identify with and participate in any number of legal discourses. These can take place anywhere from a micro level of transitory personal interaction, such as nightly interactions between bouncers and clubbers, to a macro level of enduring public interaction such as religious communities.[220] Legal discourse is stable or transitory, systematic or improvised, to the same extent these qualities are found in the contextual and lived normative experiences of the participants.

Legality in this sense is not only ubiquitous but also inescapable, notwithstanding claims raised to the contrary that any particular community has no self-acknowledged concept of law. This might be the case when what we are looking for as law is that which we already recognize as law in our own, familiar legal communities, particularly if our concept of law includes a formal system of symbolically expressed rules. But to propose the possibility of a legal community where participants act in common to order their interactions in a manner consistent with their shared normative understandings of their existence, yet do so in the absence of law, is contrary to strong *prima facie* historical evidence supporting the intuition that law is distinct from other forms of normative ordering.[221]

On this point, Melissaris returns to his argument that we intuitively distinguish between law and other normative orders,[222] as evidenced by our linguistic practices. As part of everyday life, we can intuitively differentiate between prescriptive utterances that are legal in nature as opposed to moral utterances or simply utterances that refer to habitual practices. Melissaris's argument on this point appears to differentiate based on the significance of the content of the utterances as well. "You must brush your teeth" self-evidently is not a legal utterance, while "You must not rape" self-evidently is a legal utterance. I assume this stark dichotomy is provided for the purposes of illustration,[223] particularly given my own experience regarding the effectiveness of hyperbolic hypotheticals in teaching law. Nonetheless, Melissaris argues that across the range of possibilities, the weight of evidence is sufficient that the burden of proof should be on those who would argue that communities who do not use the word "law" as we know it operate without a conception of law. This is, after all, why we need a sufficiently thin transcontextual definition so that we do not overlook instances of legal discourse that differ significantly from our own.

To think of law as both ubiquitous and inescapable, however, is not to imagine an oppressive dystopia of overburdened legal subjects. Law is indeed everywhere, but not as a fretting, exogenous force that by design negates the possibility of legal subjects' constructive capacities, particularly with respect to the nature and extent of their agency. Institutionalized legal discourse is indeed autonomous, but not in the sense of being vacantly self-referential. Melissaris is adamant that legal imputation is distinct from moral imputation, this being a necessary consistency with his criticism of postmodern theories of legal pluralism that fail to distinguish between law and norm. Legal imputation involves the merging of material facts and relevant norms, which in turn is predicated upon certain necessary presuppositions by participants in legal discourse, that is to say, their shared normative experience.[224]

The specificity of legal imputation that characterizes legal discourse is a consequence of participants' shared experience of transforming their world from real to ideal through their commitments to their normative beliefs. Law in this sense is no longer a relationship of power whereby an addressor imposes duties upon an addressee.[225] The emancipatory potential of Melissaris's definitional contextualism, similar to the emancipatory potential of Macdonald's critical legal pluralism, is the acknowledgment (or at least the argument) that rule-following is not obsequious passivity but rather a central aspect of human nature. Accordingly, Melissaris argues that we should understand a transcontextual definition of law, when contextually instantiated in plural legal communities, as incorporating the lived experiences and commitments of the participants themselves.

In discussing the significance of shared normative experiences, Melissaris engages in what he refers to as a detour into normativity, law, and morality. The point is not fundamental to his theory but does helpfully bookend the discussion of the methodological problems of conventional legal theory in terms of the endless antinomy and oscillation between law and justice, which informs the first part of my discussion in Chapter 2. Definitional contextualism specifies a connection between law and normativity, although given the nature of contextualism, precisely how this connection takes place in diverse *nomoi* cannot be specified as a matter of theoretical exposition. Melissaris's transcontextual definition of law does not specify normative content, and we might well wonder if this is either possible or desirable.[226] In subsequent analysis, Melissaris argues that in addition to consistency with a transcontextual definition of law, the validity of a community's legal claim must meet an additional requirement of internal public justification. The requirement, however, is procedural and not substantive in nature.[227] Nonetheless, Melissaris acknowledges that law and morality are necessarily interconnected, with implications for interperspectival communication and critique, including as always self-critique, among members of diverse and plural *nomoi*.

I do not want to distort the significance of this issue relative to his theory of definitional contextualism. I have also concluded, for reasons discussed below, that critical legal pluralism provides more viable theoretical support for my proffered concept of law, a conclusion Melissaris may well prefer, although I would like to pursue at a later date the transcontextual aspects of my hypothesis. The reason, however, that I direct attention to an admittedly non-integral issue is that I rely upon Melissaris's discussion here to provide additional support for the concept of the narrative/*nomos* obligational self I develop in Chapter 4.

As will become evident in Chapter 4, the efficacy of conceiving of legal subjectivity as a narrative/*nomos* obligational self depends on support for both narrative and *nomos* aspects of identity formation. The narrative/*nomos* obligational self is an elaboration of the jurisgenerative subject of critical legal pluralism, and Macdonald is explicit but not extensive in his explanation of the inherently normative aspects of our identity.[228] Bruner's work in cognitive psychology and McAdams' work in personality psychology also support an understanding of our senses of self that incorporates normative evaluation and justification. Add to this Melissaris's arguments regarding the possibility of substantive normative agreement, and a persuasive case has been made.

To demonstrate the possibility of universal obligations that contain substantive content, that is to say, of universal morality, Melissaris refers to Korsgaard's argument that our consciousness is reflective in nature, which means that rather than acting on the basis of unexamined impulses or desires, we require reasons for our actions, which in turn leads us to form conceptions of the right. To acknowledge our identity as human means acknowledging the reflective nature of our subjectivities. With power, of course, comes responsibility.[229] If we have the power to evaluate, we have the responsibility for the conclusions we reach. Membership in humanity thus entails certain universal obligations, although the extent of these is a matter of discussion.[230]

Note that Melissaris is careful to restrict these obligations to a very thin and limited sense of universality, minimally sufficient to establish a common vocabulary of ethics across diverse *nomoi*. This is consistent with his theoretical account of legal pluralism as contextualism. Melissaris is adamant that identifying what constitutes the shared normative experiences of different communities cannot be answered through conceptual analysis. The only way to determine how normative experiences come to be formed, shared, and applied is by engaging with the self-understanding of participants in legal communities. This requires a forum for interperspectival dialogue and critique that is political rather than legal in nature and that privileges the participants of legal communities themselves rather than expert legal culture.

Potential for re-imagining law

I have now explained the premises of these two discursive theories of legal pluralism, albeit by focusing on those that are most relevant for providing potential theoretical support for exploring my hypothesis of law and culture as mutually constitutive discourse. As I noted in the introduction, my intention was to locate a discursive theory of legal pluralism that accorded narrative a significant function. An appropriate theoretical approach would also incorporate an understanding of law as alternity, to recall Cover's formulation, as a bridge that takes us from worlds as they are to worlds as we think they ought to be. I also noted the value of encounter and exchange that occurs when evaluating these two theoretical approaches not only as they relate to my own hypothesis, but also in light of each other. This produces the additional insight that the scope of the project can include a more ambitious re-imagining of law.

I came to understand, in a way that needed to be demonstrated and not simply expressed as a conclusion, that my objective is not to define law (positivism), evaluate law (normativism), or even critique law (critical legal theory). Instead, my objective is to develop an analytical framework capable of exploring mutually constitutive discourse between law and popular culture as an ongoing process of knowledge, meaning, and commitment. The focus is on how we come to understand our jurisgenerative ability as both opportunity and responsibility. I am not providing a prescriptive account of how eco/animal activists might operationalize cultural legal authority, so that state law defenses may be transformed into a conflict of law analysis instead. A programmatic approach would contradict the emancipatory potential of understanding law as a capacity exercised by legal subjects themselves.

As for the process of evaluation, I first address the question of differentiation and definition. As I noted in the discussion above, the most significant and relevant concepts I identify for Macdonald's critical legal pluralism are knowledge and narrative, while the most significant and relevant concept for Melissaris's definitional contextualism is shared normative experience. The theories are compatible in many important respects. Both emphasize the jurisgenerative abilities of legal subjects. Both locate emancipatory potential in this constructive capacity, which liberates legal subjects from law conceived as a unidirectional imposition of legal authority from addressors to addressees. From each perspective, the ubiquity of law, to adopt Melissaris's term, is a function of how we may potentially find law in any number of interactional activities that have normative aspects. The one irreconcilable difference is the question of definition. I agree with Melissaris that we cannot say anything meaningful about law unless we differentiate the subject of our discussion from that which is not law. My preference, however, is for Macdonald's approach, wherein differentiation need not take place by way of definition. I also agree with Macdonald that using a definition to distinguish *a priori* between law and other forms of normativity is prescriptive, not descriptive.

From the perspective of critical legal pluralism, legal analysis does not require that we first demonstrate that whatever normative circumstances we are examining meet threshold definitional criteria. This requirement is not rendered more palatable simply by expanding the definition to a broader range of contextual instantiations. We can begin instead with how legal subjects themselves might, if they so choose, understand the legal significance of their normative beliefs and behaviors. I do not deny the emancipatory nature of definitional contextualism. When a transcontextual definition, however, is placed in service of law as an outcome, this limits the greater emancipatory potential made possible by re-imagining law as a verb rather than as a noun.

After addressing the issue of differentiation and definition, I turn next to assess the extent to which each theory provides elements of discourse, narrative, and alternity. As a necessary preliminary point, I discuss how to reconcile Melissaris's reference to law as institutionalized legal discourse with my concerns regarding the mistaken assumption that we can extract and isolate law from the culture in which it is created and maintained. After clarifying this issue, I address the requirement of a discursive approach to legal pluralism. I conclude that both theories demonstrate sufficient discursive potential and are actually compatible in many important respects concerning the constructive capacity of legal subjects and, to use Melissaris's term, the ubiquity of law. Consideration of this factor is thus not determinative.

As for narrative, critical legal pluralism is more relevant in this regard, given that narrative is directly incorporated into the account of how legal subjects exercise their jurisgenerative capacity, both as a means of communication and as a means of identity formation. While Melissaris relies upon Cover's theoretical support to begin his own development of a theory of definitional contextualism, he adopts alternity but discards narrative. This is somewhat surprising given that Cover's work specifically addressed the relationship between *nomos* and narrative. On the other hand, as many have observed, this objective was not necessarily achieved, as the nature of the relationship is stated in ambiguous terms. While Melissaris is not adamant on this point, he is inclined to conclude that narratives embody or reveal but do not create *nomos*. Nonetheless, the potentially constitutive role of narrative is not definitively excluded. Melissaris does not specify, and thus does not limit, the substantive content of shared normative experiences in any particular or possible context.[231] Thus our shared understandings of how we might transform our worlds in common through our normative commitments could include a narrative component. This would be a creative solution but one for which the theoretical materials do not provide any guidance. On this metric, critical legal pluralism is a more amenable approach than definitional contextualism.

As for the requirement of alternity, the positions are reversed. Melissaris's concept of shared normative experiences as the bedrock of legality is predicated upon Cover's notion of alternity, the ability to bridge the gap between the real and ideal by normatively linking material facts. For Macdonald's critical legal pluralism, the concept of alternity is arguably present, albeit implicit, in how legal subjects seek to create an ongoing narrative of normative meaning in their lives. If we are engaged continually in exploring and evaluating possible worlds and possible selves, I would argue this exploration is implicitly a purposive attempt at alternity, to move between the world we live in to the world we ought to live in. As with Melissaris and narrative, I acknowledge I am engaged in a creative reading at this point. On the other hand, alternity, unlike narrative, is a fairly self-contained concept, and thus amenable to adoption without further elaboration. Consideration of this requirement favors definitional contextualism, but only slightly, and less than the marked difference between the two approaches to narrative. Having considered these three factors, critical legal pluralism provides a superior theoretical foundation, although not without elaborating upon the role of narrative in relation to identity, as discussed in Chapter 4.

Differentiation and definition

A fundamental challenge for legal pluralism as a theoretical approach to law is how to take pluralism seriously. As noted above, a significant question to be resolved is whether, in order to take account of plural legal communities, a theory of legal pluralism must begin with an *a priori* definition of law. Both Macdonald and Melissaris acknowledge the necessity, if we are to say anything meaningful about law, of differentiating law from that which is not law. As a preliminary point, this is an aspect of an overarching concern with panjuridism, a critique directed at some theories of legal pluralism on the basis that if everything is law, then nothing is law. But as Macdonald notes, a subtler and potentially more disruptive aspect of panjuridism is concern over the colonizing effect of legal discourse.

Law tends to be a privileged discourse that, once applied, erases or displaces other types of discourse. Macdonald addresses this concern as applicable to an instrumental concept of law, such as the political state engaged in command-and-control regulatory authority. Legal pluralism actually addresses this concern by seeking to displace the exclusive authority of state law.[232] More specifically, critical legal pluralism's anti-prescriptivist approach focuses on the constructive agency of legal subjects, thus liberating them from the passive subjectivity found in the binary options of obedience/disobedience to state law.[233] Melissaris also addresses this concern, taking care to explain that ubiquitous law is inherent in our human nature, and thus not the oppressive threat to human agency posed by overreaching institutions of the political state.[234]

Nonetheless, the point of disagreement between these two approaches is whether differentiation must proceed by way of definition. Melissaris faults post-modern theories of legal pluralism, including critical legal pluralism, for failing to provide a transcontextual definition of law. Absent such a definition, law collapses into normativity more generally, with the result that all that remains is "a vague and wholly indeterminate conception of legality."[235] When law is characterized in such vacuous terms, we cannot establish the necessary conditions for mutual recognition or critique between dispersed legal discourses.[236] Indeed, Macdonald explicitly rejects any attempt to articulate *a priori* definitions of law based on characteristics, whether structural or functional in nature, as misguided definitionalism.[237]

Criticism based on a lack of definition is unfounded. Implicit in this criticism is the assumption that normativity can and should be understood in hierarchical terms, with reference to privileged definitions, rather than the relevance of any particular norm to those involved. We need a transcontextual definition of law so that we can limit our consideration to commensurate legal claims while excluding from consideration mere normative claims that do not meet the definition of law. Acknowledging and responding to normative heterogeneity is thus a two-stage process, whereby we first distinguish between laws and norms so that we can exclude the latter, and only then proceed to engage in transcontextual communication and critique. That which is law is understood to prevail over that which is not law.

My difficulty with this argument is that it assumes what must be decided. The claim is that without a meaningful definition of law, legal inquiry collapses into normative inquiry without any way to identify and analyze the unique characteristics of law. Of course, this critique depends upon the unexamined presupposition that law has sufficiently unique characteristics that distinguish it from norms, which is the case only if we first define law, in a circular fashion, as having the very characteristics that demonstrate its unique status. To simply say that we need to distinguish between law and norms because otherwise we cannot talk meaningfully about law, since it is distinct from norms, is to rely, incorrectly, on a definitional defense.

Melissaris argues that our linguistic practices reflect our fundamental intuition that more than trivial differences exist between legal utterances and prescriptive but non-legal utterances. He acknowledges Kleinhans and Macdonald's argument that this intuition is actually nothing more than our language of law being overdetermined by an exclusive association with the state.[238] I find Kleinhans and Macdonald more logically compelling on this point. If the state, for example, desires to claim exclusive legal authority, what necessarily follows is an attempt by the state to differentiate the norms it claims as its own from norms originating elsewhere. In the process, law becomes a word that differentiates and imposes hierarchy on the basis of definition alone. Melissaris's response, however, apart from reiterating that his transcontextual definition of law has no necessary connection with the political state, is to repeat his insistence that our intuitive differentiation merits examination in order to determine if we are indeed referring to a non-ideological concept of law.[239]

Perhaps one point upon which we can all agree is that to think in terms of legal pluralism is to call into question our unexamined assumptions as to what constitutes law. If the boundaries of our legal imagination are defined by the characteristics of the law of the political state, we have no need of engaging in this enquiry. We do not question the veracity of the presuppositions upon which this concept of law is predicated, because we are always already situated in normative conditions that take these presuppositions for granted, giving them the appearance of being intuitive and timeless.[240] Kleinhans and Macdonald argue that reliance upon unexamined assumptions does not indicate our belief in the truth of these assumptions. Their status as unexamined means that we have yet to investigate their veracity. Consider, for example, the implications of the presupposition that law is singular and centralized, a relationship of force between addressors and addressees. If upon further examination we find ourselves unconstrained by this presupposition, we can locate (or, perhaps more aptly, regain) the emancipatory potential of law with respect to our own jurisgenerative capacity without losing the ability to bind ourselves by law.

Consider next the implications of relying on the presupposition that law is distinct from mere norms. This means that law exists precisely in the distinction we think we must draw, and thus do draw, between law and other types of normativity. Without this distinction, law cannot exist, and hence the necessity of incessant definitional projects. This explains why I locate the thematic basis of Melissaris's definitional contextualism in perspective and definition. Melissaris argues that conventional legal theories and empiricist-positivist legal pluralism present falsely universal perspectives that lead to deficient definitions of law. The difficulty with postmodern legal theories in contrast is that they lack any sense of perspective, failing to provide a definition of law as distinct from other normative orders. Postmodern theories, such as critical legal pluralism, thus contain inherently contradictory claims, for they proffer to be theories of legal pluralism as opposed to value pluralism, thus defining the nature of their enquiry as legal in the absence of defining what constitutes law.

But simply because we distinguish law from norm, no matter how intuitive this presupposition may be, does not mean we need to assume this presupposition is universal, nor are we in a position to argue that without first defining law, critical legal pluralists cannot speak of legal rather than value pluralism. If anything, given the inability of legal theory to define law, perhaps we should be questioning not the methodology of our enquiries but rather the efficacy of the presuppositions upon which our enquiries are based. As Tamanaha notes, legal pluralists are hardly unique in failing to agree upon a definition of law. The same difficulty exists in legal theory more generally, although he agrees that the question of what is law must be resolved.[241] As I stated above, presumably this is a point upon which everyone agrees. The disagreement between Macdonald and Melissaris is whether this question can and should be answered with a definition.

Macdonald agrees that differentiation is necessary for theorizing about law but that differentiation need not take place by means of a definition.[242] In fact, Macdonald explicitly warns legal pluralists against the dangers of definitions as political acts directed toward political purposes.[243] This is in contrast to Melissaris's faith in a concept of law "undiluted by ideology."[244] Nonetheless, Macdonald also explicitly rejects the argument that whatever participants in a presumptive legal community choose to consider law should be recognized as such.[245] Law is distinct in that its content necessarily references not only aspirations, but also modalities and procedures through which these aspirations may be realized.

Instead of definition, Macdonald argues for differentiation based on the nature of the analytical perspective rather than the object being analyzed. When we conceive of law as a way of making sense of human behavior, we do not need to focus on definitional criteria so that we may know law when we see it. Instead, the focus is on the types of questions that are of interest from a legal perspective by "attending to a particular manner of imagining how human beings negotiate their relationships with others."[246] We theorize, contemplate, and communicate about law whenever our attention is directed toward "the endeavour of symbolizing human conduct and interaction as governed by rules." Other symbolizations of human conduct are possible. Economists, for example, symbolize human conduct and interaction as motivated by self-interest in pursuit of efficient market transactions. No need exists to define what is economics, just as there is no need to define what is law. What matters is what kinds of questions should be asked by those engaged in economic or legal analysis (which I would add arguably includes participants themselves) and the implications of these questions for understanding human interaction.[247]

In arguing against a prescriptivist account of law, that is to say, an understanding of law as a social fact that exists separate and apart from the legal subjects whose conduct it regulates, Macdonald and Sandomierski raise another concern about legal theory's reliance on definition. Once we define what constitutes law, we have a tendency to focus on the end product of legal subjects' jurisgenerative activity, being the rules themselves, rather than how legal subjects understand and determine for themselves the relevant normative standards that guide their behavior. Definitional criteria constitute legality rather than the goals (aspirational or alarming) that a norm seeks to achieve[248] or its efficacy in relation to how people govern their lives.[249]

If we want to understand how and why people act as they do, we cannot simply examine the subset of norms that meet threshold definitional criteria as law.[250] Law does not exist prior to recognition by legal subjects, which means the question of what constitutes law can only be answered by legal subjects[251] even if their understanding contradicts theoretical assertions of the definition of law. Universal application of a theoretical concept of law for analytical purposes cannot compel legal subjects to recognize the concept's existence or validity.[252] The key question is not whether a norm raises a legal claim but what is the relevance and effect of this norm in the context in which it is used by the people who use it.[253]

Despite this fundamental difference, I am intrigued by the degree of correspondence between Melissaris's understanding of law as necessarily based on the shared normative experiences of the participants and Macdonald's understanding of law as necessarily based on the hypotheses of law created by legal subjects as a function of their self-narration and interaction.[254] Both locate law in the jurisgenerative capacities of legal subjects engaged in either institutionalized legal discourse (Melissaris) or the endeavor of symbolizing human conduct and action as governed by rules (Macdonald). For Melissaris, the thin, universal aspect of legal discourse consists of specifying the conditions for the application of norms that in turn constitute the demarcation of the boundaries of what constitutes law. We cannot further specify how norms actually apply in diverse *nomoi*.[255] This is consistent with Macdonald's argument that if the experience of living in a hypothesized legal community is also the experience by which this community is hypothesized, then the recognition of plural legal communities is context-specific and contingent.[256]

Nonetheless, the question of definition persists and influences the evaluation of emancipatory potential. The unspecified and open-ended nature of the concept of shared normative experiences offers potentially unlimited scope for analyzing law and popular culture as mutually constitutive discourse. The characterization of law as institutionalized and autonomous legal discourse does not isolate law from culture; shared normative experiences are the culture that constitutes the conditions of legal discourse, and thus scope exists for a constituting role for popular culture. Nonetheless, I agree with Macdonald's argument that conceptual definitions as to what constitutes law can be a distraction from relevant and meaningful inquiry.[257] After all, the effect of a definition (and in many cases the intention as well) is to exclude some participants from the benefits the definition confers, otherwise a definition would not be required.[258]

Critical legal pluralism is less concerned with the presumptive pedigree of norms than examining our reactions to them in everyday life, and I find this argument compelling. If the obligational force of a norm is a function not of its consistency with an *a priori* definition of law but of the normative significance accorded by legal subjects,[259] then should we be using definitional criteria to exclude even considering the validity of *prima facie* claims in the processes of interperspectival dialogue envisioned by definitional contextualism? Why emphasize the inclusion and perspective of members of plural legal communities if the legal claims being discussed do not include those that participants may find more relevant in their normative relations with others? The possibility that participants may accord more normative significance to non-legal claims excluded from a process intended to manage the complexity of normative heterogeneity raises questions about the efficacy and relevance of this process. This possibility is also at odds with the emphasis Melissaris places on the commitments of participants themselves, with respect to their shared normative experiences, as the common bedrock of legality.

Thus criticisms regarding a collapse into value pluralism might be revealed instead as a misguided concern for the pedigree, function, or structure of norms rather than their relevance. This places arguably unwarranted conditions on which normative experiences can be considered as *prima facie* legal claims. This potential exclusion does not trouble Melissaris, as he answers the question of what is law with a definition. This is law as a noun, the result of an inquiry impelled by a desire to address the outcome of acknowledging legal authority other than the state. This potential exclusion would trouble Macdonald because he answers the question of what is law with differentiation. This is law as a verb, the result of an inquiry impelled by a desire to understand how legal subjects understand and respond to normative claims,[260] including how they conceive of these claims in the context of normative heterogeneity.

Discourse, narrative, and alternity

In terms of the requirement of a discursive theory of law, little discussion on this point is required. Both critical legal pluralism and definitional contextualism were examined on the basis that they provide a discursive account of law, sufficient in this regard to provide theoretical support to a hypothesis of law and popular culture as mutually constitutive discourse. Both theories amply demonstrate the legitimacy of locating law in the discourse of participants, which means we needn't consider whether popular culture can successfully approximate the modalities of state law, such as legislatures and courts. As discursive theories, they are similar in many key respects, such as emphasizing the constructive capacity of legal subjects. To use Melissaris's term, the ubiquity of law is that it may potentially be located in any number of associational activities. Both Macdonald and Melissaris emphasize the emancipatory potential of an approach to law that rejects a unidirectional imposition of authority by centralized and exclusive addressors, such as the state, upon passive legal subjects.[261]

I do, however, need to acknowledge and address in more detail a point alluded to above. An apparent contradiction may exist among Melissaris's explanation of legal discourse as institutionalized and differentiated from other types of normativity and social practices, my own hypothesis of law and popular culture as mutually constitutive discourse, and my rejection of assumptions of law as autonomous and thus distinct from culture. I reconcile these two hypotheses of law with reference to Melissaris's concept of shared normative experiences. As noted, legal discourse is institutional and autonomous but not in the sense of being isolated from culture. Instead, shared normative experiences are the necessary cultural conditions of presupposition that are an integral aspect of legal discourse itself.

The advantage of conceiving of law as shared normative commitments is the ability to acknowledge the legitimacy of shared self-understandings as these arise in the cultural context of the participants. In his explanation of how shared normative experiences can account for the autonomy of law, Melissaris distinguishes legal imputation from moral imputation. I have addressed this aspect, however, with reference to the emancipatory potential of law as verb rather than noun, in that no need exists for *a priori* distinctions between law and mere norms. In terms of the institutionalization of legal discourse, legal imputation cannot be desegregated from the shared normative experiences that constitute the conditions of its application.[262]

Melissaris acknowledges that the shared normative experiences that make legal utterances intelligible are contextual and dynamic, subject to affirmation and amendment consistent with the social conditions in which they originate. The resulting institutionalized legal discourse in turn shapes the beliefs of participants by specifying the available criteria for distinguishing that which is normatively imaginable from that which is not. The system is described as relatively closed.[263] But the way in which Melissaris conceives of a relatively closed discourse does not describe law as isolated from culture and in fact is more expansive than other discursive examples that attempt to reconstruct relationships between law and society, specifically Tuebner's systems-theoretical approach.

Admittedly, Melissaris is somewhat ambiguous on this point. In his survey of the development and nature of theories of legal pluralism, he introduces two classifications, both of which he discredits. The first are theories based on empiricism-positivism, and the second are postmodern/critical theories. Melissaris includes Teubner's systems-theoretical approach within this second category, but his attitude here is more ambivalent.[264] He explicitly critiques Manderson, Davies, Kleinhans, and Macdonald, all of whom he classifies as postmodern legal pluralists, on the basis that their theories fail to distinguish between law and other normative orders and thus are unable to comment meaningfully about law.[265] But as McKee notes, whether this critique includes Teubner is unclear.[266] McKee also finds puzzling Melissaris's lack of engagement with Teubner in developing his theory of definitional contextualism given his earlier support for aspects of his theory.[267]

Nonetheless, my own (perhaps creative) reading is that Teubner's theory falls short of acknowledging the constitutive significance of the social (cultural) context of law. As Melissaris notes, a binary code of legal/illegal is inescapably positivist in the way it draws a line of demarcation between law and the social environment, although he notes that in Teubner's case, the legal discourse itself assumes the task of defining the boundaries of law.[268] This is also a feature of Melissaris's definitional contextualism. Perhaps the more significant limitation, and I am reading a great deal here into a few paragraphs of commentary, is that adaptable linkage institutions connecting law and social processes do not conceive of the relationship between law and society in quite the same way as Melissaris approaches the constitutive function of shared normative experiences. Again, I stress this is not an argument Melissaris presents, but shared normative experiences do not create a relationship between legal discourse and participants' experiences in a way that is analogous to structural coupling through adaptive linkage institutions. Melissaris describes law as being bound to shared normative experiences, which are often tacit and silent, but nonetheless constitutive.[269] Shared normative experiences do not merely inform law through a productive misreading; they constitute the very conditions of its existence to such a degree that they become the bedrock principle of a transcontextual concept of law.

Law is indeed an institutionalized discourse, distinct from moral discourse, to the extent we accept other than in an *a priori* definitional manner a distinction between law and norms. But while legal discourse is differentiated, it does not involve sterile self-reference. This is in contrast to state law, for example, which Melissaris argues may not be law at all, given that it operates on the basis that facts and norms are two different, self-contained, and coherent realms.[270] Melissaris argues that institutionalized legal discourse demarcates its boundaries with reference to the shared normative experiences of the participants. This is why the concept of shared normative experience provides such strong potential for analyzing law and popular culture as mutually constitutive discourse, notwithstanding the reference to institutionalized (and autonomous) legal discourse. Law is embedded in the shared normative experiences, and thus the cultural context, of the participants. Melissaris is specific in his claim that law is constituted by these experiences.[271]

As for the requirement of narrative, assessment recalls the trajectory of this question across different modes of inquiry, as discussed in Chapter 2. Analyzing the function of narrative in each theory recalls Cover's unanswered question about the nature of the relationship between narrative and *nomos*. Does narrative create law or merely represent law in narrative form? Cover as noted is somewhat ambiguous on this point, and a close reading of the text does not settle the question. Initially, Cover appears to suggest that narratives are *nomos*, as when he states that "the very imposition of a normative force upon a state of affairs, real or imagined, is the act of creating narrative."[272] But he is not always consistent on this point, as when he later says that narratives "create and reveal the patterns of commitment, resistance and understanding."[273] As I stated in Chapter 1, my motivation for this project is to provide an answer in the form of both a hypothesis and the necessary analytical framework for exploring this hypothesis. The point of departure is the characterization of law and culture as "seamless web of authority."[274] I do not dispute the metaphorical guidance provided by this characterization but seek a specific answer at a more granular level of analysis.

An interesting aspect of Melissaris's approach is that while he relies on Cover's concept of alternity, he does not assign a function to narrative in his theory of definitional contextualism. This is somewhat at odds with Cover's insistence on the significance of narrative in relation to *nomos*, notwithstanding the ambiguity of his explanation. Melissaris dispenses with the relationship between narrative and *nomos* in a footnote, stating that the answer to this question is not relevant for his analysis. His own position, while not adamant, is that narratives embody and reveal but do not create *nomos*.[275] Since definitional contextualism does not specify an explicit function for narrative, I could try to locate one by implication, but this does not appear promising given Melissaris's comment that the question of narrative is irrelevant. If theoretical support for this project is to be found within Melissaris's definitional contextualism, it will have to be by elaboration, not implication, most likely with reference to the contextualized content of shared normative experiences. This is not necessarily determinative, since as I explain below, Macdonald's critical legal pluralism lacks explicit reference to alternity, although reference by implication in this case is an easier task.

In contrast, Macdonald is explicit in his use of narrative, although the discussion is not extensive. Within critical legal pluralism, the function of narrative is both as a means by which legal subjects communicate legal information as well as a means by which they constitute their self-identity. Admittedly, Macdonald does not provide extensive argument on these points. The entry point for understanding the function of narrative is Macdonald's characterization of the life of a legal subject, multiply identified, as a "continuing narrative of meaning."[276] An earlier reference by Kleinhans and Macdonald raises the possibility only in passing that we can conceive of this process with reference to a theory of narrative identity formation.[277] On the other hand, narrative identity formation finds implicit affirmation in their statement that law is autobiographical in nature, with legal subjects engaging in inter- and intra-subjective evaluation of alternatives proffered by their narrating selves.[278]

We can then proceed to Macdonald's succinct characterization of law as a consequence of personal narration and interaction,[279] which I interpret as incorporating both narrative communication and narrative identity formation. To explain this in greater detail, we can hypothesize our understandings of legality, and communicate these understandings, through narratives. These narratives constitute the legal knowledge that creates and maintains what we recognize as the reality of law. Macdonald is quick to respond to any potential objections that inter- and intra-subjective narration is characterized by unconstrained agency. He acknowledges the predominance of dominant narratives imposed by either ideology or force. But since the legal subject is the sole (not joint) author of self-narrative, any narrative of law must be sufficiently persuasive to attract the legal subject's commitment.[280] In our constant re-narrations of our identities, we both receive and engage the narrative imaginations of other legal subjects. Through this process of narration and interaction, legal subjects narrate and are narrated by their hypotheses of law.[281]

These are admittedly brief explanations when we take into account the significance of narrative for understanding the jurisgenerative capacity of legal subjects to hypothesize law and for understanding how their hypothesis of law constitutes them as legal subjects. Accordingly, I take the liberty in the next section of more fully developing critical legal pluralism's concept of legal subjectivity, with reference to cognitive and psychological theories of narrative. Drawing upon the work of Bruner and McAdams, I elaborate upon the jurisgenerative capacity of legal subjects to develop the concept of a narrative/*nomos* obligational self. Our identity, the way we conceive of ourselves as selves (always understood as multiply identified, non-unitary, and non-essential), is a function of narrative construction. Not only do we make sense of our experiences based on the ways in which we narrate the stories of our lives, but also we are always in the process of becoming the persons in the stories we narrate.[282] A theory of narrative identity formation affirms and more fully specifies Macdonald's statement of law as a consequence of personal narration and interaction. We constitute our inherently normative identities, and our legal subjectivities, through a process of telling stories to explain "who and what we are, what's happened, and why we're doing what we're doing."[283] These are the narrative/*nomos* obligational selves that both inherit and amend prevailing hypotheses of law.

As for the requirement of alternity, the case is the reverse of the position of the two theories in regard to narrative. In developing his theory of definitional contextualism, Melissaris explicitly adopts and integrates Cover's conception of law as alternity. The unique claim of legal discourse is the ability to mediate between the real and the ideal by evaluating and authorizing action. Shared normative experiences, meaning participants' common experiences of transforming their world through their normative commitments, account for the institutionalization of legal discourse by defining its boundaries. Cover's political liberalism provides theoretical support for Melissaris's definition of plural law as contextualism, but more specifically, his concept of law as alternity is directly integrated into the definition of institutionalized legal discourse.

Macdonald, on the other hand, does not explicitly identify alternity in hypothesizing law as the endeavor of symbolizing human conduct as governed by rules. Nor is alternity explicit in his description law as a function of personal narration and interaction. Nonetheless, the concept of law as alternity is implicit. First, recall that the implication of the word "endeavor" is that law is purposive aspiration in the sense that we must commit to its achievement. Note as well the implications of the word "conduct," which requires both belief and action to constitute law. As I discussed earlier, Cover also specifically addresses the significance of action in reference to alternity; we cross the bridge from real to ideal not by virtue of belief alone but with committed behavior.[284]

At this point, my reading of Macdonald becomes somewhat creative, although not inconsistent with the fundamental premises of critical legal pluralism. As a necessary prelude, recall that Macdonald rejects a reified understanding of law as an entity or essence and argues instead for an understanding of law as a process of legal knowledge that creates and maintains legal reality. Recall as well that legal subjects themselves hypothesize the legality that constitutes their legal subjectivity. The process is social in that legal subjects' multiple subjectivities both constitute and are constituted by relations with others. The process is also psychological in that legal subjects exercise agency in according normative significance to claims as they arise in contextual and contingent circumstances of normative heterogeneity. The process is psychosocial in that sustained normative significance among participants in legal communities is a process of accretion of individual affirmations, modifications, and denials, all of which reflect and refract these same processes as carried out by others.[285]

With this in mind, I locate alternity in the way people use narrative in their reciprocal constructions of law and legal subjectivity. Macdonald argues that legal subjects are motivated to create an ongoing narrative of meaning in their lives.[286] As noted, Melissaris refers to legal subjects in similar terms, in that the ubiquity of law is an acknowledgment of the centrality of rule-governed behavior in human nature,[287] which as I noted provides additional support for my development below of the concept of the narrative/*nomos* obligational self. Admittedly, Macdonald does not press this point with any further explanation, but this ongoing narrative is understood as a process of self-narration.[288] This process of creating meaning involves exploring possible worlds and possible selves, seeking in our relations with others and in our own narratives the evaluative criteria we need to decide which possible worlds and which possible selves to inhabit.[289] We are the nexus of normative heterogeneity, given that our inter- and intra- subjective relations are characterized by evaluation and judgment.[290]

Thus our inter- and intra-subjective relations can also be characterized with reference to alternity. The exploration of possible worlds and possible selves implies a movement from the worlds and selves we are to the worlds and selves we would like to be. The purpose of seeking criteria for evaluation and judgment is specified somewhat differently from Cover's alternity. Cover, perhaps not surprisingly, describes law as alternity with reference to a more singular destination, notwithstanding the actual definition of alternity, which refers to multiple alternatives. Nonetheless, his explanation conveys that what we have in mind is an imagined future in a preferred ideal and that we would like to begin our journey in that direction from our current location in the real. Macdonald, again not surprisingly, has a more plural conception in that we inhabit present worlds and present selves and through self-narration and interaction adopt and employ criteria of evaluation and judgment to choose between the alternative worlds (and presumably alternative selves) that are open to us.[291]

This is indeed a rather fulsome reading of very brief references to personal narration and interaction as alternity. The result is nonetheless consistent with Cover's articulation of law as the bridge between real and ideal as well as Melissaris's account of the ability of legal discourse to evaluate and authorize action. While Melissaris is explicit on this point, the implication required to locate alternity in critical legal pluralism is less of a departure from theoretical premises than the possibly contradictory elaboration required to inject narrative into an account of definitional contextualism. I acknowledged that while the role of narrative within critical legal pluralism is foundational, it also requires elaboration. I also noted the opportunity to build upon critical legal pluralism's concept of legal subjectivity, incorporating a psychological theory of narrative identity formation to conceive of a narrative/*nomos* obligational self in a way that is complementary rather than contradictory to theoretical premises. Accordingly, based on evaluation of the three requirements of discourse, narrative, and alternity, critical legal pluralism provides a more appropriate theoretical foundation for this project of re-imagining law and popular culture as mutually constitutive discourse.

Notes

1 See, for example, Geertz' well-cited explanation of law as "meaning . . . not machinery": Clifford Geertz, *Local Knowledge: Further Essays in Interpretive Anthropology* (Basic Books 1983) 232.

2 Manderson, for example, refers to Cover in arguing against a strict demarcation between law and culture and in favor of a more plural and discursive understanding. See: Desmond Manderson, 'Memory and Echo: Pop Cult, Hi Tech and the Irony of Tradition' (2013) 27 *Cultural Studies* 11, 12.

3 See, for example, Melissaris's explanation on this point: Emmanuel Melissaris, *Ubiquitous Law: Legal Theory and the Space for Legal Pluralism* (Ashgate Publishing Company 2009) 53.

4 West classifies approaches to law and literature, and subsequently law and culture, into the literary, hermeneutic, and jurisprudential approaches. With the literary approach, when culture references law, we can study culture for insights regarding the nature of law. With the hermeneutic approach, law and culture are sufficiently similar that we should apply to law methodologies currently used to study culture. The jurisprudential approach, and the one adopted in this analysis for popular culture, is that culture might presently or in the past have the normative force of law. See: Robin West, 'Literature, Culture, and Law at Duke University' in Austin Sarat, Catherine O. Frank, and Matthew Daniel Anderson (eds), *Teaching Law and Literature* (Modern Language Association of America 2011). Mezey rejects the idea of law as autonomous from culture and refers to different possibilities for the nature of the relationship. When referring, however, to how culture might operate as regulation independently of state law, a perspective closest to this analysis, she characterizes this as social norms. When referring to law as culture and culture as law, the relationship appears to be more reciprocal than mutually constitutive, arguably because her use of the term "law," based on chosen illustrative examples, refers to state law. See: Naomi Mezey, 'Law as Culture' (2001) 13 *Yale Journal of Law and the Humanities* 35.

5 See, for example: Jerome Bruner, *Actual Minds, Possible Worlds* (Harvard University Press 1987); Jerome Bruner, 'The Narrative Construction of Reality' (1991) 18 *Critical Inquiry* 1; Jerome Bruner, *Making Stories: Law, Literature, Life* (Harvard University Press 2002); Jerome Bruner, 'Life as Narrative' (2004) 71 *Social Research: An International Quarterly* 691.

6 Robert M. Cover, '*Nomos* and Narrative' (1983) 97 *Harvard Law Review* 4, 9, citing George Steiner, *After Babel: Aspects of Language and Translation* (Open Road Media 2013).

7 Since I reject the idea of law's necessary isolation from culture, I also reject Günther Teubner's systems theory approach. See: Gunther Teubner, 'The Two Faces of Janus: Rethinking Legal Pluralism' (1992) 13 *Cardozo Law Review* 1443. As Melissaris notes, positivism remains a fundamental characteristic, the difference being that the demarcation of legal from non-legal is delineated by the discourse itself in relation to its environment. See: Melissaris (2009) 36.

8 For development of the theory of critical legal pluralism, see primarily: Martha-Marie Kleinhans and Roderick A. Macdonald, 'What Is a Critical Legal Pluralism?' (1997) 12 *Canadian Journal of Law and Society* 25; Roderick A. Macdonald, 'Critical Legal Pluralism as a Construction of Normativity and the Emergence of Law' in Andrée Lajoie, Roderick A. Macdonald, Richard Janda, and Guy Rocher (eds), *Théories Et Émergence Du Droit: Pluralisme, Surdétermination, Effectivité* (Éditions Thémis 1998); Roderick A. Macdonald, 'Here, There and Everywhere: Theorizing Legal Pluralism; Theorizing Jacques Vanderlinden' in Nicholas Kasirer (ed), *Étudier Et Enseigner Le Droit: Hier, Aujourd'hui Et Demain – Études Offertes À Jacques Vanderlinden* (Éditions Yvon Blais 2006); Roderick A. Macdonald and David Sandomierski, 'Against Nomopolies' (2006) 57 *Northern Ireland Legal Quarterly* 610; Roderick A. Macdonald, 'Custom Made – For a Non-Chirographic Critical Legal Pluralism' (2011) 26 *Canadian Journal of Law and Society* 301.

9 Emmanuel Melissaris, 'The More the Merrier? A New Take on Legal Pluralism' (2004) 13 *Social & Legal Studies* 57; Emmanuel Melissaris, 'The Limits of Institutionalised Legal Discourse' (2005) 18 *Ratio Juris* 464; Emmanuel Melissaris, 'The Chronology of the Legal' (2005) 50 *McGill Law Journal* 839; Emmanuel Melissaris, 'Perspective, Critique, and Pluralism in Legal Theory' (2006) 57 *Northern Ireland Legal Quarterly* 597.

10 Melissaris (2009).

11 Emmanuel Melissaris, 'From Legal Pluralism to Public Justification' (2013) 6 *Erasmus Law Review* 173.

12 See, for example, Macdonald's extensive list of his application of critical legal pluralism to other contexts and situations: Macdonald (2006). See also: Roderick A. Macdonald and Thomas McMorrow, 'Wedding a Critical Legal Pluralism to the Laws of Close Personal Adult Relationships' (2007) 1 *European Journal of Legal Studies* 1; Roderick A. Macdonald, 'Three Metaphors of Norm Migration in International Context' (2008) 34 *Brooklyn Journal of International Law* 603; Roderick A. Macdonald, 'Pluralistic Human Rights? Universal Human Wrongs?' in René Provost and Colleen Sheppard (eds), *Dialogues on Human Rights and Legal Pluralism* (Springer Science & Business Media 2013).

13 By "legitimacy," I mean whether in a context of normative heterogeneity a particular claim is acknowledged as a legal claim, as opposed to the legitimacy of the substantive content of the claim.

14 Melissaris (2009) 39.

15 Macdonald (2013) 28. See also: Kleinhans and Macdonald (1997) 33, citing HW Arthurs, *Without the Law: Administrative Justice and Legal Pluralism in Mid 19th-Century England* (University of Toronto Press 1985) 3.

16 Macdonald (2006) 393.

17 Note, for example, that Macdonald sees some similarity between these two approaches, specifically with respect to the significance and function of human agency and social interaction. See: Macdonald (2011) 309.

18 As Tamanaha states: "The question 'what is law?' however, has never been resolved, despite innumerable efforts by legal theorists and social scientists." See: Brian Z. Tamanaha, 'Understanding Legal Pluralism: Past to Present, Local to Global' (2007) 29 *Sydney Law Review* 375, 391.

19 See, for example: Macdonald (2006) 408; Melissaris (2009) 25.

20 My use of the word "radical" here is meant to indicate an inquiry that focuses on the fundamental and constitutive aspects of a concept, as opposed to matters of application. Macdonald describes critical legal pluralism in similar terms, taking care to note that his "fundamental" inquiry does not involve essentialism. See: Macdonald (1998) 402.

21 Victor M. Muñiz-Fraticelli, *The Structure of Pluralism* (Oxford University Press 2014). "The roots of and antipathy towards positivism."

22 Melissaris (2009) 34. Interestingly, based on his earlier scholarship in this field, both Davies and Webber characterized Melissaris as a critical legal pluralist. See: Margaret Davies, 'The Ethos of Pluralism' (2005) 27 *Sydney Law Review* 87, 107; Jeremy Webber, 'Legal Pluralism and Human Agency' (2006) 44 *Osgoode Hall Law Journal* 167, 181. Based on subsequent work by both Macdonald and Melissaris, this characterization is no longer apt, although commonalities persist in terms of locating law's origin and expression in legal subjectivity, as discussed below. See: Melissaris (2009). More recently, Muñiz-Fraticelli also characterizes Melissaris as a "self-described critical legal pluralist," although no doubt Melissaris would not agree. See: Muñiz-Fraticelli (2014).

23 Desmond Manderson, 'Beyond the Provincial: Space, Aethetics, and Modernist Legal Theory' (1995) 20 *Melbourne University Law Review* 1048, 1066.

24 Desmond Manderson, 'From Hunger to Love: Myths of the Source, Interpretation, and Constitution of Law in Children's Literature' (2003) 15 *Law and Literature* 87. See also: Amar Khoday, 'Prime-Time Saviors: *The West Wing* and the Cultivation of a Unilateral American Responsibility to Protect' (2009) 19 *Southern California Interdisciplinary Law Journal* 1.

25 Kleinhans and Macdonald (1997).

26 Macdonald (1998); Macdonald (2006); Macdonald and Sandomierski (2006); Macdonald and McMorrow (2007); Macdonald (2011); Macdonald (2013).

27 In my discussion of critical legal theory, I focus throughout on the work of Macdonald, although I do refer at one point to subsequent work by Kleinhans. See: Martha-Marie Kleinhans, 'Plural Corporate Persons: Displacing Subjects and (Re)forming Identities'

(2006) 57 *Northern Ireland Legal Quarterly* 634; Martha-Marie Kleinhans, 'Rewriting Outsider Narratives: A Renaissance of Revolutionary Subjectivities' (2007) 2 *Charleston Law Review* 185. This is not, however, to overlook Kleinhans's contributions in developing this theoretical perspective.

28 Kleinhans and Macdonald (1997) 42, citing Geertz (1983) 232.

29 Macdonald (2013) 24.

30 Webber (2006) 181.

31 Melissaris (2009) 46.

32 Macdonald and Sandomierski (2006) 617. Macdonald and Sandomierski reject Tamanaha's non-essentialist approach wherein law is understood as whatever people identify as law and treat as such through their social practices. See: Brian Z. Tamanaha, 'A Non-Essentialist Version of Legal Pluralism' (2000) 27 *Journal of Law and Society* 296, 313.

33 Note that while Melissaris refers to legal communities, he does not raise any claims as to their ontological or normative status. Law is not co-extant with uniform communities of legal subjects. People's shared normative commitments are as fragmented as their identities. Nor does every aspect of identity necessary correlate with a shared normative experience. See: Melissaris (2009) 24.

34 Melissaris (2009).

35 Melissaris (2009) 4.

36 Melissaris (2009) 91.

37 Melissaris (2013).

38 For Melissaris, see, for example: Melissaris (2009) 25; Melissaris (2013). For Macdonald, see, for example: Macdonald and Sandomierski (2006) 611.

39 Melissaris (2009) 60.

40 Derek McKee, 'Review Essay: Emmanual Melissaris' Ubiquitous Law: Legal Theory and the Space for Legal Pluralism' (2010) 11 *German Law Journal* 573, 582.

41 Macdonald (2006) 408.

42 Melissaris (2009) 53.

43 Macdonald (2006) 406–407.

44 McAdams argues that narrative identity is used to explain past, present, and future, "a moral justification of how a person was, is, and will be." See: Dan P. McAdams, 'Narrative Identity' in Seth J. Schwartz, Koen Luyckx, and Vivian L. Vignoles (eds), *Handbook of Identity Theory and Research* (Springer 2011) 100.

45 Melissaris (2006) 609.

46 Macdonald (2006) 403.

47 Macdonald (2006) 407.

48 Melissaris (2009) 25.

49 Melissaris (2009) 25.

50 Macdonald (2006) 409.

51 Melissaris (2009) 25.

52 Macdonald (1998) 22.

53 Melissaris argues that if we recognize legal orders other than state law, the problem of how to manage plural legalities will arise. We will need to find a way to reconcile diversity and order, or to refer to de Sousa Santos, emancipation and regulation. See: Melissaris (2009) 2, citing Boaventura de Sousa Santos, *Toward a New Legal Common Sense: Law, Science and Politics in the Paradigmatic Transition (After the Law)* (Routledge 1995).

54 Melissaris (2006) 600.

55 Melissaris (2009) 71. Melissaris emphasizes this point in a subsequent article wherein he adds to the definition of law a procedural requirement for public justification. Participants must be offered an opportunity to assess and agree upon reasons for legal rules, but this procedural requirement does not extend to transcontextual substantive requirements of the content of law in addition to its concept. See: Melissaris (2013).

56 Melissaris (2013) 174.

57 I do not want to digress here into debates about whether Gregory Bateson defined information as difference that makes a difference or whether this is a valid argument regardless of the source. Whether we refer to information and difference, or figure and ground, surely we can accept that to talk about something, we need to distinguish this from everything that is not this something.

58 As Tamanaha notes, given that legal theory to date has yet to produce a satisfactory answer to the question of what is law, the lack of consensus regarding a definition is not a problem unique to legal pluralism. This does indicate, however, that theoretical accounts of legal pluralism would be more productive if this question could be set aside. Tamanaha's solution is to proceed on the basis of a non-essentialist approach. See: Tamanaha (2000) 297.

59 Macdonald (2006) 393. Macdonald derives this hypothesis of law initially from Fuller and then as subsequently developed in his own work. See: Macdonald (2006) 393 n15, citing Lon L. Fuller, *The Morality of Law* (Yale University Press 1969) 106; Roderick A. Macdonald, *Lessons of Everyday Law* (Published for the Law Commission of Canada and the School of Policy Studies, Queen's University by McGill-Queen's University Press 2002) 3.

60 Kleinhans and Macdonald (1997) 42.

61 I owe this insight to David Sandomierski, SJD Candidate, Faculty of Law, University of Toronto. His conversations clarified and guided my thoughts on this point in relation to legal pluralism.

62 Kleinhans and Macdonald (1997); Macdonald (2006).

63 Macdonald (2011) 309.

64 Kleinhans and Macdonald (1997) 33.

65 Kleinhans and Macdonald (1997) 33. Bal also makes this point in advocating for the utility and relevance of narratological analysis. See: Mieke Bal, *Narratology: Introduction to the Theory of Narrative* (Third Edition, University of Toronto Press 2009) 12.

66 Recall that Kleinhans and Macdonald do not characterize their own approach as definitive. See: Kleinhans and Macdonald (1997) 38 n43.

67 Macdonald (2013) 30.

68 Cover (1983) 9.

69 Macdonald (1998) 406.

70 Macdonald and Sandomierski (2006) 617.

71 Desmond Manderson, 'Modernism and the Critique of Law and Literature' (2011) 35 *Australian Feminist Law Journal* 107, 125.

72 Macdonald (2013) 35.

73 Melissaris (2009) 26.

74 Melissaris (2009) 77.

75 See, for example, Geertz's well-cited explanation of law as "meaning . . . not machinery:" Geertz (1983) 232.

76 Geertz (1983) 184.

77 Macdonald and Sandomierski (2006) 617.

78 As Macdonald and Sandomierski note, a non-prescriptivist approach to law, such as critical legal pluralism, does not lead to anarchy. Legal subjects cannot conceive of themselves independently of the social structures in which they exist. See: Macdonald and Sandomierski (2006) 630.

79 Macdonald and Sandomierski (2006) 616.

80 Cover (1983).

81 Macdonald (2006) 408.

82 Macdonald (2006) 406.

83 Kleinhans and Macdonald (1997) 38.

84 I adopt the term "jurisgenerative" from Cover's work on *nomos* and narrative: Cover (1983). Kleinhans and Macdonald refer to the ways in which legal subjects are law-creating, not merely law-obeying. See, for example: Kleinhans and Macdonald (1997).

85 Macdonald (2013) 22.
86 Macdonald (2011) 308.
87 Macdonald (2011) 308.
88 Macdonald (2006) 391; Macdonald (2011).
89 Macdonald (2011).
90 Macdonald (2011) 309.
91 Macdonald (2011) 309.
92 Muñiz-Fraticelli argues that legal pluralists have mistakenly rejected positivism when it could be helpful to support their arguments. See: Muñiz-Fraticelli (2014).
93 Macdonald (2011) 309; Macdonald (2013) 23.
94 Macdonald (2006) 402. Macdonald explains that by "radical," he is referring to the nature of the inquiry as fundamental but does not mean to imply a sense of essential or inherent with respect to the object of the inquiry.
95 Kleinhans and Macdonald (1997) 34.
96 Kleinhans and Macdonald (1997) 37.
97 Cover (1983) 18.
98 Bal (2009) 156.
99 Macdonald (2013) 24.
100 Macdonald and Sandomierski (2006) 614.
101 Macdonald and Sandomierski (2006).
102 Macdonald (2006) 407.
103 Macdonald and Sandomierski (2006) 619.
104 Macdonald and Sandomierski (2006) 621.
105 Macdonald and Sandomierski (2006) 616.
106 Macdonald (2011).
107 George Orwell, *Nineteen Eight-Four* (Random House 1992).
108 Margaret Atwood, *Oryx and Crake* (McClelland & Stewart 2003) 93.
109 As discussed below, Melissaris's approach to legal pluralism also rejects an understanding of law as a relationship between addressor and addressee. See: Melissaris (2009) 45.
110 Macdonald (2006) 394.
111 Macdonald (2006) 406.
112 Macdonald and Sandomierski (2006) 617.
113 Kleinhans and Macdonald (1997) 35, citing Pierre Schlag, 'The Problem of the Subject' (1990) 69 *Texas Law Review* 1627.
114 Schlag (1990).
115 Macdonald and Sandomierski (2006) 617.
116 Wendy A. Adams, '"I Made a Promise to a Lady": Critical Legal Pluralism as Improvised Law in *Buffy the Vampire Slayer*' (2010) 6 *Critical Studies in Improvisation*, n5.
117 Cover (1983).
118 Elaine Scarry, 'The Made-Up and the Made-Real' (1992) 5 *The Yale Journal of Criticism* 239.
119 Macdonald and Sandomierski (2006) 614.
120 Manderson (1995).
121 For an extensive discussion of how various modes of legal thought construct our legal subjectivity, see: Schlag (1990).
122 Macdonald and Sandomierski (2006) 611.
123 Macdonald (2006) 408.
124 Macdonald and Sandomierski (2006) 618.
125 Macdonald (1998) 15.
126 Macdonald and Sandomierski (2006) 619.
127 Macdonald and Sandomierski (2006) 616.
128 Macdonald and Sandomierski (2006) 620.
129 Manderson (1995) 123.

130 Macdonald and Sandomierski, for example, argue that reliance on the exclusivity of state law allows people to deny their own participation (and perhaps complicity) in the creation and maintenance of legal rules. See: Macdonald and Sandomierski (2006) 620.
131 Macdonald (2006) 406.
132 For example, see Macdonald's discussion of this point with respect to formal legal texts and institutions associated with international human rights: Macdonald (2011) 30.
133 Kleinhans and Macdonald (1997).
134 Macdonald (2006) 408.
135 Kleinhans and Macdonald (1997) 42; Macdonald (2006) 406.
136 Kleinhans and Macdonald (1997) 42.
137 Kleinhans and Macdonald (1997) 42.
138 Cover (1983).
139 Macdonald (2006) 407.
140 Macdonald and Sandomierski note that Cover's work is subject to different interpretations. Not everyone interprets Cover as arguing for the hierarchical superiority of state law. If Cover is interpreted as allowing for plural legality, his work is consistent with the argument advanced by critical legal pluralism with respect to the creative capacity of legal subjects. See: Macdonald and Sandomierski (2006) 614.
141 Macdonald (2006) 407.
142 Kleinhans and Macdonald (1997) 42.
143 Kleinhans (2006) 634.
144 Bruner (2002).
145 Bruner (2002).
146 Adams (2010).
147 Kleinhans and Macdonald (1997) 43; Macdonald and Sandomierski (2006) 630.
148 Macdonald and Sandomierski (2006) 616.
149 Melissaris (2009) 90.
150 Melissaris (2009) 105.
151 Melissaris (2009) 4.
152 Melissaris (2006) 609.
153 Melissaris (2009) 57.
154 Melissaris (2009) 58.
155 Melissaris (2009) 115.
156 "Whether it refers to something which somehow exists in the world or a universally shared concept, what I call the universal sense of law is a universalist claim raised in the course of the enquiry into the legal." See: Melissaris (2009) 50.
157 Melissaris (2009) 61.
158 Desmond Manderson, 'Judgment in Law and the Humanities' (2013) 1 *Revista Forumul Judecatorilor* 43.
159 Melissaris (2009) 25.
160 Melissaris (2009) 58.
161 Melissaris notes the frustration of being asked to provide instructions to operationalize communication and co-ordination between context-sensitive plural legalities, which are shaped by participants' experiences and must be communicated by the participants themselves. Context-sensitive interaction, in other words, cannot be specified in advance of the experience of the context in which the interaction takes place. See: Melissaris (2009) 152.
162 Melissaris (2009) 1.
163 Melissaris (2009) 124.
164 Melissaris (2009).
165 Cover (1983).
166 Melissaris (2009) 84.

167 Melissaris (2009) 54.
168 Melissaris (2009) 89.
169 Deciding that a claim, based on a transcontextual definition of law, is legal in nature involves evaluating internal procedural legitimacy but does not extend to transcontextual evaluation of substantive content. See: Melissaris (2013).
170 Melissaris (2009) 115.
171 Melissaris (2009) 61.
172 The objection is not only that they cannot account for plural law but also that they should be able to account for plurality in order to constitute a valid legal theory. Absent an account of plurality, a purported legal theory is nothing more than a first-person account of internal coherence. See: Melissaris (2009) 76.
173 Kleinhans and Macdonald (1997) 34.
174 Melissaris (2009) 45.
175 Melissaris (2009) 26.
176 Melissaris (2009) 3.
177 Melissaris (2009) 51.
178 Macdonald and Sandomierski note that disagreement exists as to whether Cover advocates for or acknowledges the superiority of state norms. See: Macdonald and Sandomierski (2006) 614.
179 Melissaris (2009) 52.
180 Cover (1983) 18.
181 Melissaris (2009) 57.
182 Melissaris (2009) 57.
183 Whereas Macdonald explicitly rejects reification, Melissaris claims that one can develop a universal sense of law "without needing to take a stance on whether this sense is part of the fabric of nature or purely socially constructed and yet constant through time." See: Melissaris (2009) 60.
184 Melissaris (2009) 51.
185 Melissaris (2009) 59.
186 Melissaris (2009) 51.
187 Melissaris (2009) 53.
188 Melissaris (2009) 79.
189 Institutions are different from social practices in that they are self-regulating. An institution not only provides a socially constructed frame of thought and action but also requires that that we think and act within this frame if we want to be considered as participants in the discourse. See: Nelson Phillips, Thomas B. Lawrence, and Cynthia Hardy, 'Discourse and institutions' (2004) 29 *Academy of Management Review* 635, 637.
190 Melissaris (2009) 90.
191 Melissaris (2009) 91.
192 Melissaris (2009) 93.
193 Melissaris (2009) 100.
194 Melissaris (2009) 105.
195 Melissaris (2009) 121.
196 Melissaris (2009) 58.
197 Melissaris (2009) 126.
198 Melissaris (2009) 152.
199 Melissaris (2009) 91.
200 See, for example: McKee (2010); Seán Patrick Donlan and Richard Bronaugh, 'Ubiquitous Law: Legal Theory and the Space for Legal Pluralism (2009)' (2012) 25 *Canadian Journal of Law & Juris* 177.
201 Melissaris (2009) 126. Macdonald argues a similar point that our agency may be constrained by fluctuating patterns of power within legal discourse, but it is not fixed as a binary obey/disobey response to immutable standards of behavior. See: Macdonald and Sandomierski (2006) 620.

202 Melissaris (2009) 115.
203 Melissaris (2009) 25.
204 Melissaris (2009) 152.
205 Melissaris (2009) 61.
206 Melissaris (2009) 113.
207 Melissaris (2009) 61.
208 Melissaris (2009) 117.
209 Melissaris (2009) 71.
210 Melissaris (2009) 68; Macdonald and Sandomierski (2006) 616.
211 Macdonald and Sandomierski (2006) 617.
212 Macdonald (1998) 22.
213 Macdonald (1998) 18.
214 Macdonald (2006) 406.
215 Macdonald and Sandomierski (2006) 616.
216 Macdonald (2006) 404.
217 See, for example: McKee (2010).
218 Melissaris (2009) 152.
219 Melissaris (2013) 152.
220 Melissaris (2009) 125.
221 Melissaris (2009) 112.
222 Melissaris (2009) 112.
223 Melissaris (2009) 124.
224 Melissaris (2009) 123.
225 Melissaris (2009) 126.
226 The problem of wicked legal systems is not unique to legal pluralism. See, for example: David Dyzenhaus, *Hard Cases in Wicked Legal Systems: Pathologies of Legality* (Oxford University Press 2010). The relationship between legal pluralism and universal human rights was an issue of interest to Macdonald. See, for example: Macdonald (2013).
227 Melissaris (2013).
228 See, for example: Kleinhans and Macdonald (1997) 42; Macdonald (2006) 406.
229 While many sources exist for variations on this theme, my preference is Uncle Ben, speaking to his nephew Peter Parker, a.k.a. Spiderman. "With great power there must also come great responsibility." See: Stan Lee and Steve Ditko, 'The Amazing Spider Man' (1962) 15 *Marvel Comics: Amazing Fantasy*. "With great power comes great responsibility." See: *Spider-Man* (Sam Raimi 2002).
230 Melissaris (2009) 116, citing Christine M. Korsgaard and Onora O'Neill, *The Sources of Normativity* (Cambridge University Press 1996).
231 Melissaris (2009) 124.
232 Macdonald (2006) 400.
233 Macdonald and Sandomierski (2006).
234 Melissaris (2009) 126.
235 Melissaris (2009) 5.
236 Melissaris (2009) 26.
237 Macdonald (2006) 391.
238 Melissaris (2009) 46.
239 Melissaris (2009) 47.
240 Kleinhans and Macdonald (1997) 41.
241 Tamanaha (2000) 297.
242 Macdonald (2006) 391.
243 Macdonald (2013) 28. See also: Kleinhans and Macdonald (1997) 33, citing Arthurs (1985) 3.
244 Melissaris (2009) 47.
245 Macdonald and Sandomierski (2006) 617.
246 Macdonald (2006) 393.

247 Macdonald (2006) 395.
248 Macdonald and Sandomierski (2006) 617.
249 Macdonald and Sandomierski (2006) 618.
250 Macdonald and Sandomierski (2006) 614.
251 Macdonald and Sandomierski (2006) 616.
252 Macdonald and Sandomierski (2006) 616.
253 Macdonald and Sandomierski (2006) 618.
254 Macdonald (2006) 408.
255 Melissaris (2009) 123.
256 Macdonald (2006) 404.
257 Macdonald (2013) 27.
258 For a discussion of definition and legal personhood, see: Wendy A. Adams, 'Human Subjects and Animal Objects: Animals as Other in Law' (2009) 3 *Journal of Animal Law & Ethics* 29.
259 Macdonald and Sandomierski (2006) 617.
260 As noted, this does not mean that whatever legal subjects claim as law must be recognized as such. Law is explicitly hypothesized as "the endeavour of symbolizing human interaction as being governed by rules". See: Macdonald and Sandomierski (2006) 617.
261 For Melissaris, see, for example: Melissaris (2009) 25. For Macdonald, see, for example: Macdonald and Sandomierski (2006) 611.
262 Melissaris (2009) 123.
263 Melissaris (2013) 178.
264 Melissaris (2009) 27.
265 Melissaris (2009) 43.
266 McKee (2010) 584.
267 McKee (2010) 584, citing Melissaris (2004).
268 Melissaris (2009) 35, citing Teubner (1992).
269 Melissaris (2009) 93.
270 Melissaris (2009) 106.
271 Melissaris (2009) 106.
272 Cover (1983) 10.
273 Cover (1983) 17.
274 West (2011) 6.
275 Melissaris (2009) 53.
276 Macdonald (2006) 407.
277 Kleinhans and Macdonald refer in passing to identity formation through narrative. See: Kleinhans and Macdonald (1997) 42. Kleinhans is more explicit in arguing that "[legal] subjectivity is best understood through the lens of narrative." See: Kleinhans (2006) 634.
278 Kleinhans and Macdonald (1997) 46.
279 Macdonald (2006) 408.
280 See, for example: Macdonald (2013) 24.
281 Macdonald (2006) 406.
282 Bruner (2002).
283 Bruner (2002).
284 Cover (1983) 9.
285 Macdonald (1998) 22; Macdonald (2006) 406.
286 Macdonald (2006).
287 Melissaris (2009) 126.
288 Kleinhans and Macdonald (1997) 42. See also: Macdonald (2006) 406.
289 Macdonald (2006) 406.
290 Macdonald (2006) 406.
291 Macdonald (2006) 406.

4 Obligation and identity

Introduction

As noted in Chapter 2, I have been unable to locate within the relevant scholarship a more precise explanation of how popular culture might function as legal authority without the necessity of translation into state law.[1] I propose to answer this question by hypothesizing law and popular culture as mutually constitutive discourse and by developing the necessary analytical framework pursuant to which inquiry can proceed. Critical legal pluralism provides the necessary theoretical foundation not just as a discursive theory of plural law but by locating the nexus of law in the jurisgenerative capacity of legal subjects. Legal subjects themselves hypothesize the conceptions of law that inaugurate their legal subjectivity, albeit in a context in which their legal imagination is always already conditioned by hypotheses of law that prevail in their communities. Legal subjects themselves conceive, create, and interpret legal rules, again albeit in a context in which the nature of proffered claims is conditioned by prevailing hypotheses of law. Finally, legal subjects accord normative status to proffered claims by instantiating through action those they consider to be obligational, again influenced by the normative understandings that prevail in their community.[2]

As noted above, Macdonald describes law as a function of personal narration and interaction, and in the absence of further elaboration, I have organized his commentary on this issue as specifying two conceptions of narrative. The first way that narrative functions is as a means of communicating and understanding the legal knowledge that creates and maintains legal reality. The second way that narrative functions is as a means by which we constitute our sense of our self as self, that is to say, our identities. This creates the template for what in this section I more fully articulate as the narrative/*nomos* obligational self, understood always as multiply identified, non-unitary, and non-essential. At this point I am effectively reading in to Macdonald's extensive scholarship in this area, and for my own purposes as well, but hopefully in a way entirely consistent with his work. Having established critical legal pluralism as the theoretical foundation, I now further develop the analytical framework by incorporating cognitive and psychological theories of narrative, and more specifically narrative identity, with reference to Bruner and more particularly McAdams. Critical legal pluralism locates the nexus of law in the jurisgenerative capacity of the legal subject. With reference to narrative identity thesis, I elaborate upon this constructive capacity to locate the nexus of mutually constitutive law and popular culture discourse in the self-narration of the obligational self.

The narrative/*nomos* obligational self thus provides a more specific conception of the legal authority of popular culture, unmediated by translation into state law. The direct normative force of popular culture is a function of the ways in which collective popular culture narratives are implicated in the self-narration of the obligational self. As emancipatory potential rather than programmatic imposition, the same process also accounts for the authority of state law. Popular culture as law is simply one aspect of the complexity of our normative understandings. In each case, law's origins are found not in legal rules but in the normative significance accorded these rules by narrative/*nomos* obligational selves. This is not to say that law becomes the totality of our selves; rather, it is the aspect of ourselves that is most relevant when we engage in rule-governed behavior in our relations with others. Simply stated, law is not something we obey but something we become.

In terms of narrative as a means of communicating and understanding legal knowledge, our comprehension of the worlds in which we live is a function of what Bruner has called a narrative construction of reality. Bruner argues that we use narrative, both as a particular manner of cognition as well as a particular manner of discourse, to make sense of our world. How we understand our experiences, and how we communicate these understandings among ourselves, is a function of narrative thought and communication. In terms of narrative as a means of constituting our identity, and with respect to law, our legal subjectivity, the way we conceive of ourselves as selves, or more accurately as multiple selves, is a function of narrative identity formation. McAdams argues that we make sense of our experiences based on the ways in which we narrate the stories of our lives and furthermore that we are always in the process of becoming the person in the stories we narrate.[3]

Thus the legal subject of critical legal pluralism, when informed by theories of narrative communication and narrative identity formation, becomes a more fully realized narrative/*nomos* obligational self. If we understand subjectivity as a function of a psychological process of self-narration, taking place in a social context where meaning is also communicated by narrative, we understand the significance of narrative/normative self-identity rather than reified rules as the origin of normative authority.[4] If we conceive of subjectivity as constituted by self-narration, then the selves we narrate are inherently normative, which in turn affirms our understanding of law as alternity, as inherently normative aspiration. As McAdams argues, narrative identity is not just a descriptive account of our past, present, and future selves, but also a moral justification of how we were, how we are, and how we will come to be.[5] Accordingly, questions of obligation are also questions of identity.

Our response to circumstances of normative heterogeneity is a function of our inherently normative identity, which we self-narrate with reference to cultural narratives, as we affirm, deny, resist, ignore, reject, or otherwise react to the necessity of choice in a way that reconciles who we think we are with what we think we are obliged to do. The concept of the narrative/*nomos* obligational self is simply an acknowledgment that that the question of what kind of person I am cannot be disaggregated from the question of what I am obliged to do. A narrative theory of self-identity also raises and responds to the logical question of how one acquires the narratives, which arguably include popular culture narratives, that are implicated in self-narration.[6] We negotiate boundaries between social and psychic aspects of popular culture as we self-narrate our obligational identities with reference to collective cultural narratives.[7]

The concept of the narrative/*nomos* obligational self may evoke at this point comparisons to the significance of character in virtue ethics.[8] Briefly stated, pursuant to virtue ethics as a moral theory, the normatively correct choice is assessed with reference to the characteristics that constitute a virtuous person. This can be contrasted with deontological normative theories, in which the right action is one that corresponds to an *a priori* moral standard, and consequentialist theories, in which the right action is one that produces the morally desired result. The echo of virtue ethics is not surprising and originates in the nature of jurisgenerative capacity as emancipation, but also assumption of responsibility. As Macdonald notes, when human beings are both law makers and law appliers, legal claims are hypotheses of law, the legitimacy of which must be confirmed by legal subjects themselves. Hence his characterization of a legal subject's jurisgenerative capacity as an aretaic concept.[9] Perhaps normative responsibility is subject to a law of conservation similar to that of energy; if we relocate the authority and legitimacy of law not in the political state but in the agency of legal subjects themselves, however constrained and contextualized, then responsibility for law and its consequences must logically follow accordingly. Possible connections to and integration with virtue ethics would be an intriguing line of enquiry, albeit one not within the scope of this project.

A summary of the developing analytical framework would be helpful at this point. Briefly stated, the analytical framework comprises: (a) adoption of critical legal pluralism as the most appropriate theoretical framework, being a discursive theory of law as alternity, as verb rather than noun, as capacity rather than outcome, in which narrative is accorded a constitutive function; and (b) incorporation of cognitive psychology and personality psychology theories of narrative identity formation to elaborate upon the jurisgenerative legal subject as a narrative/*nomos* obligational self, in that the selves we narrate are inherently normative. In the discussion that follows, I explain this concept of a narrative/*nomos* obligational self in greater detail.

Next, I consider issues of identity that inevitably arise in discussions of legal subjectivity.[10] First, I seek to avoid any potential misunderstanding that this project of re-imagining law involves a claim that those who do not share that which is being imagined are laboring under the delusion of false consciousness. In other words, if the eco/animal activists considered in the case study in Chapter 5 understand their actions as resistance to state law, this is a false consciousness that can and must be remedied in a programmatic fashion. To propose, however, that we might hypothesize legality, in some manner and to some extent, in a way that accords legal authority to popular culture is not a claim that we must proceed in this fashion. As I have emphasized throughout, the emancipatory potential of this project exists in the acknowledgment of our constructive capacity and not in any particular configuration of the outcome of normative heterogeneity. From the perspective of critical legal pluralism, and as informed by the concept of the narrative/*nomos* obligational self, an activist's understanding of acts of resistance as moral rather than legal claims might be an unexamined assumption, but it is not false consciousness.

Second, I differentiate the concept of the narrative/*nomos* obligational self from scholarship concerning legal consciousness, which may be defined here in brief as how people experience and understand law in everyday life.[11] While false consciousness raises concerns of overdetermination, legal consciousness raises concerns of underdetermination. Not surprisingly, research in this field reflects people's understandings of the prevailing (albeit arguably unexamined) hypothesis of law as the exclusive legal authority of the political state. That our legal imaginations might consider alternatives to this hypothesis, even if the end result is to affirm the legitimacy of state law, is still at this point an exercise in theoretical re-imagination rather than everyday application.

The next topic is also a familiar theme, being the tension between determination (or structure) and agency. In this discussion, I return to Macdonald's theory of critical legal pluralism to attend more closely to how he reconciles jurisgenerative capacity with constraints on agency. Macdonald's sensible position on this topic is that legal subjects do exercise agency, however constrained this might be. A worldview informed by critical legal pluralism is not a naive utopia in the sense that power and domination no longer determine how we hypothesize and respond to claims of legality. Nonetheless, dominant legal hypotheses can and do change over time as multitudes of legal subjectivities affirm, modify, or reject multitudes of proffered claims of legality.

Finally, I address another potential misunderstanding that the concept of the narrative/*nomos* obligational self is an atomistic approach, one which presupposes essential, unitary, and autonomous legal agents who are able to independently exercise their constructive capacity without regard for others. I do not want to digress here into a detailed discussion of theories addressing legal obligation as a function of our existence in relation to others. I do argue, however, that the concept of a narrative/*nomos* obligational self does not ignore the significance of community as an aspect of our jurisgenerative capacity.

First, although ultimately I did not adopt Melissaris's definitional contextualism as the theoretical foundation for developing the necessary analytical framework for this project, I nonetheless identify significant potential in his concept of shared normative experiences for exploring law and popular culture as mutually constitutive discourse. As I noted in Chapter 3, Melissaris is understandably reluctant to provide a detailed specification of this concept in the absence of interperspectival dialogue involving participants themselves. The jurisgenerative capacity of legal subjects provides the emancipatory potential of ubiquitous law, wherein law is no longer conceived as the unidirectional authority of addressors commanding addressees. Univocal command is replaced with multi-vocal legal discourse, the success of which depends upon presuppositions of relationships between facts and norms embedded within a legal community's shared normative experiences. At the risk of overly simplifying his work, while individual humans exercise constructive capacity with respect to legal discourse, law is constituted by shared experiences.[12] Accordingly, the concept of the narrative/*nomos* obligational self, being consistent with Melissaris's exploration of the foundation of law as shared normative experience, is arguably not an atomistic approach.

Second, the narrative/*nomos* obligational self, being an elaboration of the legal subject of critical legal pluralism, is necessarily consistent with Macdonald's approach to the nature of the relationship between legal subjectivity and social relations. Recall Macdonald's succinct statement of law as a function of personal narration and interaction. Again at the risk of oversimplifying a complex body of work, this statement arguably assigns equal significance to both functions. Throughout his work, Macdonald emphasizes the relational nature of jurisgenerative capacity and thus the relational nature of law. Our narrative/*nomos* obligational selves engage in normative evaluation precisely because we are embedded in social relations. We need to decide how to live in this world in relation to others, just as others need to decide how to live in this world in relation to us. One might even wonder if normative evaluation would be possible, or whether a concept of law would be necessary, in the absence of living in relation to others.[13] To refer to our narrative/*nomos* obligational selves as a nexus of mutually constitutive discourse of law and popular culture does not mean that communal understandings of law fracture into plural legalities of one, in which case law ceases to exist.[14] Whether through wisdom[15] or force,[16] we are influenced by the legal meanings produced by those around us.[17] The narrative/*nomos* obligational self, in the conduct of committed behaviors, does not vacillate between unrealistic utopian aspiration and equally unrealistic dystopian relativism.

The nexus of narrative/*nomos*

I have organized Macdonald's characterization of law as a function of personal narration and interaction with reference to two functions of narrative, the first as a means of communicating legal knowledge, and the second, less fully articulated, as a means of constituting the identity of legal subjectivity. To further elaborate upon the nature of the jurisgenerative legal subject as a narrative/*nomos* obligational self, I incorporate into this developing analytical framework theories of cognitive and personality psychology, with reference to the work of Bruner and McAdams respectively. As with critical legal pluralism, my objective is not to assess the merits of these theories from a disciplinary perspective, particularly as I venture beyond my own discipline's modes of thought. Instead, I adopt the principles and concepts most relevant for incorporation into the developing analytical framework for hypothesizing popular culture and law as mutually constitutive discourse. As before, I take care not to distort the meaning or thematic coherence of substantial bodies of work in the process.

The function of narration as a means of communication is arguably non-controversial and thus less in need of extensive discussion. Simply stated, with reference to Bruner's work in cognitive psychology on this point, narrative is both a cognitive process we use to make sense of our experiences and a symbolic system of discourse we use to communicate with each other about these experiences.[18] Bruner initially argued that we make sense of the world with two different systems of thought, paradigmatic and narrative, wherein the function of narrative is to propose that which paradigmatic thought then affirms or denies. In the narrative mode, our comprehension of experience is a matter of making sense of our needs, desires, and goals, with the objective being to produce a coherent explanation.[19] In the paradigmatic mode, our comprehension of experience is a matter of observation, logical analysis, and proof, with the objective being cause and effect explanations. Bruner has since repudiated his earlier subversion of narrative to paradigmatic modes of thought, wherein narrative imagination provided hypotheses of the human condition that could and should be tested and verified by the scientific method.[20] His work since then has legitimated the power of narrative to influence what we perceive as reality and thus emphasized the importance of narrative as a way we make sense of ourselves in relation to others.

Before proceeding further, I should explain why I refer to Bruner's work in cognitive psychology rather than his more recent scholarship in law and literature.[21] In particular, his work with Amsterdam, a legal scholar, would appear to be more on point.[22] The difficulty is the appearance of a by now familiar obstacle, in that the concept adopted is that of the exclusive legal authority of the state. I also rely less on Bruner than McAdams for elaborating more fully upon the function of narrative in constituting subjectivity even though Bruner's arguments regarding the narrative construction of reality also address the narrative construction of identity. No insufficiency or difficulty of application exists on this point. Rather, I adopt McAdams as authority on this issue based on his assertion, which does not appear to be disputed, that he provided the first fully developed theoretical model of narrative identity.[23]

As for the constitutive function of narrative communication, recall Macdonald's argument that knowledge creates and maintains realities and that legal knowledge is the reality of law created and maintained by legal subjects.[24] Bruner provides support for this assertion from the field of cognitive psychology. He argues that we are all inherently storytellers who make use of narrative, including narrative fiction, to structure our experience of reality.[25] Narrative accomplishes this to such an extent that we conceive of what we call the "real" world in a manner consistent with the stories we tell.[26] Neither life nor fact can be isolated from each other. Bruner's discussion on this point would provide further support for Melissaris's theory of definitional contextualism, given the echo here of shared normative experiences, wherein the merger of fact and norm is a necessary presupposition of legal discourse. Bruner argues that every story is predicated upon certain normative presuppositions regarding a given state of affairs; we know to be concerned when the Big Bad Wolf appears because we know this is not something that should happen when a child such as Little Red Riding Hood visits her grandmother.[27]

As Bruner acknowledges, the argument that reality is represented in the act of knowing itself, which led to a "cognitive revolution" in psychology and other human sciences, continues a debate that originated in literary theory. Subsequent to this cognitive revolution, psychologists began to examine how narrative might not simply represent but actually constitute reality, with similar inquiries taking place in other disciplines such as anthropology, linguistics, and philosophy of language. Bruner's argument regarding the nature of this constitutive activity is that narrative is both a mode of thought, that is to say a mental process, as well as a form of discourse that expresses this mental process. The constitutive function of narrative is found in the way we organize our experience and memory of human activity in the form of narrative. Our fluency is such that we are able to engage in narrative from a very young age.

Bruner's work on narrative from the perspective of cognitive psychology integrates the narrative construction of life per se with the narrative construction of our own lives in the form of our self-identity. While I rely on McAdams to support the narrative/*nomos* aspects of the obligational self, I include a brief account of Bruner's arguments here as additional support for the relevance of collective cultural narratives. According to Bruner, not only is selfhood a function of self-narration,[28] but also narrative self-construction draws upon the same narrative models of construction available for stories in our culture more generally. We are able to make sense of our own actions and intentions, and convey this sense to others, because we share the same cultural knowledge of narrative. Reality is represented in the act of knowing, but the act of knowing is a function of how we communicate as well. Since narrative creates the categories of comprehending reality such as objects, actors, and relationships, what we narrate with reference to our collective cultural narratives is what we become.[29] In other words, in the process of telling our stories, we become the person in the stories we tell.[30] We become variations of canonical forms,[31] a point similar to that raised by McAdams and discussed below. McAdams conceives of our self-narrations as stories populated by imagoes, being a range of characters who are all idealized personifications of aspects of ourselves and who function as protagonists in the stories of our lives.

Having provided additional theoretical insight into narrative as a means of communicating legal meaning, and thus creating and maintaining legal reality, I now proceed to address the more complicated function of narrative as a means for constituting identity and thus legal subjectivity. I adopt a theory of narrative identity formation in order to elaborate upon the jurisgenerative capacity of the legal subject, which in turn leads to the concept of the narrative/*nomos* obligational self. To understand the explanatory power of the self-narrated identity of the obligational self, recall Cover's claim that jurisgenerative and jurispathic functions are a necessary consequence of the bifurcation of law into two distinct aspects, being the social organization of law as power and the (arguably also social) organization of law as meaning.[32] By rejecting singularity in favor of plurality, critical legal pluralism can locate both aspects of law in the jurisgenerative capacity of legal subjects, notwithstanding the jurispathic tendencies of political states.

Jurisgenerative capacity is explained as the ways in which legal subjects themselves create, understand, and respond to what constitutes the relevant legal rules in any given situation of normative heterogeneity. A common theme found throughout Macdonald's work is that both law and inter-legality are noumenal rather than phenomenal in nature.[33] The social power of law thus depends upon the emergence of collectively persuasive normative self-understandings, or social meanings, specific to any given legal community. Similarly, by integrating social meaning and social control within constitutive processes of narrative/*nomos*, the obligational self provides a more specific concept of the constructive capacity of inherently normative self-narration.

The narrative/*nomos* obligational self, embedded in the always already cultural context of narrative meaning that includes popular culture narratives, is a facilitator of the legal knowledge that creates and maintains the reality of law for legal subjects. These provide conditions of possibility for the reflections, representations, and refractions implicated in the ways we narrate our inherently normative identity, which in turn provide the conditions of possibility for the ways we respond to proffered claims of legality, and consider ourselves bound by law. As a facilitator of legal knowledge, the narrative/*nomos* obligational self is thus also the origin of law's social power, even if a jurisgenerative legal subject understands the nature of that power as a top-down imposition of state legal rules. This apparent paradox is resolved by keeping in mind the fundamental insight of critical legal pluralism, which is that legal subjects themselves hypothesize the form and content of laws by which their legal subjectivity is constituted and which operate as external reference points for rule-governed behavior.[34]

Simply stated, we are not governed by an exogenous entity, a concept of legality that brings to mind a metaphorical rule book in the sky, imposing a normative grid upon otherwise unstructured human behavior from above. Our experience of law is not the imposition of rules and their modalities bestowed upon us by abstract and autonomous authority. As Macdonald and Sandomierski argue, in a point which really should be non-controversial, law does not pre-exist human recognition of that which we understand to be law.[35] Rejecting a prescriptivist understanding, they argue in favor of human agency, however constrained by modes of social relations, on the basis that law is imagined, given expression, experienced, modified, resisted, and rejected by human beings as active legal subjects.[36] What I conceive of as our narrative/*nomos* obligational selves are facilitators of legal knowledge and thus legal reality, contributing to the "collective normative field"[37] of rules, institutions, and practices of law as we know them.[38] Even if we conceive of law as the rules and modalities of the political state, we are the ones who create the legal reality of state law as autonomous and distinct from social relations. Should the opportunity and desire arise, we can conceive otherwise.

To return to the specifics of the inherently normative obligational self, wherein subjectivity is constituted through self-narration, I incorporate into the developing analytical framework a psychological theory of narrative identity formation. McAdams provides a life-story model of identity.[39] His work is situated in a branch of psychology known as personality theory, wherein the objective is to account for the structure and function of personality. Two premises of McAdams's work are particularly relevant. The first is that narrative identity is evaluative; identity formation is a function of our ongoing creation of our life story in a way that provides both a persuasive and purposive sense of our lives to others and to ourselves.[40] The second is that narrative identity is a psychosocial construction, a joint authorship contextualized by social relationships, discourse, and culture.[41] This context provides the conditions of possibility for the kinds of stories that constitute a good and meaningful life.[42]

McAdams defines narrative identity as a person's "internalized, evolving, and integrative story of the self."[43] Our narrative identity is an ongoing, internalized story we create, maintain, and rely upon to provide sense and meaning to the events and people in our lives, including the selves we are in the process of narrating. There is a strong echo of alternity in the way this story, like any story, involves selective reconstruction and editing. We use narrative to combine elements of our autobiographical past with our anticipated future in a way that serves to explain, to ourselves and others, how we came to be and where our life is going.[44] Our narrative identity thus both defines and justifies to others and ourselves who we are and who we are going to be.[45] This affirms my proposition that obligation is, at least in significant part, a function of identity, in that the question of who I am cannot be disaggregated from the question of what I am obliged to do.

At this point, I should distinguish between what might be called representational and constitutive aspects of narrative identity. By representation, I refer to narration that represents the self, to the self and others. By constitutive, I refer to narration that actually constitutes the self that is always already in the process of narrating its own conditions of existence. The latter constitutive aspect is more closely aligned with how Macdonald conceives of the constitutive nature of legal subjectivity, wherein the legal subject hypothesizes the concept of law that calls into being its own legal subjectivity.

McAdams is perhaps less explicit than Bruner is in accounting for not just the representational but also the constitutive aspects of self-narration. Recall that for Bruner, in the process of telling our stories, we become the person in the stories we tell. As McAdams notes, however, narrative identity is now "a psychological first among equals" in terms of the psychological senses whereby humans "make identity."[46] In the field of personality psychology, life stories are a distinct domain of personality structure and function, separate from and yet related to the more familiar personality domains of disposition traits and characteristic adaptations. A full account of psychological individuality must incorporate all three domains.[47] Accordingly, I interpret McAdams as providing a constitutive theory of narrative self-identity as required to support the concept of the narrative/*nomos* obligational self as an elaboration of the jurisgenerative legal subject of critical legal pluralism.

McAdams's focus on narrative integration across one's lifespan describes our search for an integrative narrative capable of providing a sense of unity to our sense of self. This might appear to be at odds with the concept of a narrative/*nomos* obligational self predicated upon critical legal pluralism as a postmodern account of non-essential, non-unitary, and multiply identified legal subjects. An explicitly postmodern theory of narrative identity thus might be more appropriate for integration into this developing analytical framework. Not surprisingly, the dialogic nature of identity as a negotiation between psychic and social has been explored, as for example in Hermans's account of the dialogic self. According to Hermans, our narrative identity is polyphonic in the same manner as a novel authored by different characters who engage with each other within our own narrative identity as well as with persons in the external world.[48]

McAdams's theory of narrative identity formation, however, does not contradict the postmodern aspects of the narrative/*nomos* obligational self as multiply identified rather than unitary and essential. The first important aspect is multiplicity, in that McAdams conceives of contemporary selves as characterized not by unity of purpose but rather by fragmentation and multiplicity of identity.[49] Another aspect is the function of social construction and agency in the narrative construction of self-identity. The self is not a stable identity that accumulates over the course of a lifetime but rather is a fluctuating identity situated in social locations and constructed through discourse. The interesting inversion provided by theories of self-narration, including Bruner as well as McAdams, is that stories do not exist inside our narrated selves but rather our selves exist in the stories that circulate throughout culture.[50] Arguably, this is the narrative identity formation equivalent of inverting prevailing notions of law and legal subjectivity we see as a foundational premise of critical legal pluralism. For the purpose of this analysis, the important point to note is that McAdams's understanding of coherence is not dependent on an essential unity.[51] In fact, as discussed below, McAdams's concept of the imago is an explicit acknowledgment of the multiplicity of self.

This acknowledgment of the multiplicity of a sense of self is necessary if psychological theories of narrative identity are to coexist with developments in literary theory at least with those that accept either explicitly or implicitly the foundational premises of Bakhtin's theory of the novel as a broader theory of knowledge more generally.[52] The discursive plurality of narrative defies any attempt to disaggregate the voices of characters, narrators, and authors from each other or from the social context in which narrative is created and performed. Intersubjectivity of meaning is not confined to the characters, the narrator, or even the author.[53] Self-narration is therefore not exempt from the operation of discursive plurality. Analytical separation can be applied to undifferentiated discourse, which is the whole point of methodologies such as narratology, but as Bal notes, this is done precisely in order to account for intersubjectivity and its implications.[54] Accordingly, I do not find it necessary to explicitly adopt postmodern perspectives on narrative identity formation. Given the significance of cultural narratives in McAdams's work as discussed below, his theoretical approach is not inconsistent with an understanding of discursive plurality.

McAdams conceives of narrative identity as a psychosocial construction, and thus incorporating his theory into this developing analytical framework addresses a potential objection that locating the nexus of mutually constitutive law and popular culture discourse in the narrative/*nomos* obligational self creates an irresolvable contradiction between individual constructive capacity and the collective nature of both narrative and *nomos*. The concept of the narrative/*nomos* obligational self informed by McAdams's theoretical approach to narrative identity formation is consistent with Macdonald's reference to a legal subject's narrating selves as being both inter- and intra-subjective as well as Macdonald and Sandomierski's recognition that the emancipatory potential of agency has limits, as for example, our susceptibility to the coercive influence of dominant narratives.[55] Self-narration is necessarily interactional, not idiosyncratic, in nature.[56] No aspect of the narrative/*nomos* obligational self is meant to suggest the isolation of essentialism, a concept of self explicitly rejected by Kleinhans and Macdonald.[57]

On the other hand, the collective nature of narrative and *nomos* should in turn not lead to essentialized abstractions of law. As Kleinhans and Macdonald aptly note, the modern self is indeed a construct, but the constructive capacity of this construct creates the inter-normative character of legal pluralism. This is why a critical legal pluralist analysis is not simply a matter of recalibrating for a micro rather than macro perspective on an essentialized entity. This would presuppose the empirical existence of conflicting legal orders, examined through a zoom lens, so to speak, to reveal otherwise imperceptible details. This fails to take into account the constructive capacity of legal subjects and the collective nature of their narratives as they acknowledge and respond to normative heterogeneity.[58]

McAdams's theory of narrative identity formation as interactional in nature also demonstrates a relationship between popular culture narratives and the self-narration of the narrative/*nomos* obligational self. No life story begins with a blank page. The narratives we draw upon to construct our identity are the cultural narratives in which we always already exist.[59] In our ongoing self-narrations, or to be more colloquial, in the ongoing process of telling our life stories, we incorporate cultural norms, images, characters, plots, and themes that we encounter in the collective narratives of our cultural contexts, including the self-narrations of others.[60] McAdams's perhaps most sustained exploration of how cultural narratives influence narrative identity is provided by his analysis of redemptive life stories.[61] McAdams analyzed the life stories of what he referred to as generative adults, meaning middle-aged persons who were committed to promoting the development and well-being of successive generations. This was demonstrated by a desire to pass on fundamental values acquired through life experience (hence the relevance of middle age) and by actions such as community involvement.

McAdams found that the life stories of generative adults were characterized by the theme of self-redemption. They narrated quintessentially American stories of heroic individuals who overcome obstacles in pursuit of upward mobility, in other words, typical Horatio Alger stories. These are the redemptive stories of people fulfilling the manifest destiny of American exceptionalism,[62] which is to make a positive difference in the rest of the less fortunate world (whether by invitation or otherwise). I do not want to confer legitimacy on the invasive concept of manifest destiny. This specific example, however, can be applied to other contexts in order to demonstrate that self-narration incorporates prevailing and predominant cultural narratives, including those widely distributed through works of popular culture. The point to be made is that life stories are psychosocial constructions, reflecting not only an individual's authorial intentions, but also the canonical stories that form a distinct part of our different cultural heritages.[63]

To return to Bruner on this matter of cultural psychology, the cultural aspect of self-narration is consistent with what Bruner refers to as the "distributed self." What we might understand as our essential and unitary sense of self is not an inner truth or core of pre-social existence but rather a product of social construction in which we all participate. What is innate is our drive to interpret, through narrative, the "collective text" of our cultures. In abstract terms, we experience culture as knowledge, in the sense that meaning is derived from the way in which we interpret our cultural experiences.[64] Whether as McAdams's reference to narrative identity as a psycho-social construction or Bruner's reference to the distributed self, these theories demonstrate the importance of collective narratives, including popular culture narratives, in establishing the narrative/*nomos* of the obligational self.[65]

Having argued that the narrative/*nomos* obligational self is an identity formed through self-narration, that this psycho-social construction of self draws upon collective narratives, and that these necessarily include narratives of popular culture, the next step is to provide additional support for my claim that the self-narration of the obligational self is inherently normative in nature. Bruner and McAdams both focus on the normative aspects of narrative identity, albeit in different ways. Burner's argument is more implicit in that the focus is on narrative as a mode of discourse. Narrative discourse is based on breaches of expectation, and these instances of breach presuppose the existence of a norm.[66] He cites in support of this argument narrative scholars who propose that a fundamental concern of narrative is cultural legitimacy.[67] McAdams, as expected, focuses more specifically on personality in arguing that the central function of self-narrative in respect of the modern self is to confer moral legitimacy. Just as normative standards exist in cultural narratives, so too will they be incorporated into self-narrative.[68] The culturally recognized narratives we draw upon in self-narration provide the various perspectives and standards for judging the moral value of our lives.[69] Since we are moral agents, our life stories always provide a moral perspective of our actions, wherein we reference cultural standards of right and wrong behavior.[70]

As is the case with narrative more generally, we tell stories for particular reasons. McAdams argues that when we tell the story of our life, meaning the stories that constitute our sense of self, we do so with reference to normative standards. Consistent with Bruner, McAdams argues that all narratives presuppose a normative understanding of the world. Just as we need an understanding of the good to make sense of fictional stories, we need this same understanding to make sense of our lives. Our normative understanding as an orientation toward the good is an integral aspect of how we understand our lives as protagonists of our own continually unfolding and constitutive life story.[71] There is an almost exact correspondence here among the life story as moral justification, Cover's concept of law as alternity,[72] and Kleinhans and Macdonald's account of legal subjects engaged in exploring possible worlds and possible selves.[73] The life stories we narrate address both our reconstructed past and our imagined futures.[74] These internalized life stories provide a moral justification that integrates an explanation of the person we were with an aspiration of the person we want to become.[75]

As noted above, our orientation toward the good is necessarily influenced by the normative standards that originate and are revealed in our interactions with others. We construct a story of our lives not just to communicate our experiences to others, but also to create and understand our own identity by creating continuity between our past, present, and future.[76] The intra- and inter-subjective context in which we narrate our multiple selves provides us with the means to recognize and evaluate normative alternatives, and in the act of telling our story, we become the person in the story we are telling. In making this point, I return again to my claim, succinctly stated, that obligation is a function of identity. Our understanding of who we are is a function of our understanding of our obligations in relation to others.

To return to the jurisgenerative narrative/*nomos* obligational self as a nexus for the mutually constitutive discourse of law and popular culture, the most relevant normative aspect of McAdams's theory of narrative identity formation is his concept of the imago. He defines the imago as "an idealized personification of the self that functions as a protagonist in the narrative."[77] Beginning in adolescence, we start to create a life story for ourselves that assumes a mythic quality. Whereas cultural myths express the fundamental concerns and basic truths of a society, our personal myths delineate our identity and express our fundamental values.[78] Our personal myth becomes an ongoing psychological quest across our lifespan. We strive to create an integrative life story, constitutive of our sense of self, which explains how our past produced our present. This narrative task, and thus the self-narration of our identity, is inherently normative in that explanation involves evaluation and judgment.[79]

McAdams's concept of the imago explains how our personal stories can create a sense of unity and purpose and yet also account for the multiplicity of selves that are a more accurate characterization of our existence. Our life stories, our personal myths, contain multiple characters, or imagoes, each of which represents an idealization, either hero or villain, of the various roles we play (or have played) in everyday life. Each imago is a different personification of an aspect of self, reflecting differing and even contradictory aspects of identity. Our identity is the story we tell ourselves that includes, as all stories do, a cast of characters in the form of imagoes, positive and negative, common and unique. They are all aspects of our selves, and thus the better we understand the characters of our life story, the better we understand ourselves.[80]

Any aspect of self, including who we are, who we were, who we aspire to be, and who we fear we might become, can be incorporated into the personal myths of our life stories as imagoes. As character types, they are created with reference to the larger cultural context of what McAdams describes as stock characters[81] as well as people we perceive as role models.[82] Note, however, that in exploring the normative implications of collective narratives, I am not arguing that the significance of narrative either implies or requires a causal relationship whereby collective narrative X, instantiated in imago Y of a narrative/*nomos* obligational self, results in behavior Z. Such an approach would confine the significance of popular culture to mimesis while at the same time reducing the complexity of narrative to syllogism.[83]

The explanatory value of McAdams's imagoes for the concept of the narrative/*nomos* obligational self is the constitutive and inherently normative nature of self-narration, as informed by collective cultural narratives. First, as discussed above, the imago is evocative of Cover's understanding of law as alternity. McAdams compares imagoes to the "possible selves" articulated by Markus and Nurius to refer to our ideas of what kind of person we might become and what kind of person we are afraid of becoming. Possible selves provide both an interpretive and evaluative context for one's current view of self.[84] We tell a story of our life, and thus create our sense of self, by integrating these multiple protagonists in a way that provides a sense of unity and purpose.

Second, our imagoes are self-defining aspects of our life story. Recall that narrative identity for McAdams is not simply representative, in the sense of how we describe ourselves to ourselves and to others, but also constitutive, not in the sense of creating an essence that exists but in the sense that our internalized life story is the understanding we have of our selves (which is not to say our understanding would be perceived by others as accurate). Imagoes are expressions of personal desires and goals and, more significantly, the individual and cultural values that characterize the mythic quality of our life story.[85] Our normative understandings (referred to by McAdams as our ideological setting) may be expressed to a significant degree in our imagoes.[86] To the extent that our narrative understanding of our selves is both constitutive of our identity as well as an explanation of how we perceive our behavior, we act in a manner consistent with, or at least not fundamentally contradictory to, the type of person we understand our selves to be. Again, this is not a claim that others agree with our perspective as we tell the stories of our lives, but on the other hand, complete social consensus is not necessary to demonstrate the normative force of imagoes with respect to the narrative/*nomos* obligational self. As Kleinhans and Macdonald argue, any concept of law, however influenced by the conceptions of others, is necessarily autobiographical.[87]

Nor does this mean we will always act in accordance with the characteristic and personalized properties of our imagoes. This does not affect the explanatory value of that which is proposed. First, we often fall short of meeting our normative aspirations in our everyday lives. Second, our imagoes do not provide the entirety of the story of our lives. As with any story, character is merely one narrative element along with plot, theme, setting, and so on.[88] Third, when we reconstruct our past, we are very selective in the editing process. The narrative identities we seek to create are not objectively true in the sense that others would necessarily agree with our self-assessment,[89] nor can we be assured that we will consistently realize our narrative/*nomos* aspirations. Nonetheless, the very act of attempting to explain divergence in the continued redrafting of our life stories presupposes the existence of a narrative/*nomos* standard that has relevance in our lives.

In terms of understanding the diversity of our accounts of self, no agreed-upon or widely validated typology of imago exists.[90] McAdams provides an initial classification of types based on the properties of agency and communion, which he has identified through empirical research as central themes in people's life stories. He then further identifies character types based on combinations of representative properties. A warrior, for example, tends more toward agency than communion, while a lover represents the opposite configuration. Some characters, such as teachers and healers, combine both properties, while others, such as escapists and survivors, possess little of either.[91]

In addition to achieving a greater understanding of specific people, commonalities may exist between the self-narrated life stories of people with common imagoes, however defined.[92] In other words, we might expect to find common imagoes based on shared cultural narratives in the self-narrated identities of eco/animal activists, as evidenced by accounts of their normative beliefs and behaviors.[93] Accordingly, I will require an appropriate typology of imago to analyze collective narratives in popular culture as instantiated in the narrative/*nomos* obligational selves of eco/animal activists. In contrast to McAdams's empirical work, my typology will need some other method of verification for its utility. Also in contrast to McAdams's work, while many first-person accounts of the beliefs and behaviors of eco/animal activists exist, the explanations provided are unlikely to reference their life stories. Given that they are engaged in what we all tend to perceive as acts of transgression against state law, however justified, the basis of any explanation of belief and/or behavior is likely to be framed as moral imperatives taking precedence over illegitimate legal rules.[94] These explanations, if sufficiently consistent, will serve as a proxy for examining the recursive integration of popular culture narratives and self-narrations of narrative/*nomos* obligational selves.

In the case study presented in Chapter 5, I explain the validity and utility of analyzing imagoes with reference to a typology of character alignment, which is fundamental to table-top role-playing games such as Dungeons and Dragons.[95] In doing so, I further specify the participation of the narrative/*nomos* obligational self in mutually constitutive discourse with reference to a character alignment termed "neutral good." The relevant property of a neutral good identity formation is a willingness to follow moral imperatives when faced with illegitimate claims advanced by state law. While many people may disagree with state law, not all of these narrative/*nomos* obligational selves are oriented toward the normative orientation of neutral good. For a person who has a neutral good imago, meaning an idealized sense of an aspect of self that has these relevant properties, adverse consequences of unlawful behavior do not provide relief from performance of the obligation, as would be the case for those who disagree with the law but either do not believe that morality takes precedence over law or, more prosaically, do not believe that the consequences are something they are obliged to bear.

As a preliminary caution, the issue of typology raises an important point, arguably self-evident, that different cultures provide different shared narratives that condition the possibilities of narrative identity. Different kinds of narrative identity do not necessarily make sense across different cultures,[96] and thus life stories will reflect the culture in which they originate.[97] Significantly, they will also reflect divisions predicated upon gender, race, and class constructions. This not only shapes narrative identity, but also indicates that privileged narratives will prevail over those that are more marginalized.[98] In recognizing these limitations on authorial agency, McAdams's account of narrative identity is consistent with Macdonald's caveat concerning the emancipatory potential of critical legal pluralism. In processes of personal narration and interaction, capacity and resources are not evenly distributed among legal subjects. Neither inter- nor intra-subjective life is either democratic or egalitarian. Through either dominance or ideology, those with power will be able to impose their narratives on others.[99] Nonetheless, the emancipatory potential of critical legal pluralism, and thus the emancipatory potential of the narrative/*nomos* obligational self, is the recognition that counter-hegemonic power is possible not by resisting state law, which simply confirms its legitimacy through cooption, but by denying its exclusivity in relation to the word "law."[100] McAdams similarly calls attention to the construction of counter-narratives that exist apart from and resist dominant cultural narratives.[101]

In summary then, the narrative/*nomos* obligational self is an elaboration of the jurisgenerative legal subject defined by Macdonald with reference to two narrative functions, being narrative as a means of communicating the legal knowledge that creates and maintains legal reality and self-narration as a means of constituting the identity of legal subjectivity. References to these narrative functions in Macdonald's work were illuminating but nonetheless brief, particularly in terms of narrative identity. By incorporating into the developing analytical framework theories of narrative meaning and narrative identity formation from cognitive and personality theories of psychology, I elaborate upon the jurisgenerative legal subject of critical legal pluralism by proposing the concept of a narrative/*nomos* obligational self.

Obligation is a significant function of our self-narrated identity in that our understandings of our selves cannot be disaggregated from our understandings of our obligations in relation to others. The obligational self is inherently normative, as demonstrated by McAdams's theory of narrative identity. As we narrate the ongoing life story that creates and maintains a unified and purposive sense of self, we engage is a process of moral justification as part of the process of explaining the person we were, the person we came to be, and the person we hope to become. More specifically, the inherently normative nature of the obligational self is demonstrated by McAdams's concept of the imago as an idealized aspect of self, represented as a character in our life story. The obligational force of imago is a function of the mythic quality of our life stories. Imagoes express both individual and cultural values, and the inherent logic of narrative identity is that we seek to act, although we may not always succeed, in ways that are consistent with who we think we are and, perhaps more importantly for this re-imagination of law, who we aspire to be.

Collective narratives, including popular culture narratives, exert a significant influence on our identity, as we draw upon these narratives in our own constitutive self-narrations of our life stories, and thus our understandings of our selves. To return to Bruner on this point, the stories we tell of ourselves, the stories we use to constitute our sense of self, are taken from the culture in which we exist. Our own cognitive capacity for narrative makes possible our acts of self-narration, but Bruner is nonetheless explicit in stating that "we are virtually from the start expressions of the culture that nurtures us."[102] The integrated narrative/*nomos* nature of the obligational self is a function of the incorporation of aspects of collective narratives, including popular culture narratives, into self-narration generally and as informing the development of imagoes more specifically. When we narrate the life stories that give us our sense of identity, we refer to both prevailing cultural norms and common narrative devices, including images, metaphors, themes, characters, and plots.[103] When we understand imagoes as individualizations of so-called stock cultural characters, and understand their obligational force as our desire to act in ways consistent with the sense of self we create and maintain through our ongoing life story, we have a means for hypothesizing with sufficient specificity the legal authority of popular culture, unmediated by translation into state law.

Critical legal pluralism locates the nexus for law in the jurisgenerative capacity of the legal subject, who is responsible for creating and responding to proffered claims of legality. With reference to narrative identity formation, I elaborate upon this constructive capacity to propose a narrative/*nomos* obligational self. I locate the nexus of popular culture and law as mutually constitutive discourse in the self-narrations of our obligational selves as we create and respond to proffered claims of legality. In narrating our identities, we draw upon broader cultural narratives and common narrative characters,[104] instantiating them in our imagoes as idealized representations of different and at times conflicting aspects of our selves. When we encounter normative heterogeneity in our everyday lives, we will aspire to act in a manner consistent with our inherently normative self-identity, albeit one which is multiply identified and also potentially normatively heterogeneous.

When we re-imagine legality based on an analytical framework that incorporates both critical legal pluralism and a psychological theory of narrative identity formation, resulting in a conception of a narrative/*nomos* obligational self, we can understand with specificity how popular culture might function as legal authority. Our narrative/*nomos* obligational selves are participants in a mutually constitutive discourse of law and popular culture wherein legality is conceived not by reference to the source of the claim but by reference to the inherently normative aspects of our self-narrated identities and the manner in which we seek to govern ourselves accordingly.

Before proceeding to the next section, note that I do not claim that the now-developed analytical framework represents a reflection of an observable external reality. I adapt and apply Macdonald's theoretical account of critical legal pluralism as a cornerstone of this analysis, and as Macdonald notes, he did not develop his theory as a systematic observation of law as a verifiable entity. Law, and ways of thinking about law, are constantly made and remade as we use this term to announce, explain, and justify our interactions with others. Macdonald's claim is that if we adopt critical legal pluralism as a way of thinking about law, we are better able to understand, rhetorically employ, and refer to the full emancipatory potential of law.[105] I am also mindful of the significance accorded by Melissaris to an interperspectival approach to analyzing legal pluralism.[106] In recognizing the contingency of my own hypothesis, and avoiding a programmatic approach by suggesting but not imposing a framework for re-imagining law, I hope that I am following appropriately their example.

The subjectivity of obligational selves

The necessary analytical framework for analyzing popular culture and law as mutually constitutive discourse is now in place. What remains before proceeding to Chapter 5, in which I provide an illustrative case study as proof of concept for the application of this analytical framework, is to address recurring questions of identity. These questions arise whenever we consider the nature of legal subjectivity, which I characterize in this analysis as a narrative/*nomos* obligational self, understood always as non-essential, non-unitary, and multiply identified. As Schlag observes, contemporary modes of legal thought increasingly engage directly with what he refers to as the problem of the legal subject.[107] In addition, any particular mode of thought necessarily presupposes, albeit often in an unexamined manner, precisely those characteristics of a legal subject that provide coherence and validity to the concept of law being advanced.[108] Briefly stated, the problem of the legal subject is its absence, in that our manner of inquiry tends to treat law as acting of its own accord.[109] What is missing from legal thought is an account of the actual human beings who create, maintain, and resist the law being analyzed. As I argued in Chapter 2, this may be in part a consequence of our habit of nominalization, a process of moving from verb to noun that is not without its advantages as a means of communication.

On the other hand, the difficulty with nominalization, also discussed above, is that we tend to neglect and forget the actors who are the subjects, not to mention the objects to which (and whom) they apply their actions. Incorporating constructivist accounts of legal pluralism and narrative identity formation into an analytical framework counters this tendency. So too does the concept of the narrative/*nomos* obligational self, particularly when considered in relation to the thematic objective of re-imagining legality as verb (capacity) rather than noun (outcome). Recall that I locate the nexus for the mutually constitutive discourse of law and popular culture within the narrative/*nomos* obligational self, an assignment justified by the inherently normative nature of our self-narrated identities. This is consistent with Macdonald's claim, as a fundamental premise of critical legal pluralism, that both legality and inter-legality are noumenal rather than phenomenal in nature.[110] Reference to noumenal legality, however, could lead to potential misunderstandings about certain characteristics of the narrative/*nomos* obligational self, which I address as three related issues: (a) legal consciousness, with reference to both over- and underdetermination; (b) the exercise of agency and its constraints, in that emancipatory potential is not simply a naive utopian aspiration; and (c) narrative/*nomos* obligational selves as necessarily embedded in social relations, in that jurisgenerative capacity does not provoke a dystopian nightmare of relativism, lawlessness, indeterminacy, and indecision.

Consciousness over-/underdetermined

A significant aspect of the legal subjectivity of the narrative/*nomos* obligational self, established by reference to the legal subjectivity of critical legal pluralism, is that subjectivity is not imposed by authoritative command. Rather, legal subjectivity originates with our own jurisgenerative capacity and commitment, although we may indeed hypothesize and affirm a concept of law that imposes our subjectivity by way of authoritative command. A related premise of critical legal pluralism, one that I take seriously in providing my own hypothesis of law and popular culture as mutually constitutive discourse, is that the people involved in conceiving of, believing in, and responding to law should not be viewed as abstractions. Accordingly, I would like to devote some attention to the issue of consciousness, which I organize with respect to overdetermination and underdetermination. The former involves the fine line between proposing alternative conceptions of law while not assuming that those who believe in a traditional concept of law are possessed of false consciousness. The latter involves legal consciousness scholarship, which to the extent that the focus remains on the exclusive legal authority of the state, may underdetermine the scope of our legal imagination.

With the problem of overdetermination, I want to pre-empt a potential misunderstanding that the hypothesis of a narrative/*nomos* obligational self implies false consciousness on the part of those who do not perceive their legal subjectivity in these terms. This would be a programmatic overdetermination of consciousness that contradicts the emancipatory potential of re-imagining law in a way that emphasizes the agency and constructive capacity of legal subjects. As stated earlier, the emancipatory potential for the eco/animal activists analyzed in the case study below does not take the form of legal advice. The objective is not to provide instruction on how to transform a reimagined concept of law into drafting the types of legal documents required to successfully present state courts with a conflict of laws analysis. The emancipatory potential is that they may, if they so choose, call upon the full signifying power of law to understand their beliefs and behaviors. From their perspective, their normative claims may well be legal claims, as state law would no longer have a monopoly on legal authority. On the other hand, they may choose instead to affirm their belief in the exclusive authority of state law, in which case the emancipatory potential is still realized, given that the hypothesis of state law is no longer an unexamined assumption.

With respect to the overdetermination of false consciousness, the theoretical foundation of critical legal pluralism arguably guards against this type of programmatic result. Recall that Macdonald's theory is both a first-order hypothesis that accounts for plural law and a second-order hypothesis that accounts for plural understandings of law.[111] In other words, critical legal pluralism is an argument for understanding law as plurality and at the same time an argument that accounts for understandings of law held by others. The question of what is law cannot be hypothesized in the abstract or in advance or by anyone other than the person who is in the process of understanding circumstances of normative heterogeneity as they arise in relation to themselves. This resolves the apparent paradox whereby a theory of legal pluralism can nonetheless recognize the legitimacy of monist conceptions of law. From a critical legal pluralist perspective, belief in the exclusivity of state law is not an instance of false consciousness.

As a related issue, and one that becomes evident in the case study presented in Chapter 5, I do not need to demonstrate a proof of concept by claiming that eco/animal activists currently understand legality, not to mention their own jurisgenerative potential, consistent with the concept of the narrative/*nomos* obligational self. Nor do I claim this is the case, as evidence of a re-imagined law on the part of those who have yet to re-imagine law in these terms would be an extraordinary coincidence. Eco/animal activists have produced extensive literature in which they provide their reasons for action. A recurring theme is that moral imperatives provide justification for transgression of state legal rules.[112] That moral imperatives might constitute their own, alternative legality is not considered; the relevant circumstances of normative heterogeneity are understood as the actions of a resistance movement against valid but unconscionable state law. This is consistent with a critical legal pluralist approach to normative heterogeneity in that a valid hypothesis of law is one that attracts the beliefs and committed behaviors of legal subjects themselves. A critical legal pluralist approach does not also require legal subjects to adopt critical legal pluralism in order to validate their monist understanding of law, which would be a contradiction in terms.

Nonetheless, moving from theory to proof of concept, how can I analyze their beliefs and behaviors in a way that is inconsistent with their understanding of state law, and furthermore, how can I do this in a way that does not impute false consciousness with respect to their beliefs? The resolution is that the emancipatory potential of re-imaging law is a matter of capacity, not outcome. The analytical framework I have developed, including most specifically the concept of the narrative/*nomos* obligational self, does not require a programmatic overdetermination of legal consciousness. The beliefs and behaviors of eco/animal activists do not provide evidence of a re-imagined hypothesis of law that does not yet exist in the imaginations of legal subjects themselves. This does not discount, however, the explanatory power of the concept of the narrative/*nomos* obligational self as a more specific account of how we might understand popular culture as legal authority. As to whether eco/animal activists themselves choose to reconceive of moral justifications as legal claims, the choice is theirs, as is the choice to affirm their belief in state law.

Beliefs and behaviors are amenable to different explanations. Assume for example that eco/animal activists hold a set of beliefs concerning the appropriate nature of relationships between humans and animals. These beliefs reject the assumption, embedded in economic as well as legal relations, that humans are hierarchically superior to animals as a matter of nature, morality, or theology. Assume as well that the eco/animal activists engage in a set of behaviors that instantiate commitment to these beliefs, such as arson or other acts that damage the property of people and corporations engaged in exploiting animals for human gain.

Nothing in this project of re-imagining law seeks to assess eco/animal activists' normative understandings, including not only how they understand human-animal relationships, for which significant commentary exists, but also how they conceive of law and legal subjectivity. Pursuant to the prevailing hypothesis of law, an eco/animal activist is likely to understand transgressive actions as morally right/legally wrong acts of resistance. Nonetheless, these beliefs and behaviors could be analyzed independently from activists themselves, as information to be considered from the alternative perspective of a re-imagined legality, wherein the narrative/*nomos* obligational self incorporates into identity formation, and thus the formation of obligation, popular culture narratives of resistance. Furthermore, popular culture narratives may also convey understandings of law that are consistent with the exclusive authority of the political state and that acts of resistance are morally justified acts of transgression. Again, this does not affect the utility of the concept of narrative/*nomos* obligational self, since fictional accounts of law can also be analyzed as information, independently from the narratives in which they are conveyed. For a proof of concept of the narrative/*nomos* obligational self, what is required is evidence of shared normative understandings of resistance, more specifically, the rules of resistance as they pertain to the nature and extent of violence permitted. My argument, which is not causal in nature, is that these shared normative understandings are an indication of how we draw upon popular culture narratives as we narrate our inherently normative selves. This is the process whereby we can understand our narrative/*nomos* obligational selves as the nexus of jurisgenerative capacity and normative heterogeneity. Our narrative/*nomos* obligational selves exercise this jurisgenerative capacity by hypothesizing and responding to hypotheses of law.

When an eco/animal activist explains her actions with reference to justified transgression or resistance to state law, she is not surprisingly referencing the hypothesis of law that has the greatest command by far of our legal imaginations. The same normative beliefs and behaviors, however, can be understood with reference to range of different hypotheses of law. Legality is located in these beliefs and behaviors, not in the label attached. As Macdonald and Sandomierski argue, normative inquiry begins with the significance of the standards to which we refer in our interactions with others, what Melissaris would refer to as our shared normative experiences, and not with the symbolic expressions themselves.[113] That we tend to explain ourselves with reference to state law is a reflection of the superior reputation of these norms relative to others.[114]

The recurring theme of moral imperatives that trump state law is yet another instance of the endless oscillation between law and justice I discussed in Chapter 2. As I argued, the hierarchical distinction in status between law and mere norms is not inevitable. This simply reflects an intentional and conceptual extraction of presumptively autonomous law from the domain of culture. All external reference points not extracted from culture in this manner are consigned to the status of mere norms. Should eco/animal activists choose to understand their beliefs and behaviors as normative but unlawful, this understanding is not a consequence of an inevitable distinction between law and norm. Nor does their own inquiry into what constitutes law begin with the symbolic expressions of state law. This should be a logically obvious conclusion; the meaning people derive from symbolic expressions of law cannot precede the hypothesis of law pursuant to which meaning is established. If eco/animal activists understand their belief and behavior as morally justified illegal acts, this is a consequence of a hypothesis of law as state law, affirmed by the relevant community of eco/animal activists who consider themselves bound by law accordingly.

I may appear to be laboring the point here, but objections of false consciousness are common and persistent, and exorcising them requires an emphatic discussion. To label any person's understanding of law as false consciousness would actually contradict the fundamental premises of critical legal pluralism and would thus be incompatible with the concept of the narrative/*nomos* obligational self. Disagreement may exist as to whether a dominant concept of law is affirmed or imposed, but this is a question of power, not truth. I do not dispute the relevance of the question of truth when posed from the perspective of other legal theories, other disciplines, or other modes of thought. The question is simply not relevant to the concept of a narrative/*nomos* obligational self. The emancipatory potential of this project is the invitation (not prescription) accorded to legal subjects to re-imagine their understanding of law as one in which they possess creative capacity, particularly in relation to the prospective legal authority of popular cultural narratives in which they are always already immersed. Whether this invitation is desirable, detrimental, or delusional is something that can only be determined by eco/animal activists themselves.

Moving to the problem of underdetermination, I want to distinguish the narrative/*nomos* of the obligational self from scholarship on legal consciousness. Legal consciousness scholarship explores the normative implications of how people understand law. The approach appears similar to the extent that the focus is on how people understand law. The difference, however, is that legal consciousness scholarship is an inquiry into how people understand state law and how these understandings in turn contribute to the meaning of state law. State officials do not have exclusive control over the meaning of law, but nonetheless, the meaning of law remains that of the exclusive authority of the state. This is not a deficiency of legal consciousness scholarship, which could not be otherwise given the predominance of the hypothesis of state law. People believe in the exclusivity of state law because no alternative image prevails. For this reason, however, legal consciousness is a project of understanding how people understand a dominant hypothesis of law. To the extent our legal imaginations are overdetermined by a single image of law, this will be reflected in legal consciousness scholarship. The concept of the narrative/*nomos* obligational self is a project of re-imagining how people might understand an alternative hypothesis of law, one that resists the overdetermination of monist conceptions of state law.

As Lobel explains, there are at least two different approaches to legal consciousness. As a question of legal theory, legal consciousness simply refers to a particular society's understanding at a particular time of the concept and function of law. On the other hand, empirical research in socio-legal studies adopts a constitutive approach in examining how citizens experience, understand, and evaluate law in their ordinary lives, including decisions regarding compliance and transgression.[115] The constitutive aspect is the reciprocal nature of people's participation, in that as legal meanings proliferate and circulate, they stabilize into patterns that become institutionalized discourse, which in turn determine the scope of what constitutes legitimate legal meaning.[116] Socio-legal analysis may also be critical in nature, in the sense of seeking to understand why people who are so ill-served by law continue to abide by legal rules, although Silbey argues that recent scholarship has lessened the critical potential of the concept. Focusing on the thoughts and actions of individuals may assist in policy reforms targeted toward specific groups but does not disturb the underlying status quo. She argues instead for a broader focus on the relationships among legal consciousness, power, and hegemony.[117]

Legal consciousness scholarship provides evidence of baseline understandings of the normative failure of state law. In earlier work, Ewick and Silbey set out a trifold categorization of how people conceive of law in relation to their everyday lives. Note that the categories apply to modes of thought, not people themselves, whose responses and reactions may be partial, overlap, and change over time. The most remote category is that of "before the law," in which people who have little or no experience of legality conceive of law as an exogenous and objective abstraction. In other words, those who have never had to deal with law in their everyday lives, for better or for worse, never experience the disillusion that accompanies the gap between the image of law and the reality of its instantiation. The other two categories include people who have experienced law at some point in their everyday lives. In the category of "with the law," people conceive of law as a mechanism to be exploited, if possible, to achieve their desired ends. In contrast, in the category of "against the law," people conceive of law as an instrument of power rather than justice, incapable of providing equitable outcomes for vulnerable people who lack resources.[118] At no time do people imagine, as an aspect of their legal consciousness, the possibility of an alternative to state law.

A possible connection between legal consciousness scholarship and the concept of the narrative/*nomos* obligational self may be found in Fritsvold's work on the legal consciousness of radical environmentalists. I discuss the results of Fritsvold's work in more detail below, as part of the case study of bio-punk critical dystopia narratives of resistance and the beliefs and behaviors of eco/animal activists. For now, I note Fritsvold's argument that the extensive body of analysis and commentary concerning radical social and activist movements would benefit from legal consciousness's constitutive approach to law and society.[119] He elaborates upon Ewick and Silbey's trifold categorization to analyze the legal consciousness of radical environmentalists engaged in civil disobedience. Radical environmentalists associated with a "deep ecology" perspective develop what he has categorized as an "under the law" legal consciousness. Like the legal consciousness of "against the law," people in the category of "under the law" reject the aspirational premises of state law as capable of delivering justice. The difference is one of response.

Radical environmentalists understand our world as a corrupt social order, which inevitably produces a corrupt legal system that operates solely to perpetuate exploitative social relations. Powerful interests are affirmed, dissent is repressed, and ostensible opportunities to achieve justice through legal means are illusory at best. While the legal consciousness of "against the law" understands law as failing to achieve social justice, the legal consciousness of "under the law" understands this failure as a product of intentional design. The objective of radical environmentalists who are "under the law" is nothing less than to subvert both the illegitimate legal system and the unjust social relations of modern industrial capitalism that law is designed to protect.[120]

In terms of the potential for reconceiving of law with respect to a narrative/*nomos* obligational self, the difficulty is determining whether "under the law" rejects illegitimate law in a specific instance or rejects the concept of law more generally. Radical environmentalists act pursuant to a well-considered analysis of the role of law in sustaining a particular model of social relations, as is evident in their strong resistance to being labeled terrorists by state legal authorities. If anything, the state is more deserving of the label, given its unsustainable exploitation of nature and unconscionable exploitation of animal life.[121] By their own understandings, radical environmentalists don't simply oppose state law; they engage in revolution. Successful revolution will lead to new normative systems, but whether any of these will be conceived as law is an open question. My assessment on this point is tentative, given Fritsvold's statement that the category of "under the law" is a point of departure for new and further inquiry.[122] As a provisional solution, however, we can assume that even if radical environmentalists are opposed to law generally, this opposition is directed toward prevailing understandings of state law. The potential remains to consider alternative hypotheses of law. I discuss this issue in more detail as part of the case study provided in Chapter 5.

Agency exercised and constrained

The concept of the narrative/*nomos* obligational self, as a proposal regarding the constructive capacity of legal subjectivity, raises concomitant issues of agency. The nature of the relationship between agency and structure (or determinism) is a recurring theme across different disciplinary inquiries. Bruner, for example, addressing the concept of self from the perspective of cognitive psychology, succinctly states, "It can never be the case that there is a 'self' independent of one's cultural-historical existence."[123] He argues that when we represent ourselves to others and ourselves through stories, we are always in the process of balancing both autonomy and commitment. On the one hand, we desire autonomy, the freedom to make our own choices, and the ability to act unimpeded on our own desires. On the other hand, for those of us who are social beings (Bruner arguably assumes we are all social beings), we also desire relations with others, and our commitments to others have the effect of limiting our autonomy.[124] He also refers to the nature of our identity as a distributed self, in the sense that identity formation is relational, both a product of our interpretations of our selves as well as others' interpretations of our interpretations. Our selves are "highly negotiable," responding to the price mechanisms operating in our preferred reference groups just as goods and services respond to price mechanisms in free markets.[125]

To take a more specific example from legal theory, recall the discussion of legal consciousness above. Coombe notes the contributions of law and society scholarship in identifying the ways in which law shapes consciousness. She notes, however, that the relationship between structure and agency, which would be a logical line of inquiry, remains largely unexamined. Somewhat paradoxically, social constructionist accounts of legal consciousness (along with social-constructionist and identity-based legal scholarship more generally) tend to tilt toward either structure or agency as determinative. Engels provides similar observations, noting that legal consciousness scholarship tends to be one of two different models. In the "power and resistance" model, less powerful people attempt to retain some small degree of autonomy among the categories and meanings imposed by law. The "communities of meaning" model is at the opposite pole, wherein different groups seek to capture the signifying power of law to create their own versions of categories and meanings.[126] As Coombe argues, a more dynamic or dialogical approach would better inform people's understandings of how to recognize and respond as desired to structural domination.[127]

An investigation of the relative strengths of structure and agency in regard to the jurisgenerative capacities of our narrative/*nomos* requires detailed enquiry beyond the scope of this project. As noted above with more recent aspects of legal consciousness scholarship, this would be an ideal line of inquiry to which the open-source nature of this analytical framework is well suited. Nonetheless, discussion on this point is sufficient to demonstrate that the concept of the narrative/*nomos* obligational self affirms both the agency inherent in jurisgenerative capacity as well as the constraints under which this agency is exercised. Addressing this inescapable tension between agency and determination, even if the issue remains unresolved, negates any potential objections that the concept of the narrative/*nomos* obligational self is at best a naive utopian impulse.

When we conceive of law not in terms of reified abstractions but rather as a function of the jurisgenerative capacity of human beings themselves, the manner in which agency is both exercised and constrained is significant for at least two reasons. The first is one of capacity, while the second is one of responsibility. In terms of capacity, the necessary presupposition of jurisgenerative ability, whether articulated by Cover with reference to jurisgenerative communities and the jurispathic state, by Kleinhans and Macdonald as foundational to a theory of critical legal pluralism, or as elaborated here in the concept of the narrative/*nomos* obligational self, is that legal subjects exercise more than nominal agency. We are not simply the passive legal subjects contemplated by a command-and-control understanding of law such as the exclusive legal authority of political states. Even within the confines of jurispathic state law as envisaged by Cover, assuming without deciding that Cover does not advance a claim of legal pluralism, we are both "law-abiding" and "law-inventing."[128] We have both the ability and responsibility for conceiving of and creating law, even if the law we so conceive and maintain is one in which we implicitly delegate our constructive capacities to the political state.

As described by Macdonald and Sandomierski, this is a significant movement away from the artefacts of prescriptivism to the emancipatory potential of agency. In a prescriptivist account, the search for legal meaning begins, oddly enough, at the end with symbolized legal rules. The place to begin, however, is with the human beings whose normative beliefs and behaviors are ever only imperfectly captured in the form of symbolized standards.[129] Both Melissaris and Macdonald and Sandomierski make a similar argument on this point, that agency provides the emancipatory potential of an abundance of law. We no longer think of ourselves as passively subject to law as an imposition of authority, leaving us with nothing more than a binary choice to obey or transgress.[130]

Emancipatory potential, however, is indeed just that, a matter of potential. Whether and to what extent we acknowledge and subsequently pursue this potential depends, as always, on the allocation of agency and determinism with respect to our capacity to choose. As Macdonald argues, and as is discussed in more detail below, the horizons of our legal imaginations are never wholly our own creation.[131] On the other hand, Macdonald and Sandomierski also convincingly argue that unless we conceive of our lives as wholly determined, we necessarily possess agency to some extent. The relevant inquiry is thus not whether we have agency but whether we are aware of our agency, how much agency we do have, under what conditions, and for whose benefit?[132] This manner of framing the issue should dispel any misconception that conceiving of law with respect to narrative/*nomos* obligational selves represents an enthusiastic but ultimately unrealistic yearning for the emancipatory potential of agency.[133]

Macdonald and Sandomierski readily acknowledge that the mode of social relations in which we exist conditions the ways in which we might perceive of our agency with respect to jurisgenerative capacity. Macdonald in particular is consistent in his argument that critical legal pluralism's inversion of legal subjectivity, with its concomitant emphasis on the jurisgenerative capacity of legal subjects themselves, is a radical re-conception of law, not a prediction of revolutionary social outcomes. If inter-subjective life (not to mention intra-subjective life) is neither democratic nor egalitarian, simply re-orienting our understanding of legality toward jurisgenerative capacity will not necessarily alter prevailing modes of social relations. Nor should we expect the jurisgenerative capacity of narrative/*nomos* obligational selves to function contrary to prevailing patterns of power and dominance.[134]

This theme of constraint is further complicated by Kleinhans and Macdonald's recognition that subjects and communities are themselves in a constructing/constructed relationship.[135] In other words, we should be aware as always that when we discuss polarized oppositions, in this case being individual agency and communal restraint, we risk unduly simplifying the complexity of our relations with others. Socio-economic circumstances, cultural constructs, and even (as always) coercion all place limits on our emancipatory potential.[136] Nonetheless, limitations are not extinctions. As Kleinhans and Macdonald argue, we more truly grasp the power of agency when we think of it not in terms of unrealistic expectations but rather from an informed acknowledgment of its contingencies and its limitations.[137]

Both the exercise of agency and its constraint are integrated into the concept of narrative/*nomos* obligational selves through narrative, more specifically in the self-narrations of our inherently normative selves whereby we draw upon prevailing cultural narratives to tell the stories of our lives. As a means of identity formation, narrative is never constant. We never tell the same story twice, meaning that the stories we tell are not the same as these stories are told to us. Time, context, and interpretation all contribute to inescapable narrative flux. Accordingly, even dominant narratives change over time, however imperceptible this may be.[138] Just as our legal subjectivities mutate in response to dominant narratives, we in turn cause mutations to the dominant narratives we reflect and refract.[139]

The potential for narrative/*nomos* obligational selves to change dominant narratives is not confined to that provided by hegemony to safely contain resistance, which in turn nullifies threats to prevailing social, political, and economic relations.[140] Recall the discussion in Chapter 2 regarding the endless oscillation between law and justice and that the vocabulary we use to justify certain types of transgression, such as civil disobedience and defense of necessity, simply affirms the legitimacy of the state law that is being resisted. The emancipatory potential of critical legal pluralism, and thus the constructive capacity of our narrative/*nomos* obligational selves, is the ability to conceive of other, valid legalities. Counter-hegemony is a matter of denying the state "sole possession of the *sobriquet* law."[141] Normative heterogeneity, no longer limited to how the state responds to claims of plural legalities, now includes how plural legalities view claims of state law.[142]

As Macdonald argues, narratives raise issues of not only pervasiveness, but also persuasiveness,[143] which leads us to the second significance of agency as a matter of responsibility. Not all narratives are equally persuasive to the multiplicity of our narrative/*nomos* obligational selves. Admittedly, dominant narratives can be imposed by physical force or ideology, but we are also amenable to the narrative authority of what Macdonald refers to as a "wise person." We may all be law-makers as well as law-appliers, but widespread application is a matter of credibility. Others do not affirm legal claims offered by persons who lack credibility, while the claims of credible persons will attract wide support.[144] Our narrative/*nomos* obligational selves may offer to others a potentially unlimited number of claims for legal authority, but we cannot all expect to be equally successful. Those among us who are perceived as particularly wise will find that our narrative communication of legal meaning (and our narrative identity formations) are accorded more deference by others. This in turn creates the conditions of reciprocal construction that provide legitimacy to legal claims.[145]

Obligational selves in social relations

The potential misunderstanding of the concept of narrative/*nomos* obligational selves in terms of agency and constraint is that claims regarding our jurisgenerative capacity over overstated. In other words, they represent an aspirational but ultimately unattainable utopian impulse. In this section, I discuss the integration of our narrative/*nomos* obligational selves within culture as a matter of social relations, where potential misunderstandings may be more aptly characterized as concern for dystopian trajectories. Simply stated, the concept of the narrative/*nomos* obligational self, even acknowledging the limits of agency, might be criticized as excessively individualistic. In response, I address potential misunderstandings of the narrative/*nomos* obligational self as: (a) a legality of one, which has the effect of negating legality altogether; (b) an autonomous legality of one, abstracted from social context, unencumbered by responsibility, and with a predilection for lawlessness; (c) a multi-vocal legality of many, which frustrates attempts at interpretation; and (d) an indeterminate legality, which frustrates the social consensus required for transforming normative aspiration into binding law.

Locating law's origins in the jurisgenerative capacity of narrative/*nomos* obligational selves may appear counter-productive in that the potential exists that we will exercise our capacity in a way that results in plural legalities of one, albeit with reference to selves who are multiply identifying. Even taking this into account, however, the possibility exists that law as social meaning, to use Cover's term, will regress into a plurality of psychological meanings instead. The concern is that an excessively individualistic approach to constructive capacity will inevitably fracture any cohesive sense of legality into fragmented multitudes. If every narrative/*nomos* obligational self is a law unto herself, then law ceases to have any function as one of the modalities of social relations. If we are all a law unto ourselves, then this project of re-imagining law has produced lawlessness. Only by happy coincidence would we exercise our jurisgenerative capacity in a way that provides common rules that bind us as members of legal communities. Should we advance a concept of law that leaves the rule of law to chance in this manner?

This concern may be addressed in a fairly summary fashion. Recall that in the discussion above, I described narrative/*nomos* obligational selves as necessarily exercising agency but that such agency is necessarily constrained, given that we always already exist in culture, a mode of social relations, or any other term that applies to describe our existence as the antithesis of atomistic individualism. This arguably insulates the concept of the narrative/*nomos* obligational self from potential misunderstandings regarding naive orientations toward unattainable utopias. Acknowledging constraints on agency, however, does not dispense with critiques of excessive individualism. As Schlag argues, many contemporary modes of legal thought, including those which explicitly acknowledge social and cultural influences, owe their coherence to a conception of legal subjects as rational and autonomous individuals.[146] The concept of the narrative/*nomos* obligational self, however, is an elaboration of legal subjectivity as conceived by a theory of critical legal pluralism. From the perspective of this mode of legal thought, legal meaning is necessarily relational.

We cannot, as narrative/*nomos* obligational selves, claim sole authorship of the concepts of law we hypothesize and affirm, nor the beliefs and behaviors that instantiate our conception of ourselves as bound by law. Even assuming without deciding that from some perspective not yet articulated, sole authorship is a possibility, the necessarily reciprocal nature of legal authority precludes an endless regression into individual assertions of legal claims, wherein we bind no one but ourselves, and thus possibly negate the very possibility of being bound by law. A significant distinction between power and law, noted by both Melissaris and Macdonald, is that power is imposed but law is accepted. The validity of a legal claim is not in the pedigree of its source but in the satisfaction of two conditions: (a) a claim by one (or more) against another (or more) that an action is justified by law; and (b) the acknowledgment in return that the claim of legal validity is legitimate.[147]

Admittedly, acknowledging the necessity of reciprocity means that emancipation is indeed a matter of potential rather than result. As Macdonald notes, where legality is resisted, domination by violence is still possible. Nonetheless, we should not underestimate the significance of reciprocity as a condition of legitimacy. If an official authority, such as the political state, does not meet these two criteria in asserting its legal claims, then state law actually negates the concept we understand as the rule of law.[148] On the other hand, the rule of law is not a zero-sum game. If we acknowledge our own capacity to confer legitimacy through reciprocity, we can imagine as well many instances in which preferred claims of legality would be validated even in the absence of the political state. The function of the rule of law as an organizing concept for our normative relations would be strengthened, not diluted.[149] Accordingly, we should not be concerned that conceiving of jurisgenerative capacity with reference to narrative/*nomos* obligational selves will inevitably collapse into a legality of one, thus negating the possibility of law altogether.

The second potential misconception of excessive individualism is that the concept of narrative/*nomos* obligational selves (a concept which I emphasize does not comprise the totality of our subjectivities) is abstracted from social context and thus absolved of social responsibility. In other words, narrative/*nomos* obligational selves would be under no obligation, so to speak, to create obligations in their relations with others. Pursuant to this dystopian vision, we can deny, if we so choose, the inherently normative aspect of our sense of self and lapse into law's absence. This concern may be alleviated by recalling, again from the discussion above regarding agency and determination, that the emancipatory potential of our jurisgenerative capacity is subject to the conditions of possibility that reflect our always already existence in culture. To deny that our exercise of legal agency is bounded to a greater or lesser degree by culture would return us to the purported dichotomy between law and culture that this project of re-imagining law has sought to avoid.

If we accept Macdonald's argument that law is a function of personal narration and interaction,[150] we must also acknowledge that jurisgenerative capacity cannot be exercised independently of social relations. Reconciliation between self and community is simply a different but equally significant aspect of the inevitable tension between the agency and determinism discussed above. When law is conceived as noumenal in nature, every normative decision we make is indeed a door we go through alone, but we still exist on either side in relation to others. The potential legal status of any proffered claim does indeed begin with our narrative/*nomos* obligational selves, as we are the ones who encounter and respond to specific circumstances of normative heterogeneity in our everyday lives. As Macdonald and Sandomierski argue, only legal subjects themselves can answer the question of what is law.[151] As Macdonald also argues, however, this individual response takes place within a mode of social relations in which the individual is already a participant. We receive what others imagine, and in turn, others receive what we imagine in response. As we understand and communicate our understanding of both what constitutes law as well as our own relationship to law, we participate in an ongoing process of creating and sustaining what Macdonald refers to as our "collective normative field."[152]

To characterize law's origins as noumenal rather than phenomenal in nature does not mean that jurisgenerative capacity can be reduced to solipsism. As I have argued elsewhere, idiosyncratic behavior, understood as the individualized response of a singular subject, is the antithesis of critical legal pluralism.[153] Kleinhans and Macdonald expressly reject the concept of an autonomous legal subject acting in isolation.[154] A legal subject is plural rather than singularly identified and situated always within a multiplicity of discourses. The plural legal subject reflects and refracts the projected understandings of other plural selves, projecting multiple understandings to be reflected and refracted in turn. If we accept law as a process of knowledge creation, and furthermore that the relevant knowledge domain is communal in nature, then jurisgenerative legal subjects and the communities in which they exist are necessarily composed of reciprocal relationships of constructing and constructed.[155]

Given the lack of a unitary self, legal subjectivity in the absence of social relations is simply not possible. If anything, the relevant issue is not excessive individualism but rather the familiar tension between determinism and agency. Any constructivist account of self and identity will engage issues of identity formation, an important aspect of which is the extent to which our beliefs and behaviors are conditioned by cultural contexts, material conditions, and particular modes of social relations. Bruner, for example, has devoted significant attention to how we come to understand our selves as a self or, rather more accurately, as a multitude of selves,[156] as a compromise between autonomy and commitment.[157] We seek the freedom to make our own choices and act upon them accordingly, and yet we also seek opportunities to interact with and bind ourselves emotionally to others. When we commit ourselves to relations with others, which means taking account of their needs even at times at the expense of our own, we limit the extent to which we can act autonomously.

In proposing the concept of a narrative/*nomos* obligational self, I do not claim to provide an exhaustive analysis of the relative positions of agency and structure in relation to jurisgenerative capacity. Nor do I attempt to track with precision what Kleinhans and Macdonald have referred to as law's hermeneutic circle.[158] Either of these would be a productive line of inquiry to which this analytical framework could be applied, being amenable to a range of different research orientations and methodologies, so long as we seek understanding and questions rather than a definitive answer. Nonetheless, that some questions can perhaps never be fully answered, that some trajectories can perhaps never be fully mapped, does not negate the utility of the line of inquiry. Even as intellectual inquiry increasingly favors specialization and definitive answers, the inherent value of open-ended inquiry persists.

A third concern which might arise if we misunderstand the nature of the narrative/*nomos* obligational self as being excessively individualistic is a proliferation of legitimate legal meaning. However we may conceive of law, legal rules are not self-executing. They are a form of legal knowledge we use as reference points to guide our behavior, but whether explicit or inferential, the meaning and manner of application in the particular context in which they are referenced must first be ascertained. This takes us back once again to Cover's characterization of the tragic bifurcation between law as social meaning and law as social control. Cover argued that state officials could not claim superior insight over other legal communities with respect to interpretive methods. Thus the jurispathic function of courts is not to interpret ambiguous legal rules but to impose a single interpretation upon a plurality of legitimate interpretive claims regarding legal rules.[159]

Having adopted a pluralist perspective, however, the jurispathic function of state courts is not my primary concern. The difficulty is that if I locate the nexus of the mutually constitutive discourse of law and popular culture within the narrative/*nomos* obligational self, have I created an excess of jurisgenerative potential sufficient to overwhelm our collective normative fields? The potential objection is somewhat similar to that raised with respect to the rule of law, but with the problem being indeterminacy rather than plurality. When one (or more) narrative/*nomos* obligational selves raise a claim against another (or more) narrative/*nomos* obligational selves that law justifies an action, how are we to judge (respond) to such claims? If law is meaning and we are bound by law, how can we govern ourselves accordingly when valid but potentially conflicting legal meanings proliferate?

To respond to this concern, I return to Manderson's approach to judgment as polarity, discussed in Chapter 2. Recall the nature of the problem, which is the inescapable circumstance of conflicting interpretation of legal rules. In analyzing the nature of judgment in law and the humanities, Manderson argues that rather than rejecting the premise of conflicting interpretations (positivism), embracing the premise (deconstruction), or attempting to reconcile or transcend the premise (Romanticism), a preferred alternative is to welcome the opportunity to do justice that the inherent imperfection of legal judgment provides.[160]

Manderson finds in the structure of the novel an alternative vision for what judgment might look like, one which maintains the rule of law even in the face of indeterminacy. A characteristic feature of the novel is its polyphonic nature, wherein the perspectives of multiple voices and multiple characters simultaneously exist, often in tension or even contradictory with each other. An alternative for our understanding of judgment is the novel's acceptance of uncertainty as an intentional design feature.[161] Justice is not the certainty we may have thought was required but rather quite the opposite. Given the inevitability of uncertainty, we find justice in meeting our obligation to acknowledge and answer for this uncertainty, not with one perfect answer, but with reasoned deliberation for the answer we give.[162]

The role of the judge is not to protect the illusion of infallibility but to acknowledge the possibility of error as a feature rather than a failure, since the possibility of error is what creates the obligation to provide reasons for decision. These reasons are then received, discussed, assessed, and critiqued, and in the process they contribute to the legal discourse from which future decisions and reasons for decision are derived. As Melissaris and Macdonald reject the presumptive authority of legal experts, so too does Manderson. As Melissaris locates the legitimacy of law in the shared normative experiences of members of legal communities themselves, and as Macdonald locates legitimacy in reciprocal construction of legal claims between jurisgenerative legal subjects themselves, so too does Manderson locate legitimacy for law in the participation of everyday citizens in legal discourse.[163] Uncertainty invites dialogue, which is what leads Manderson to conclude that "[c]orrection is the soul of justice."[164]

With reference to the narrative/*nomos* obligational self, legal meaning will indeed proliferate. This is not only a logical consequence of jurisgenerative capacity, but also a necessary prerequisite for the emancipatory potential of conceiving of the narrative/*nomos* obligational self as a nexus for mutually constitutive discourse of law and popular culture. With reference to Manderson, however, we can characterize this proliferation of meaning as an opportunity to establish the legitimacy of re-imagining law in these terms. The emancipatory potential of our narrative/*nomos* obligational selves is not the empty claims of each to their own, nor the cacophony of competing claims, but rather the invitation to participate in legal discourse. We can accept as per Manderson's arguments regarding judgment that our responses to circumstances of normative heterogeneity will always fall short of perfection. We can adoption correction as the soul of normative assessment in our daily lives and thus appreciate the proliferation of legal meaning as opportunities for adjustment.

The final concern that the narrative/*nomos* obligational self may appear to be excessively individualistic is that no mechanism exists whereby jurisgenerative capacity can be transformed into the degree of social consensus sufficient to establish binding norms. In other words, the concept of the narrative/*nomos* obligational self privileges the capacity to create norms at the expense of the normative closure required for law. To respond to this potential objection, I examine Webber's critique of the role of agency and normative closure in critical legal pluralism. If Webber's critique is valid, then this fourth potential objection of excessive individualism might (although not necessarily) succeed as well against the concept of the narrative/*nomos* obligational self.

Webber focuses on what he sees as a lack of attention to the role of human agency in transforming normative disagreement into collective norms. He argues that the excessive individualism of critical legal pluralism is unable to provide an explanatory account of how to resolve normative disagreement, which is required if norms are to function as anything more than hypothesized aspirations. This can be seen (although not from Webber's perspective) as an aspect of a recurring problem, discussed in Chapter 2, wherein we presuppose that a necessary distinction exists between that which is law and that which is hierarchically inferior as a "mere" norm.

For Webber, one of the advantages of a critical legal pluralist perspective is in drawing our attention to how social institutions settle disagreements by imposing normative homogeneity at the expense of what may well be viable alternative courses of action.[165] The focus of analysis is on the response of individual legal subjects to intersecting and conflicting normative orders. The implicit normative evaluation is that an individual legal subject's consensual adherence to norms is preferable to non-consensual imposition of norms.[166] This means, however, that institutions tend to be viewed somewhat negatively as having a repressive effect on a legal subject's agency.[167] Such an idealistic position ignores the reality that norms are always to some extent an imposition. Legal subjects submit, whether by positive agreement or mere acquiescence, to normative options that do not necessarily reflect their preferences. This is not repression but rather a necessary compromise for peaceful social relations. But theories of legal pluralism in general, and critical legal pluralism in particular, fail to account for the fact that eventually, normative possibilities must give way to normative closure as a social (not individual) process.[168]

As an aside, I note here that Webber appears to refer to the necessity of institutionalization as a means to resolve normative disagreement as well as the means by which norms may be created and maintained. To some extent, this assumption is misplaced in a critique of critical legal pluralism, given that Macdonald argues that normativity need not be equated with institutionalization, although this may often be the case. We can also locate law in people's actions, as patterns of affirmation and denial, and in the case of violating official sources of authority, in the reasons they give in defense of these actions as legitimate.[169]

Nonetheless, to return to Webber's main argument, we may all advocate for our own normative preferences, but individual assertions such as these are merely proposed norms. Critical legal pluralism rightly draws our attention to the kinds of social experiences we use to justify the legitimacy of these claims. But these claims constitute normative alternatives, not norms in themselves. At some point, disagreement among these claims must be settled through normative closure, a social decision process that brings a norm into existence by excluding other possibilities.[170] Accordingly, proponents of legal pluralism, including critical legal pluralism, must acknowledge the practical limits of our ability to cope with normative heterogeneity. We cannot confine our attention to hypotheses of norm creation while leaving the problems of disagreements to resolve themselves.[171]

I want to address Webber's claim that even if proponents of critical legal pluralism sought to address the necessity of normative closure, the conceptual apparatus is insufficient to the task. While the objective of critical legal pluralism is to persuade us that multiple normative orders are equally worthy of consideration, a process for distinguishing between their relative merits is lacking. The end result is a theoretical prescription that is, in Webber's words, "profoundly individualistic."[172] Critical legal pluralism lacks an account of the "emphatically social, non-individual" social process required to transform mere normative assertions into actual norms.[173]

I bracket for now the problem that Webber's account is based on presuppositions concerning the nature of inter-legality that are not necessarily those of the legal subjects themselves, whose experience of normative heterogeneity constitutes the very conditions of inter-legality supposedly being analyzed. I also bracket for now that Webber's orientation toward outcome contradicts my own argument that we should conceive of law as more verb than noun, with emancipation being a matter of capacity for legal knowledge rather than the prediction of an outcome or result. Accordingly, I will address Webber's arguments on the terms in which they are presented. I agree that peaceful coexistence does require some degree of co-ordination among both complimentary and contradictory norms, although note I do not think of peaceful coexistence and normative heterogeneity as mutually exclusive. I also agree with Webber that we do need to attend to how "common positions are and should be hammered out." I disagree, however, with the way in which Webber appears to use the concept of normative closure at a social level to distinguish between proposed and actual norms. I find that the concept introduces two distinctions that lead to unnecessary complications.

The first is the distinction between mere normative claims as opposed to actual norms. As Webber argues: "It is only through such narrowing of the normative options that 'norms' come into being. Prior to that stage one has normative assertions: proposed norms."[174] I find that Webber mistakenly relies on this distinction when he argues that overcoming normative plurality is, paradoxically, an objective of legal pluralism. The second is that the reference to "emphatically social, non-individual processes" appears to assume a clear demarcation between social and psychic, community and individual. Taken together, these distinctions may explain why Webber fails to see how critical legal pluralism can account for social processes of normative closure.

As for the first distinction, I agree that not all normative claims result in norms. As Macdonald notes, law is not something that can be accomplished in isolation. As discussed above, legitimacy depends upon some degree of social relations, in that the distinction between power and law is the requirement of reciprocity among narrative/*nomos* obligational selves with respect to claims advanced as legally valid and responses that affirm this validity.[175] Affirmation may even take the form of transgression, so long as the narrative/*nomos* obligational self's characterization of transgressive acts nonetheless confirms that a law has indeed been broken.

I also agree that adjudicating between normative claims, with adjudication broadly defined,[176] does transform such claims into actual norms. My concern is rather that Webber frames the distinction between proposed norms and actual norms as a threshold issue for settling the question of how to respond to normative heterogeneity within a social order. Webber would appear to agree with this to some extent, given that he acknowledges both the provisional and contextual nature of law. Decision processes settle only specific disputes, and the hermeneutic character of normative argument means that law is always open to interpretation as old disputes recur and new disputes arise. The social decision process is able to impose collective agreement, but resolution is temporary.[177]

All of this can be accommodated within the conceptual framework of critical legal pluralism, even on Webber's terms. The only difference is that normativity would be located not in legal institutionalization (the social decision process) but in patterns of deference shown by legal subjects to proffered legal claims.[178] In relation to those who do not defer to proffered claims, and this is where I disagree with Webber, normative closure cannot be imposed. Any attempt to impose a presumptively settled norm in the face of their refusal is an imposition of power, not law. While reasons might justifiably support this imposition, depending upon the normative criteria and the perspective from which they are considered, the fact remains that "emphatically social" processes for the emergence of legal norms are not capable of producing norms that apply across the entirety of what is presumed to be the relevant social order.

Again, Webber's views would seem consistent on this point; he admits that social decision processes rarely result in substantive consensus, requiring instead a "more peremptory mechanism" to achieve a common outcome.[179] Given the reaction of those to whom such a mechanism is applied, every normative closure contains within the possibility of creating a new normative order through resistance and rebellion. Accordingly, I am not convinced that any project of legal pluralism could find a way to "overcome the radical pluralism of our normative assertions."[180] At best, normative closure is only ever partial. This is not an insignificant achievement, but we also need to consider the unintended consequences whereby plurality is actually increased. This in turn calls into question the efficacy of characterizing normative closure as an objective of legal pluralism. Perhaps the paradoxical nature of this intent should have given us pause.

I agree that all legal pluralists, including critical legal pluralists, should be as concerned with normative disagreement as we are with normative plurality, a topic I address below. As an aside on this point, I note that Macdonald and Sandomierski argue that disagreement with law may itself constitute law, the determination of which is an empirical inquiry. The answer to this empirical question, however, is of less significance to the pluralist project than is the emancipatory potential of acknowledging our own legal agency. They also refer to the familiar problem of idealized norms, in that alternative hypotheses of plural law are measured for their coherence against the presumptive unity and clarity of official law. To the extent that deficiencies in these areas negate theories of legal pluralism, so too should they negate the conception of official law, which in its real rather than ideal state is also characterized by incoherence and indeterminacy.[181]

To return to Webber's argument on this point, he identifies the value of critical legal pluralism in drawing our attention to the fact that resolving normative disagreement inevitably forecloses other normative possibilities. Acknowledgment of this fact, however, appears to be enough, as the next step for him would be to move legal pluralism beyond norm identification to the serious and significant task of establishing common positions.[182] Given the logical inconsistencies, however, I do not think any theory of legal pluralism can provide a wholly legal response to the perennial problem of normative heterogeneity. For this, we tend to rely on extra-legal mechanisms, encouraging dialogue, encounter, and exchange between legal orders.[183]

As for the second distinction, wherein an emphatically social process is necessarily non-individual, again I am not convinced these distinctions can be maintained. This means that the criticism of critical legal pluralism as "profoundly individualistic" is misguided. The inversion of legal subjectivity is a central tenet of critical legal pluralism, which might appear to indicate that normative closure is exclusively a process of individual commitment. After all, Macdonald has emphasized both law and inter-legality as noumenal rather than phenomenal in nature. But all of the characteristics of legal subjectivity identified by Macdonald need to be viewed as a whole, in which case it does not follow that critical legal pluralism mistakenly prioritizes individual subjectivity.

First, as noted above, the individual of critical legal pluralism is not the autonomous self of legal liberalism. Webber criticizes critical legal pluralism for excessive de-centering, not only displacing the state as a privileged source of law, but also equating the determinant of normative obligation with the decisions of individual legal subjects.[184] Taken at face value, this would reduce the analytical value of critical legal pluralism. What could we possibly learn from a world of infinite normative regression, where people are a law unto themselves? But legal agency is the assumption of responsibility for making choices, not a celebration of the absence of law,[185] as discussed above.

Second, legal subjects are indeed jurisgenerative but always and only in relation to other legal subjects. We participate in the maintenance of a collective knowledge domain, what Macdonald has referred to as a "collective normative field," through which we understand and symbolize our conduct toward others, and theirs toward us, as governed by rules.[186] Macdonald refers to this as an aretaic conception of law (an ethics of character rather than deontological rules or utilitarian outcomes), wherein we interact with others as legal agents, both lawmakers and law-appliers.[187] Critical legal pluralism focuses on individual normative commitment, but to whom do we turn for guidance in our normative decisions if not to each other?

No tenet of critical legal pluralism advocates in favor of an endless horizon of normative disagreement. The emancipatory potential of the theory as practice involves coordination in favor of control and, where necessary, seeking agreement through reference to consensual normative baselines. Macdonald explicitly provides scope for coordination and resolution on this basis, both in terms of the requirement of reciprocity and by embedding jurisgenerative capacity within a context of social relations. The concept of the narrative/*nomos* obligational self, as an elaboration of the legal subjectivity of critical legal pluralism, necessarily exercises normative choice as part of a larger discourse of reasons for action involving all other narrative/*nomos* obligational selves, both inter- and intra-subjective. That we all have jurisgenerative capacity does not mean we will all be equally persuasive in establishing reciprocity for our legal claims. The "manifestly foolish" among us will not attract momentum, whereas the beliefs and behaviors of the "wise human being" will be considered authoritative.[188]

In a less-than-ideal world, the world of "hard truth" that Webber acknowledges, we are more likely to acquiesce at best, which again is a possibility anticipated and addressed by Macdonald. Kleinhans and Macdonald acknowledge that our ability to exercise our constructive capacity in a way that resists prescriptivism is dependent upon how power in any particular society is distributed and exercised.[189] This is one of the reasons why I have emphasized throughout my preference for re-imagining law not only as a mutually constitutive discourse of law and popular culture, and not only with reference to the narrative/*nomos* obligational self, but also as a re-orientation toward law as a verb in terms of capacity to create legal meaning and away from law as a noun in terms of the predicted or desired outcome of normative heterogeneity.

The concept of the narrative/*nomos* obligational self is not an exercise in idealistic naiveté. I acknowledge the inevitability of normative disagreement and the severity of conflict that occurs when options are both strongly held and mutually exclusive. One can advocate in favor of the emancipatory potential of jurisgenerative capacity while still taking seriously both the potential and problems of normative disagreement. To argue in favor of the emancipatory potential of critical legal pluralism does not mean I view release from coercive forms of social control as the necessary result. Reconceiving legal subjectivity as a narrative/*nomos* obligational self is admittedly a radical departure from conventional legal thinking, including legal pluralism. The objective, however, is simply to provide an alternative for how we might understand our normative beliefs and behaviors. No claim is advanced, nor is any attempt made, to restructure social relations in the process.

Notes

1 Recall that by "translation" I mean that we understand the normative significance of popular culture as a reciprocal relationship in which popular culture influences legal officials in their expression of state law, as well as participants' understanding of state law as expressed by legal officials, which in turn influences legal officials in their expression of state law, and so on.

2 This is a concise statement of the non-prescriptivist understanding of law articulated by Macdonald and Sandomierski. See: Roderick A. Macdonald and David Sandomierski, 'Against Nomopolies' (2006) 57 *Northern Ireland Legal Quarterly* 610.

3 Jerome Bruner, *Making Stories: Law, Literature, Life* (Harvard University Press 2002).

4 Wendy A. Adams, '"I Made a Promise to a Lady": Critical Legal Pluralism as Improvised Law in *Buffy the Vampire Slayer*' (2010) 6 *Critical Studies in Improvisation* 1.

5 Dan P. McAdams, 'Narrative Identity' in Seth J. Schwartz, Koen Luyckx, and Vivian L. Vignoles (eds), *Handbook of Identity Theory and Research* (Springer 2011) 100.

6 Jerome Bruner, 'A Narrative Model of Self-Construction' (1997) 818 *Annals of the New York Academy of Sciences* 145, 155.

7 This is evocative of the nature of dialogism as a negotiation between social and psychic aspects of culture. See, for example: Rosemary J. Coombe, 'Objects of Property and Subjects of Politics: Intellectual Property Laws and Democratic Dialogue' (1990) 69 *Texas Law Review* 1853, 1878.

8 For a sustained account of virtue ethics, see, for example: Rosalind Hursthouse, *On Virtue Ethics* (Oxford University Press 1999).
9 Macdonald (2013 #152 @24). On the relationship between Macdonald's work and the concept of virtue in legal education, see: David Sandomierski, 'Pursuing Virtue: Human Potential, Citizenship, and a Research Agenda for Legal Education' in Richard Janda, Rosalie Jukier, and Daniel Jutras (eds), *The Unbounded Level of the Mind: Rod Macdonald's Legal Imagination* (McGill-Queen's University Press 2015). See also: Roderick A. Macdonald, 'Pluralistic Human Rights? Universal Human Wrongs?' in René Provost and Colleen Sheppard (eds), *Dialogues on Human Rights and Legal Pluralism* (Springer Science & Business Media 2013) 24, note 23 citing Lawrence B. Solum, 'Virtue Jurisprudence: An Aretaic Theory of Law (Working Paper)' (2004) Unpublished paper 105; Lawrence B. Solum, 'Virtue Jurisprudence A Virtue-Centred Theory of Judging' (2003) 34 *Metaphilosophy* 178.
10 As Coombe notes, identity, narrative, and justice are "thematic preoccupations" in cultural perspectives of law. See: Rosemary J. Coombe, 'Is there a Cultural Studies of Law?' in Toby Miller (ed), *A Companion to Cultural Studies* (Blackwell Reference Online Edition, Blackwell Publishing 2005) <http://www.blackwellreference.com/subscriber/tocnode.html?id=g9781405141758_chunk_g97814051417584> accessed April 12, 2016.
11 See, for example: Patricia Ewick and Susan S. Silbey, *The Common Place of Law: Stories from Everyday Life* (University of Chicago Press 1998).
12 Emmanuel Melissaris, *Ubiquitous Law: Legal Theory and the Space for Legal Pluralism* (Ashgate Publishing Company 2009) 106.
13 Nicholas Kasirer (ed) *La solitude en droit privé* (Montréal: Éditions Thémis 2002).
14 Macdonald and Sandomierski (2006) 616.
15 Macdonald (2013) 24.
16 Roderick A. Macdonald, 'Here, There and Everywhere: Theorizing Legal Pluralism; Theorizing Jacques Vanderlinden' in Nicholas Kasirer (ed), *Étudier Et Enseigner Le Droit: Hier, Aujourd'hui Et Demain – Études Offertes À Jacques Vanderlinden* (Éditions Yvon Blais 2006) 408.
17 Macdonald (2006) 409.
18 Jerome Bruner, *Actual Minds, Possible Worlds* (Harvard University Press 1987).
19 Jerome Bruner, *Acts of Meaning* (Harvard University Press 1990).
20 Jerome Bruner, *On Knowing: Essays for the Left Hand*, vol 67 (Harvard University Press 1979).
21 Bruner (2002).
22 Anthony G. Amsterdam and Jerome Bruner, *Minding the Law* (Harvard University Press 2002).
23 McAdams (2011).
24 Macdonald (2006) 406.
25 Bruner (2002) 8.
26 Bruner (2002) 103. See also: Elaine Scarry, 'The Made-up and the Made-real' (1992) 5 *The Yale Journal of Criticism* 239.
27 Bruner (2002) 6.
28 Jerome Bruner, 'The Narrative Construction of Reality' (1991) 18 *Critical Inquiry* 1; Bruner (1997); Bruner (2002).
29 Jerome Bruner, 'Life as Narrative' (2004) 71 *Social Research: An International Quarterly* 691, 694.
30 Bruner (2002). See also Fludernik on this point: Monika Fludernik, 'Identity/Alterity' in David Herman (ed), *The Cambridge Companion to Narrative* (Cambridge University Press 2007) 263.
31 Jerome Bruner, 'Life as Narrative' (1987) 54 *Social Research* 11, 15.
32 Robert M. Cover, '*Nomos* and Narrative' (1983) 97 *Harvard Law Review* 4, 18.
33 See, for example: Roderick A. Macdonald, 'Critical Legal Pluralism as a Construction of Normativity and the Emergence of Law' in Andrée Lajoie, Roderick A. Macdonald,

Richard Janda, and Guy Rocher (eds), *Théories Et Émergence Du Droit: Pluralisme, Surdétermination, Effectivité* (Éditions Thémis 1998) 21.
34 Macdonald (2006) 406.
35 Macdonald and Sandomierski (2006) 616.
36 Macdonald and Sandomierski (2006) 614.
37 Macdonald and Sandomierski (2006) 617.
38 No clear consensus exists as to whether Cover's work provides support for a pluralistic perspective. See, for example: Macdonald and Sandomierski (2006) 614.
39 McAdams (2011) 100.
40 See, for example: Dan P. McAdams, 'Personality, Modernity, and the Storied Self: A Contemporary Framework for Studying Persons' (1996) 7 *Psychological Inquiry* 295.
41 See, for example: Dan P. McAdams, 'The Redemptive Self: Generativity and the Stories Americans Live By' (2006) 3 *Research in Human Development* 81.
42 Dan P. McAdams, 'Self and Identity across the Lifespan' in Richard M. Lerner, Michael E. Lamb, and Alexandra M. Freund (eds), *The Handbook of Life-Span Development: Social and Emotional Development*, vol 2 (John Wiley & Sons 2010) 169.
43 Dan P. McAdams, 'Personal Narratives and the Life Story' in Oliver P. John, Richard W. Robins, and Lawrence A. Pervin (eds), *Handbook of Personality: Theory and Research* (Third Edition, Guilford Press 2008) 242.
44 McAdams (2011) 99.
45 McAdams (2011) 99.
46 McAdams (2011) 103.
47 McAdams (2008) 257.
48 Hubert J.M. Hermans, 'Voicing the Self: From Information Processing to Dialogical Interchange' (1996) 119 *Psychological Bulletin* 31.
49 McAdams (2011) 102.
50 McAdams (1996) 298.
51 McAdams (2011) 102.
52 Mikhail Mikhaĭlovich Bakhtin, *The Dialogic Imagination: Four Essays* (University of Texas Press 2010).
53 Desmond Manderson, 'Mikhail Bakhtin and the Field of Law and Literature' (2012) 8 *Law, Culture, and the Humanities* 1, 6.
54 Mieke Bal, *Narratology: Introduction to the Theory of Narrative* (Third Edition, University of Toronto Press 2009) 12.
55 Macdonald (2006 #33 @ 408).
56 Bruner (2004) 699.
57 Martha-Marie Kleinhans and Roderick A. Macdonald, 'What Is a Critical Legal Pluralism?' (1997) 12 *Canadian Journal of Law and Society* 25, 44.
58 Kleinhans and Macdonald (1997) 44.
59 McAdams (2011) 99. See also Bruner on this point: Bruner (2002) 87.
60 McAdams (2011) 99.
61 McAdams (2006).
62 McAdams (2010) 197.
63 McAdams (2006) 95.
64 Bruner (1987) 67.
65 There is common ground here with dialogism, a concept developed by Holquist in reference to Bakhtin's work, in the correspondence between collective narratives as they are integrated into self-narration. See: Michael Holquist, *Dialogism: Bakhtin and His World (New Accents)* (Second Edition, Routledge 2002). As Coombe succinctly (and very helpfully) articulates, this relation between self and other is a continuum rather than a binary opposition. The psyche and a culture share the same content of social and material signs and texts through which meaning is created. See: Coombe (1990).
66 Bruner (1991) 15.

67 Bruner (1991) 15, citing Hayden V. White, *Tropics of Discourse: Essays in Cultural Criticism*, vol 70 (Johns Hopkins University Press Baltimore 1978), Victor Witter Turner, *From Ritual to Theatre: The Human Seriousness of Play* (Performing Arts Journal Publications 1982), Paul Ricoeur, *Time and Narrative. Volume I* (University of Chicago Press 1984).
68 McAdams (2011) citing Charles Taylor, *Sources of the Self: The Making of the Modern Identity* (Harvard University Press 1989), A.C MacIntyre, *After Virtue* (University of Notre Dame Press 1981).
69 McAdams (2010) 169.
70 McAdams (2008) 247.
71 McAdams (2011) 110.
72 Cover (1983) 9.
73 Kleinhans and Macdonald (1997) 42.
74 McAdams (2008) 244.
75 McAdams (2011) 100. Bruner makes a similar point in arguing that we have no essential self to describe, only a construction of self that responds to the needs of the situation, guided by memories of the past and hopes for the future. See: Bruner (2002) 64.
76 See Fludernik, arguing a similar point: Fludernik (2007) 262.
77 Dan P. McAdams, 'The Psychology of Life Stories' (2001) 5 *Review of General Psychology* 100, 106.
78 Dan P. McAdams, *The Stories We Live By: Personal Myths and the Making of the Self* (Guilford Press 1993) 34.
79 McAdams (1993) 102.
80 McAdams (1993) 122.
81 McAdams (1993) 124.
82 Dan P. McAdams, 'The Development of a Narrative Identity' in David M. Buss and Nancy Cantor (eds), *Personality Psychology: Recent Trends and Emerging Directions* (Springer 1989) 169; McAdams (1993) 130.
83 See, for example, Manderson's concerns on the use of literature as proposition: Desmond Manderson, 'Modernism and the Critique of Law and Literature' (2011) 35 *Austrilian Feminist Law Journal* 107.
84 Hazel Markus and Paula Nurius, 'Possible Selves' (1986) 41 *American Psychologist* 954.
85 McAdams (1993) 127.
86 McAdams (1993) 129.
87 Kleinhans and Macdonald (1997) 46.
88 McAdams (1993) 124.
89 Fludernik (2007).
90 McAdams (1996) 313.
91 McAdams (1993) 124.
92 McAdams (1996) 314.
93 See, for example: Erik D. Fritsvold, 'Under the Law: Legal Consciousness and Radical Environmental Activism' (2009) 34 *Law & Social Inquiry* 799.
94 See, for example: Fritsvold (2009).
95 For a discussion of character alignment in Dungeons and Dragons, see: TV Tropes, 'Character Alignment' <http://tvtropes.org/pmwiki/pmwiki.php/Main/CharacterAlignment> accessed October 11, 2015.
96 McAdams (2010) 197.
97 McAdams (2008) 246.
98 McAdams (2008) 247.
99 Macdonald (2006) 408.
100 Macdonald (2006) 409.
101 McAdams (2008) 247.
102 Bruner (2002) 87.
103 McAdams (2011) 99.

104 Bruner provides additional support for the incorporation of collective narratives within the self-narration of identity. See: Bruner (2002) 87.
105 Macdonald (2006) 384.
106 One of Melissaris's critiques of Hartian positivism, for example, is that those with legal expertise are not describing the normative commitments of a legal community so much as they are projecting their own experience of law onto the participants. See: Melissaris (2009) 8.
107 Pierre Schlag, 'The Problem of the Subject' (1990) 69 *Texas Law Review* 1627.
108 Schlag argues, for example, that notwithstanding an increasingly postmodern orientation in scholarship, which emphasizes plurality and difference, a certain sameness is pervasive in the way even contradictory approaches conceive of the legal subject. Contemporary modes of legal thought revolve around a paradigmatic liberal legal subject. See: Schlag (1990) 1631.
109 Schlag (1990) 1628, citing Pierre Schlag, 'Fish v. Zapp: The Case of the Relatively Autonomous Self' (1987) 76 *Georgetown Law Journal* 37, 42; Pierre Schlag, 'Le Hors de Texte, C'est Moi: The Politics of Form and the Domestication of Deconstruction' (1990) 11 *Cardozo Law Review* 1631, 1667.
110 Macdonald (1998) 21.
111 Macdonald (2006) 408.
112 See, for example: Steven Best and Anthony J. Nocella, *Terrorists or Freedom Fighters?: Reflections on the Liberation of Animals* (Lantern Books 2004); Steven Best and Anthony J. Nocella (eds), *Igniting a Revolution: Voices in Defense of the Earth* (AK Press 2006).
113 Macdonald and Sandomierski (2006) 619.
114 Macdonald and Sandomierski (2006) 617.
115 Orly Lobel, 'The Paradox of Extralegal Activism: Critical Legal Consciousness and Transformative Politics' (2007) 120 *Harvard Law Review* 937, 939.
116 Ewick and Silbey (1998) 39.
117 Susan S. Silbey, 'After Legal Consciousness' (2005) 1 *Annual Review of Law and Social Science* 323. Analyzing the narrative/*nomos* obligational self from this perspective would be an interesting line of inquiry in legal consciousness scholarship.
118 Ewick and Silbey (1998).
119 Fritsvold (2009).
120 Fritsvold (2009) 806.
121 Fritsvold (2009) 812.
122 Fritsvold (2009) 818.
123 Bruner (1987) 67.
124 Bruner (2002) 78.
125 Jerome Bruner, 'Self-making and World-making' in Jens Brockmeier and Donal Carbaugh (eds), *Narrative and Identity: Studies in Autobiography, Self, and Culture* (John Benjamins 2001) 34. Not surprisingly, Bruner has an interest in L. S. Vygotsky. See, for example: Bruner (1987).
126 Coombe (2005) "Identity," citing David Engel, 'How Does Law Matter in the Constitution of Legal Consciousness' in G. Garth Bryant and A. Sarat (eds), *How Does Law Matter* (Northwestern University Press 1998) 138.
127 Coombe (2005) "Identity."
128 Kleinhans and Macdonald (1997) 38, citing Boaventura de Sousa Santos, 'Three Metaphors for a New Conception of Law: The Frontier, the Baroque, and the South' (1995) 29 *Law and Society Review* 569, 573.
129 Macdonald and Sandomierski (2006) 617.
130 Macdonald and Sandomierski (2006) 624.
131 Macdonald (1998) 16.
132 Macdonald and Sandomierski (2006) 623.

133 Coombe, for example, cautions against overly optimistic assessments of our constructive capacity (affected by intellectual property rights) for creating the meanings that maintain our realities. See: Coombe (1990) 1860.
134 As Macdonald notes, dominant narratives such as the exclusivity of state law will continue to be imposed by force, either physical or ideological. See: Macdonald (2006) 408.
135 Kleinhans and Macdonald (1997) 38 n44.
136 Macdonald and Sandomierski caution against an overly optimistic account of human agency that ignores the realities of typical modes of social relations. See: Macdonald and Sandomierski (2006) 620.
137 Macdonald and Sandomierski (2006) 630.
138 Kleinhans and Macdonald (1997) 43.
139 Macdonald (2006) 408.
140 Macdonald (2006) 409.
141 Macdonald (2006).
142 Macdonald (2006) 410.
143 Macdonald (2006) 409.
144 Macdonald (2013) 24.
145 Macdonald argues that law is legitimate only if produced by reciprocal construction within and among legal subjects. See: Macdonald (2006) 407.
146 Schlag (1990) 1630.
147 Macdonald and Sandomierski (2006) 616.
148 Kleinhans and Macdonald refer to changing conceptions of the rule of law. The concept no longer simply means that state officials refer to external standards to provide justification for their actions. The more sophisticated understanding that now prevails is that state officials must find justification for their actions in the same understandings of what is right and just held by those whom they purport to govern, which is a community to which they belong as well. Legal pluralism promotes rather than diminishes the rule of law. See: Kleinhans and Macdonald (1997) 34.
149 Kleinhans and Macdonald (1997) 34.
150 Macdonald (2006) 408.
151 Macdonald and Sandomierski (2006) 615.
152 Macdonald and Sandomierski (2006) 617.
153 Adams (2010).
154 Kleinhans and Macdonald (1997) 42.
155 Kleinhans and Macdonald (1997) 38.
156 See, for example: Bruner (1997); Bruner (2002).
157 Bruner (2002) 78.
158 Kleinhans and Macdonald (1997) 44.
159 Cover (1983) 40.
160 Desmond Manderson, 'Judgment in Law and the Humanities' (2013) *Revista Forumul Judecatorilor* 43, 56.
161 Manderson (2013) 56.
162 Manderson (2013) 58.
163 Manderson (2013) 59.
164 Manderson (2013) 59.
165 Jeremy Webber, 'Legal Pluralism and Human Agency' (2006) 44 *Osgoode Hall Law Journal* 167, 182. Cover reminds us of this tendency by referring to the function of state courts as "jurispathic." See: Cover (1983) 40.
166 Webber (2006) 181.
167 Webber (2006) 182. Perhaps I have misunderstood Webber's analysis at the point, but I disagree with his argument that critical legal pluralists necessarily view legal institutions as repressive simply because legal legitimacy is predicated upon individual

commitment to normative standards. Kleinhans and Macdonald, for example, argue that legal subjects and legal institutions are mutually constitutive. See: Kleinhans and Macdonald (1997) 43. Subsequent to Webber's analysis, Macdonald has elaborated upon this point. See: Roderick A. Macdonald, 'Custom Made – For a Non-Chirographic Critical Legal Pluralism' (2011) 26 *Canadian Journal of Law and Society* 301.
168 Webber (2006) 181.
169 Macdonald (1998) 15.
170 Webber (2006) 181.
171 Webber (2006) 182.
172 Webber (2006) 182.
173 Webber (2006) 182.
174 Webber (2006) 182.
175 Macdonald and Sandomierski (2006) 616 n20.
176 Webber (2006) 192.
177 Webber (2006) 192.
178 Macdonald (1998) 15.
179 Webber (2006) 195.
180 Webber (2006) 182.
181 Macdonald and Sandomierski (2006) 632.
182 Webber (2006) 182.
183 Webber (2006) 189; Emmanuel Melissaris, 'Perspective, Critique, and Pluralism in Legal Theory' (2006) 57 *Northern Ireland Legal Quarterly* 597; Melissaris (2009) 61.
184 Webber (2006) 189.
185 Macdonald and Sandomierski argue that the power of agency is in acknowledging its contingency and limitations, in that we exercise our agency in the context of social relations. See: Macdonald and Sandomierski (2006) 630, citing Kleinhans and Macdonald (1997) 25; Emmanuel Melissaris, 'The More the Merrier? A New Take on Legal Pluralism' (2004) 13 *Social & Legal Studies* 57.
186 Macdonald and Sandomierski (2006) 617 n22.
187 Macdonald (2011) 310.
188 Macdonald (2013) 24 n23.
189 Kleinhans and Macdonald (1997) 43. Coombe advances a similar argument with respect to the power of intellectual property law over cultural signification, albeit not in the context of legal pluralism. See: Rosemary J. Coombe, 'Critical Cultural Legal Studies' (1998) 10 *Yale Journal of Law & the Humanities* 463, 480.

5 Resistance has rules

Narratives of resistance

Having developed the necessary analytical framework for analyzing law and popular culture as mutually constitutive discourse, with reference to the narrative/*nomos* obligational self, I can now provide a proof of concept in the form of a case study. As noted in Chapter 1, this is a proof of concept, not proof of result. Having established the necessary analytical framework, including the concept of the narrative/*nomos* obligational self, subsequent analysis can provide more comprehensive information. While necessarily representative rather than comprehensive, the illustrative examples of cultural narratives and eco/animal activism chosen for the case study are nonetheless sufficient to demonstrate the efficacy of the concept of the narrative/*nomos* obligational self as well as the open-source nature of the analytical framework. The potential range of subject matter, being works of popular culture and relevant normative communities, is unlimited. So too is the method of analysis, as the analytical framework is neither discipline-specific nor constrained by any particular methodology. I hope the open-source nature of this analytical framework will be of use to others who are similarly persuaded by the argument that law and popular culture are mutually constitutive discourse, in a manner that reflects their interests and preferred methodologies. This will facilitate rigorous investigation of my hypothesis of the narrative/*nomos* obligational self as the nexus of mutually constitutive law and popular culture discourse.

To demonstrate this nexus, I analyze narrative/normative consistency in collective narratives of resistance in works of bio-punk critical dystopia, and the beliefs and behaviors of eco/animal activists engaged in what might aptly be described as resistance movements. Note the significance of behavior even in an analytical framework that locates emancipatory potential in conceiving of law as capacity for legal knowledge. As stressed by both Cover[1] and Macdonald,[2] law requires not simply belief, but also committed behavior. Within popular culture, I choose to focus on works of critical dystopia because of the relationship I see between Cover's seminal work on law as alternity, as the bridge between what is and what ought to be.[3] Critical dystopias present compelling narratives of alternity. What distinguishes critical dystopia from both dystopia and utopia is that causal explanations predominate. Both utopia and dystopia are characterized by symptomatic analysis, a detailed account of what constitutes a utopian or dystopian society. A critical dystopia, in contrast, is characterized by a causal analysis, a fictional account of a dystopian world that references our own world-that-is, but also demonstrates strategies of collective social behavior (e.g. resistance movements) for achieving worlds-that-might-be.[4]

The collective narratives I find most compelling in this context are those that reflect concerns of an increasingly oppressive social order based on private ownership of scientific and technological knowledge. Our perspectives on resistance no doubt vary significantly, particularly in cases that involve violence and property damage as a direct challenge to commodification and ownership as the means of socio-economic oppression. Eco/animal activism is often characterized as terrorism under state law in the United States, with a similar predisposition developing in Canada. Not surprisingly, this struggle over meaning and legitimacy finds expression in fictional narratives featuring eco/animal activists.[5]

But works of popular culture are, in Bakhtin's terms, both multi-vocal and ambiguous in meaning. The objective is not to find a work of popular culture that advocates for eco/animal terrorism, a reductionist exercise that attempts to translate narratives into legal propositions.[6] I am interested instead in the way resistance is framed as alternity, in the sense of participants' normative beliefs and committed behaviors intended to transform their community from their present reality to a more desirable future. Resistance as alternity means that resistance has rules, and the normative understandings of these narratives of resistance have the potential to be reflected and refracted in the self-narration of our narrative/*nomos* obligational selves.

Hence the relevance of McAdams's concept of the imago, which guides my analysis of collective narratives of resistance in critical dystopia. Having proposed a narrative theory of identity, both Bruner and McAdams address the next logical question, which is the origin of the content of the narratives implicated in our sense of self. If we accept a theory of identity formation through narrative, then arguably we should accept as well that our self-narrations draw upon collective cultural narratives. Bruner describes our narrative identity formation as variations of canonical forms. McAdams provides the imago as a more specific conceptualization of the process whereby aspects of collective narratives influence our self-narration and thus our identity formation.

Note that the concept of the imago, while referencing collective narratives, is not intended to suggest that identity formation is fully determined by these narratives.[7] Nor are we passive recipients who faithfully retell collective stories as they have been told to us. After all, collective narratives are by nature aggregations of individual acts of storytelling over time. The relationship is recursive, in that our ongoing self-narrations influence over time the collective narratives pursuant to which we are influenced in our ongoing processes of self-narration. Macdonald proposes a similar recursive relationship of jurisgenerative activity, in that dominant narratives of law necessarily influence legal subjects, whether imposed by direct force or more nuanced ideology. Nonetheless, we retain our narrative imagination and the ability to influence the narrative imagination of others.[8] The explanatory power of the concept of recursion is that no normative order can be fully imposed, nor can any normative order be spontaneously created. The same arguably holds true for the influence of collective narratives on the imagoes we create to populate our life stories with idealizations of different aspects of our non-unitary, non-essential selves.

Whatever one's preference in apportioning responsibility for law between structure and agency, when we create these idealized (meaning exaggerated and one-dimensional) aspects of ourselves as characters in our life stories, we draw upon conventional cultural character types. As noted, a defining property of critical dystopia is combination of causal explanation connected to aspirational suggestion. Accordingly, as an instance of a conventional character type, I argue that the genre of critical dystopia necessarily contains what I refer to, with reference to Cover, as alternity characters. These are characters whose beliefs and committed behaviors are implicated, and may even be instrumental, in the effort to transform the fictional world-that-is to the world-that-ought-to-be.

That these popular culture narratives will almost certain conceive of the beliefs and behaviors of alternity characters as engaged in resistance movements, as opposed to presenting alternative claims of legality, is not fatal to my argument. As emphasized throughout, this is a project of re-imagining law, and that which has yet to be imagined will not yet appear as such in that which is being analyzed. At the most elemental level, all hypotheses of law can be analyzed as contextual modalities of justification,[9] which is after all the necessary premise of Melissaris's insistence on the necessity and possibility of a transcontextual concept of law. The objective of this illustrative case study is to explore the hermeneutic circle, to use Kleinhans and Macdonald's image of law, of the narrative/*nomos* obligational self as a nexus of mutually constitutive discourse of law and popular culture. To what extent can we identify normative consistency (not causality) amid shared cultural narratives, narrative identity formation, and the beliefs and behaviors of eco/animal activists?

Similarly, eco/animal activists are unlikely to refer to their own reasons for action with reference to alternity characters or their own identity formation as narrative/*nomos* obligational selves. As with shared cultural narratives, the framing device is likely to be that of resistance to law, not alternative legal claims. Once again, this is an inescapable aspect of proposing different ways of explaining not the substance of our beliefs and behaviors, but rather how we might conceive of these as instances of legality, to ourselves and to each other. The undifferentiated data of narrative and normative experience, framed and referenced by familiar concepts and terminology, is reframed. Our experiences are still narrative and still normative (hence the compelling allure of Melissaris's concept of shared normative experiences), but framed and referenced by unfamiliar (for now) concepts and terminology, such as narrative/*nomos* obligational selves and alternity characters.

To identify both alternity characters and the concomitant traits that would be idealized as an aspect of self in an imago, as well as the extent to which the legal community's rules of resistance legitimate violence, I rely on Bal's theory of narratology, discussed in more detail below. As Bal aptly notes, narratives produce character effects, not people, even though the anthropomorphic qualities of these character effects are what attract our interest. What makes narrative so compelling, and its advantage over the realism of our lived experiences in this regard, is that character effects are sufficiently like us to engage our intellect and emotions, but sufficiently unlike us that they are not limited by the constraints of everyday life. For Bal, the flatness of a character, which is to say, the extent to which a character effect does not present us with the same interpersonal density we find in our relations with others, is an irrelevant measure of its significance.[10] The wonder of character effects is that we are able to see them as human, even as they behave in ways that are more (or less) than human, in the service of producing insights that are, as Bal describes, "truer than truth."[11]

Accordingly, the relevant question for character analysis is not who characters are, but rather what they are. In Bal's tripartite analytical division between text, story, and fabula, explained in more detail below, character effects are analyzed as an aspect of story. The story takes the events, actors, time, and location of a fabula, which remain consistent, and particularizes them through a manner of organization unique to that particular story. Note that these organizational processes are not the same as the author's activity in writing the story. As Bal notes, no point is served in attempting to generalize regarding the author's intentions. The organizational processes that create a unique story from a standardized fabula are hypothetical concepts, not descriptions of the writing process, and are intended to provide a systematic and thus discussable way of describing how content comes across in the story.[12]

The organizational processes of the story are what create the difference we notice between a fabula as told by Hans Christian Andersen and the same fabula as told by Disney. As part of a framework for identifying and explaining character effects, Bal proposes the use of semantic axes, meaning pairs of contrary meanings, to identity a character's relevant characteristics. She acknowledges the limitations of the structuralist aspects of oppositional meanings. Complexity is reduced to a polarizing duality that in turn creates a hierarchy between positive and negative. She also argues, on the other hand, that we commonly conduct semantic categorization by way of opposition. So long as we view the semantic labels as provisional designations, the model is a useful approach for analyzing characters.[13]

As for the specification of semantic terms, Bal argues that the selection of terms is a consequence of the ideological position of the analyst and the ideology represented in the story. Specification is not simply a descriptive task. This brings to mind McAdams's acknowledgment of a lack of consensus for creating a typology of representative imagoes for understanding people's accounts of their life stories. His own typology is based on what he identifies as recurring themes of agency and communion in his empirical analysis of life stories. I acknowledge the value of semantic axes that adopt this empirically validated typology. On the other hand, agency and communion are not particularly relevant for this inquiry. Instead, I avail myself of the wisdom of a crowd-sourced typology, being the character alignment used in role-playing table games.[14] The semantic axes are ideal for this inquiry. Adapting the common terminology to some degree, I characterize these two axes as normative orientation (good in relation to bad) and regulatory orientation (order/law in relation to chaos/illegality).

While I discuss the various combinations along these two axes in greater detail below, the alignment most representative of an alternity character is that which is termed "neutral good," meaning their normative orientation is good and their regulatory orientation is neutral. A neutral regulatory orientation means that an attitude toward either law or illegality is contingent upon the normative requirements of the circumstances. Characters oriented toward neutral good are motivated to achieve justice. They will try to achieve their objectives through legal means if possible, but if not, they will shift their regulatory orientation away from order/law and toward chaos/illegality.[15] While I am admittedly borrowing from the alignment of "chaotic good" on this fundamental point, I argue that alternity characters who are aligned as "neutral good" feel a personal responsibility to address injustice against others. They are willing to violate official legal rules in pursuit of this moral obligation.[16]

The semantic axes of character alignment are not limited to examining the normative orientations of alternity characters. I necessarily use the same metrics to examine the beliefs and behaviors of eco/animal activists, in order to demonstrate commonality among the normative understandings of alternity characters in resistance narratives and eco/animal activists in resistance movements. Adopting the semantic axes of character alignment allows me to accommodate the predominance of state law as represented in both narrative fiction and the accounts of beliefs and behaviors provided by eco/animal activists themselves. The narrative of law that prevails, whether in cultural narratives or in narrative identity formation, and whether imposed by physical force or ideology,[17] is that of the exclusive and centralized legal authority of the political state. In the critical dystopia I find most relevant here, this function has been compromised if not usurped by corporations. Nonetheless, the circumstances of dystopia themselves legitimate the narrative of state law, just as critical legal theory is capable of legitimating state law. With the use of character alignment, I can interrogate my hypothesis of the narrative/*nomos* obligational self with questions based on normative and regulatory orientations, neither of which is dependent upon any particular hypothesis of law.

As discussed above, however, I do not claim that belief in any particular hypothesis of law, including the centralized legal authority of a political state, is an instance of false consciousness. I do not analyze, but neither do I discard, references to state law in either cultural narratives or accounts by eco/animal activists of their beliefs and behaviors. Neither do I require either narrative character effects or human eco/animal activists to express their normative understanding in a way that includes references to law; references to morality, ethics, or any other normative system, including tacit and implicit references, will suffice. Throughout this analysis, I have argued against the assumption that an inherent and necessary distinction exists between laws and mere norms. I have also emphasized that the emancipatory potential of this analytical framework for re-imagining law is that we can acknowledge, if so desired, our own constructive capacity. The only programmatic aspect is my argument in favor of re-orienting our legal imaginations toward law as more verb than noun, as capacity for legal knowledge rather than prediction of or insistence upon any particular legal result.

The semantic axes are, as jurists like to say, necessary but not sufficient. For an alternity character's beliefs and behaviors to be considered transformative as opposed to disruptive and/or counterproductive, they must be consistent with Cover's conception of law as alternity. From another perspective, the purported alternity character must act in ways that are consistent, to adopt Melissaris on this point, with the shared normative experience of the community. Even if the alternity character acts alone, which is certainly a Hollywood convention for heroic people who save the world (usually men, sometimes robots, artificial intelligences, animals, aliens, or occasionally even women), what the character perceives as a moral imperative or legitimate use of violence cannot contradict the shared experiences of participants in the community regarding their ability to transform their world through their normative commitments.

I am reading into Melissaris on this point, but arguably this is possible if we understand the contextualization of law with respect to a legal community's shared normative experience to be subject to additional contextualization at a more granular level, provided that outright contradiction is not the result. Fictional resistance movements, and their cultural counterparts, often experience tension that may lead to schism when disagreement exists on ways and means to achieve desired objectives, typically along the fault lines of mainstream versus radical approaches. Nonetheless, the fact that not all participants would act with the same amount of zeal in regard to, for example, violence, does not indicate that the character does not operate with the same normative understanding of the community as those upon whose behalf action is taken.

As I explain below, how the alternity character is focalized, for example, by narrators or characters, external or internal, will provide information as to whether the relevant legal community, being that of the resistance movement, perceives the purported alternity character's beliefs and behaviors as consistent with their normative understanding of the world, or more succinctly stated, as legitimate. The nature of resistance, of course, is that the entity being resisted will have a different assessment. The nature of narrative fiction is that readers or viewers will have a variety of assessments. For the purposes of this inquiry, however, the relative normative understanding is that of the participants in the resistance.

At this point a note of caution is in order. In analyzing highly generative adults, McAdams identifies a predominant and recurring story type but acknowledges nonetheless that a range of common types of life stories might be associated with any particular identity formation. He advocates devoting greater attention to investigating the psychosocial construction of our lives from a narrative perspective. We may be able to identity types of life stories that are characteristic of common groups of people, however these cohorts may be defined. Similarly, having incorporated McAdams's theory of narrative identity to develop the concept of the narrative/*nomos* obligational self, I claim commonality and continuity, but not causality, among the alternity character as a feature of narratives of resistance in bio-punk critical dystopia, the imagoes that express and inform the narrative identity formations of eco/animal activists, and the instantiation of their narrative/*nomos* obligational selves in responding to the status quo by participating in resistance movements.

In providing a proof of concept that demonstrates narrative and normative continuity among alternity characters, imagoes, narrative identity formation, and the narrative/*nomos* obligational self, I hope to demonstrate that the emancipatory potential of my hypothesis does not result in a vague utopian impulse of unspecified normative significance. In both popular culture narratives and the beliefs and behaviors of eco/animal activists, resistance has rules, the commonality of which affirms that locating the nexus of mutually constitutive law and popular culture discourse in the narrative/*nomos* of the obligational self is both possible and plausible. The case study in this section provides a proof of concept of the application of this analytical framework to identify and account for a narrative/*nomos* of resistance.

In the absence of inquiry informed by this analytical framework, I cannot interrogate the self-narrations of eco/animal activists. Our predominant and prevailing processes of normative inquiry direct us toward giving reasons for action, not to recount our life stories, although this information occasionally emerges in an incidental fashion. I can, however, look for commonality in the normative understanding of resistance in alternity characters in collective popular culture narrative, and in the accounts of resistance provided by eco/animal activists, and extrapolate accordingly with respect to the imago of neutral good in the narrative/*nomos* identity formation of the obligational selves of eco/animal activists. This does not constitute unsubstantiated overreach into cause and effect propositional analysis. This is instead an exploration of the emancipatory potential of thinking of what we are obliged to do as a function of the narrative/*nomos* obligational self, with reference to a full range of cultural narratives and not simply those that narrate the exclusive legal authority of the political state, which then narrates us as transgressors in turn.

Bringing these different elements together, the objective is to demonstrate common narrative/normative patterns. I first analyze alternity characters in narrative fiction, adopting Bal's theory of narratology for this purpose, with reference to the character alignment of "neutral good." Following this, I analyze the beliefs and behaviors of eco/animal activists, provided in their non-fictional accounts of their participation in eco/animal resistance movements. From these instances of commonality, I extrapolate support for the plausibility of the narrative/*nomos* obligational self as a nexus for mutually constitutive law and popular culture discourse, specifically with respect to narratives of resistance.

In this circulation of legal meaning, the alternity characters of cultural narratives are incorporated into imagoes of "neutral good" in the narrative identity formation of eco/animal activists, which accounts for how narrative/*nomos* obligational selves exercise their jurisgenerative capacity when they respond to the question of what is law in circumstances of normative heterogeneity. Alternity characters in collective narratives aligned toward neutral good incorporate reflections and refractions of beliefs and behaviors narrated by eco/animal activists, who in turn incorporate into their own narrative identity formation the reflections and refraction of beliefs and behaviors narrated by alternity characters. Our narrative/*nomos* obligational selves, participating in a constructive capacity in this hermeneutic circle of law posited by Kleinhans and Macdonald, function as a nexus for the mutually constitutive discourse of law and popular culture.

I use four normative orientation questions to guide the process of analysis: (a) With reference to the normative semantic axis, is the character/activist's attitude oriented toward good in a way that involves a sense of personal responsibility or obligation for the welfare of others? (b) With reference to the regulatory semantic axis, is the character/activist's attitude toward law and illegal activity oriented toward neutral, wherein pursuing unlawful means is a necessary consequence of the failure of lawful means, and where the unlawful nature of an activity (or its repercussions) does not provide relief from performance, as it would for many of us? (c) What is the character/activist's normative understanding of violence, in terms of prescriptive limits placed on the nature and extent of violent behavior? (d) Is the character/activist's normative understanding of violence consistent with the shared normative understandings of the relevant community? The first two questions identify alternity character effects and associated traits, aligned as neutral good, which inform a corresponding imago of neutral good in the narrative identity formation of the narrative/*nomos* obligational selves of eco/animal activists. The third question provides an indication of what constitutes the rules of resistance, with a specific focus on the conditions pursuant to which violent conduct is legitimated. The fourth question establishes that a character/activist's beliefs and behaviors could constitute a viable alternative conception of law, given that they are shared by members of the relevant legal community.

The fourth question must be answered in the affirmative in order to establish the necessary conditions by which eco/animal activists might conceive of themselves as participants in a legal community. "Conceive of themselves" is a requirement that applies no matter the size or complexity of a legal community, as either a small group of activists or the citizens of a nation. In order to reconceive moral imperatives as legal claims, should participants choose to do so, the claim must be raised by a person in relation to another person, and in turn accepted by that person as a legal claim. The distinction between these circumstances and the requirements of bi-directional validity as explained by Macdonald is that the claim in these circumstances will affect third parties who are unlikely to share the participants' view of legality. Nonetheless, this would amount to nothing more (and nothing less) than what we currently conceive of as an instance of inter-legality, already addressed in state law as private international law with choice of law rules, and already acknowledged as an inevitable consequence of legal pluralism.

Note that I have no interest in disputing the efficacy or validity of state law in characterizing the actions of activists as either unlawful or even as constituting terrorism. My argument is that the activists can, if they so choose, conceive of themselves as a legal community. In the resulting plurality of *nomos*, the question of who is engaged in transgression and who is responding to transgression becomes somewhat more complicated. An affirmative answer to the fourth question, however, ensures that activists respond to state law with law of their own, and do not simply impose power in retaliation for power imposed upon them. Nor do I argue that anyone who reads or views collective narratives of critical dystopia will be sufficiently persuaded to put down his or her book or screen and proceed to join a resistance movement posthaste. I am simply hypothesizing alternity characters as one among many cultural characters available to draw upon as we create the imagoes that populate our life stories.

This discussion in this part is divided into two sections. First, I examine resistance in popular culture narrative, after first discussing in more detail the value of narratology as cultural analysis, the possible normative semantic orientations of alternity characters, and how the methodology of narratology is applied, by using character and localization to respond to the four normative orientation questions. Second, I examine eco/animal activists' accounts of their normative beliefs and behaviors, first providing background information on the activist movements analyzed, and then explaining the methodology used to respond to the questions of normative orientation.

Narratology as cultural analysis

Narrative analysis of law is well established, and thus might be considered a useful perspective from which to consider narrative as *nomos*, particularly given that most approaches are interdisciplinary in nature.[18] Bruner, for example, as briefly noted above, applies cognitive psychology to develop a theory of narrative[19] that explores the use of stories in law. This includes how lawyers arguing a case will use stories to provide support for or discredit claims,[20] as well as the use of stories to explain facts in a particular manner in judicial opinions.[21] Brooks analyzes storytelling in legal proceedings and judicial reasoning from a literary perspective, explicitly arguing the necessity of developing a narratology of law. By applying a disciplined methodology and analytic vocabulary, we are able to appreciate how telling a story differently may result in different legal outcomes.[22] Whereas the objective of many commentators is to analyze narrative as an inherent and under-theorized aspect of legal processes, others are more skeptical. Sherwood in particular appears to view narrative, or at least visual media narratives in popular culture, as a potentially harmful distraction that interferes with the capacity of litigation to objectively evaluate truth claims.[23]

As noted in Chapter 2, the difficulty with these theoretical approaches is that analysis has been confined to examples of state law, with a particular emphasis on adversarial litigation and common law reasoning. On the other hand, relying on Bal's theory of narratology to analyze narratives of resistance in popular culture could be taken as a lapse into structuralism,[24] which would be difficult to integrate into a constitutive approach to a narrative/*nomos* obligational self. I respond to this by noting that Bal's ongoing revision of her original work has resulted in a much more poststructuralist perspective, one that is attuned to ideology, context, and the role of the reader.[25] Bal anticipates objections concerning the inevitability of multi-vocal ambiguity in text, noting that interpretation has become a somewhat discredited activity, except when directed toward empirical analysis of reader response.[26] Nonetheless, she remains committed to the value of narratology, and her systematic theory is intended to facilitate interpretive processes, not with respect to objective certainty for the meaning of a text, but as a means to propose, defend, and discuss interpretation.[27] The point is not to avoid interpretation based on its subjectivity, but to account for the subjectivity of interpretation as agency exercised within cultural constraints. This situates narrative analysis within cultural analysis, in the sense of analyzing text within context.

Bal might be regarded as working within the tradition of classical narratology, in that she provides a systematic account of formal properties of narrative, organized with reference to the traditional distinction between fabula, story, and text. The first narrative element is that of the fabula, which is quite simply a series of actors and events related to each other in time and place. The elements of a fabula can then be arranged in any number of different ways, such as deciding from which point of view the elements are to be presented, the order in which they are presented, and the nature and extent of information provided with respect to the presentation of actors and events. The result of this process of arrangement is a story that conveys the fabula but in its own distinct way. As Bal notes, every story has a subjective point of view, even those ostensibly presented by an objective and external perspective.[28] This is one reason for Bal's insistence on the concept of focalization as an aspect of narratology. Every story presents us with a vision of the fabula. Focalization is a means whereby we can identify the nature of this vision as well as its origins. The story is then distinguished from the text, which is the arrangement of linguistic signs, including visual media that conveys the narrative to a reader or viewer.[29]

The three layers of analysis, however, are not defined for the purpose of categorization alone. Bal's approach is one of cultural analysis, which she distinguishes from cultural studies, both her theory of narratology as well as her scholarship dealing with a "travelling concepts" approach to interdisciplinary study. Recall as noted in Chapter 2 that Sarat and Simon also differentiate between these two approaches, referring to cultural analysis as focusing on the interpretation and analysis of symbolic processes, beliefs, and values, whereas cultural studies embeds this interpretation within analysis of the associated material conditions.[30] For Bal, the distinction is that a cultural studies approach does not involve studying culture, at least not as this would be understood from a disciplinary perspective such as cultural anthropology. Instead, cultural analysis, as an extension of prior disciplinary practice in the humanities, analyzes texts with reference to their existence in culture. In other words, they cannot be abstracted from their cultural context. They are "always-already engaged," as Bal describes them, as "interlocutors" of the culture in which they exist. The object participates in the production of meaning of which cultural analysis is itself a part.[31]

Accordingly, Bal's theory treats narrativity as a mode of cultural expression, with the tripartite division between fabula, story, and text used not to advance a structuralist claim regarding universal form, but rather as a means of analysis.

These three aspects of narrative can be identified and analyzed as distinct from each other, but they do not exist independently of each other. Indeed, the only material we have before us for the purpose of analysis is the text itself, which pursuant to Bal's narratological approach, extends to visual medial as well. Most importantly, the layers are not an attempt to speculate upon either the author's process of writing or any individual reader's process of reception.

Bal's analytical distinction between these three layers of narrative texts, being analytical rather than ontological in nature, is what makes narratology an ideal means for developing this illustrative case study. Whereas classical narratology tends to view narratives as independent, formal structures, Bal treats narratives as historically and culturally situated. The objective is not to identify and classify elements of narrative texts as a typology for its own sake, but to provide a consistent methodology to account for, *inter alia*, the effect texts have on readers.[32] Both her characterization of narrative analysis as a means of cultural analysis, as well as her systematic theory of narrative elements, are oriented toward interdisciplinary scholarship, an increasingly important characteristic given the "narrative turn" in many fields of study.

A potential criticism that Bal addresses in relation to her theory is that this explanation of reader effects is not sufficiently reception-oriented. As Bal argues, however, her theory of narratology is an analytical device focused entirely on reader expectations as they encounter, process, and respond to narrative texts.[33] The advantage of her systematic approach is that the focus is more on how structure produces content rather than on what content is produced, although this is not to characterize her approach as formal to the exclusion of substantive. Narratology, however, by placing the focus on narrative structure, avoids the lapse into text as propositional logic that so disturbs Manderson in relation to law and humanities scholarship.[34]

For example, Bal's reference to "character effects" reminds us that a realistic character should not be reduced to mere realism, a mere imitation of the non-narrative worlds we inhabit.[35] Characters, or character effects if we are to keep our focus on narrative structure, can accomplish actions and produce insights that are inconsistent with or beyond what we encounter in our interactions with other human beings.[36] Bal offers a similar explanation for her preference for the term "focalization" rather than the more familiar but less technically exact term "perspective." Again, the technical term orients us toward the constructed nature of the text, and reminds us that every story has a vision, and that every vision comes from somewhere. Every narrator, whether external or character-based, is presenting a particular, subjective, and inherently biased vision of events.[37] Focusing on a narrative's structure, on the way a narrative produces its content, reminds us that however immersed we may become in a particular world, however realistic the characters may appear to us, and however unbiased the external narrator may appear, we are dealing with a subjective presentation of character effects in a narrative text.

Bal agrees that the reader makes meaning, as demonstrated by cognitive and reception theories of language and narrative. She also affirms philosophies of language that emphasize the diversity of voice and the ambiguity of language,[38] noting their utility in reminding us of the limits of agency. Her argument for the continued relevance of narratology, one which I find persuasive, is that in a culture where creating meaning is a messy process, we should both identify and take responsibility for the choices of meaning that we make. Narrative elements are structured in a way that is intended to have reader effects. When we know how a text is structured, we can then allocate between text and reader the share and responsibility for creating meaning within our cultural constraints.

In a way, this is narratology as polarity, as an oscillation between the role of reader and text rather than a final determination of meaning. Manderson uses polarity in this way to reconcile critiques of language, objectivity, and meaning in law with the presumptive necessity of certainty and finality in the rule of law. Polarity acknowledges the productive capacity of the circuit of tension between two oppositions, which would be lost in misguided attempts to eliminate or synthesize them. Viewed through the lens of polarity, the rule of law is more meaningful as a site of endless oscillation between two irreconcilable poles of the general and particular, between prior rules and new circumstances. The resulting decision will always be unstable, but this affirms rather than discredits the productive nature of polarity. The value of legal decision-making is not finality, for no decision is definitively correct, but the continuing public discourse of justification and correction that precedes and follows.[39] Similarly, for Bal the value of narratology is not to fix objective meaning, but to provide a means to engage in a productive, ongoing discourse of justification and correction of interpretive proposals.

Bal makes no claim that narratology, her theory of narrative that provides a systemic account of aspects of narrative, provides a definitive or truthful interpretation of any particular narrative text. The objective is to provide a conceptual framework capable of facilitating not only analysis, the ability to understand and evaluate narrative texts, but also communication, in that a common vocabulary permits productive discussion. Bal fully acknowledges that textual interpretation is subjective and that the agency of the interpreter is subject to cultural influences and constraints. But for precisely this reason, because readers are subjective interpreters of meaning working with specific cultural contexts, narrative analysis is inherently cultural analysis.

Subjectivity is value-added, not a deficiency, because each interpretation, each proposal, contributes to an ongoing discussion of meaning, the objective of which is precisely the discussion itself. The provisional definitions offered by a systemic theory such as Bal's narratology are not intended to produce an account of a narrative work that is objectively right or correct. Instead, the objective provides a common language sufficient to articulate our interpretations, identify to others the evidence upon which we base our proposal, and invite discussion from others on the merits.[40] Subjectivity is inherent in any interpretive exercise, no matter which theoretical approach is adopted. As Bal notes, the failure is not the subjectivity, but the failure to acknowledge it, and open up this subjectivity itself to discussion, as part of the cultural analysis.[41]

In seeking to account for how the character effect of alternity characters comes across to the reader, I am not contradicting my statement in Chapter 1 that I am not looking to popular culture to act as law's interpreter or interlocutor. Adopting this approach would run counter to Manderson's compelling argument, discussed in Chapter 2, that inquiries in law and literature persist in reifying law. Interpretive approaches to content reduce literature to a collection of verifiable propositions, amenable to deployment in legal argument. The conjunction of law and literature not only affirms a dichotomy between two autonomous realms, but also, pursuant to the colonizing tendencies of law, places literature in the service of law.[42]

I do not dispute the interpretive nature of analyzing the character effect of alternity characters in bio-punk critical dystopia. Nor do I dispute that my objective is to demonstrate continuity between the alternity characters of collective narratives of resistance and self-narrations of imago in the hypothesized narrative/*nomos* discourse of the narrative/*nomos* obligational self. Narratological analysis is concerned with techniques and effects, that is to say, about accounting for the conditions of reception. The analysis does not seek to account for the process of writing, but for the process of reading. While the analysis is textual in nature, the relevance of context is never underestimated or ignored, in terms of the culture in which the work is situated as well as the interpretive activity of the reader. The result is an argument that is discussable, defensible, and as a consequence, amenable to amendment, of how a narrative text comes to mean something for readers.

The distinction is subtle but significant, and it is a reflection of the difficult balance between accounting for conditions of reception and specifying the reception itself. A more due diligent approach to law and popular culture would insulate analysis from potential criticism by avoiding the necessity of this distinction altogether. To account for conditions of reception would appear to circumscribe to some extent the infinite diversity in infinite combinations that characterizes reception.[43] On the other hand, we arguably need to assume some common experience to account for the pleasure we take in talking with others about our favorite works of popular culture, which includes both agreements and disagreements regarding interpretation. As Phelan has persuasively argued, shared experiences of narrative fiction, while not inevitable, are also not impossible. Different readers of the same book do not respond in the same way. On the other hand, different readers of the same book often do have a shared response, not complete but also not insignificant, to that book. To assume that readers will always have the same experience is too extreme, but then according to Phelan, so is the assumption that language is always indeterminate, or that reader response is entirely a function of ideological control of production, dissemination, and consumption. Readers do make meaning, but in the process, they respond to the way in which the text has been constructed by an author. The possibility (but not inevitability) of shared experience is located at this intersection between authorial design and reader response.[44]

While Bal is intentionally non-programmatic in regard to using narratology for cultural analysis, she is emphatic in her correction of potential misconceptions, the most relevant being that narratology is not an instrument for the "ready-made" production of knowledge. Narratological analysis cannot be instrumentalist in a way that assumes the ability of a neutral subject to stand outside and describe that which is being analyzed. I am not probing popular culture narratives for propositional truths regarding alternity characters. I am fully aware that I am the origin of the proposition being made regarding alternity characters.

A proposition is as much question as answer, but as Bal argues, that is the point of narratology, to ask meaningful questions. This admittedly sounds rather banal, but then consider the complexity of the basic question being asked: in the game of fictional make-believe, what is being proposed for us to believe?[45] The more limited scope of my question is, with respect to bio-punk critical dystopia, how are alternity characters conveyed to readers?[46] As set out in the introduction, this involves four normative orientation questions, the first two concerned with identifying an alternity character in terms of a semantic orientation toward neutral good, the third to identify the alternity character's normative understanding of violence as part of the rules of resistance, and the fourth to determine whether this normative understanding of violence is shared by members of the relevant normative (and potentially legal) community.

This is consistent with Phelan's approach (in orientation, not end result) to shared experiences in fiction, and consistent with Bal's argument that responsibility for meaning is allocated between reader and text. This is not, I argue, an interpretive approach that treats works of critical dystopia as propositional logic for the rules of resistance followed by eco/animal activists. This would involve an exogenous conception of law that contradicts the fundamental premises of my analytical framework. The nexus of the mutually constitutive discourse of law and popular culture can be found in the self-narrating identity formation of our narrative/*nomos* obligational selves, wherein questions of what am I obliged to do in any circumstance of normative heterogeneity cannot be disaggregated from questions of the kind of person I consider myself to be. To emphasize, this involves a mutually constitutive discourse of narrative/*nomos*, not a causal relationship between narrative and *nomos*. Causation is an inappropriately linear characterization, insufficient to describe legal meaning conveyed in a recursive circulation among collective narratives and self-narration of narrative/*nomos* obligational selves. These patterns defy linear alignment, and boundaries between social and psyche, communication and consciousness, are always in flux.

The objective of analyzing alternity characters with reference to the four normative orientation questions is to provide an illustrative case study for how we might hypothesize the narrative/*nomos* of the obligational self. I do not consider alternity characters to be fictional amalgams of lives lived by eco/animal terrorists. Working in the other direction, neither are near-future dystopian scenarios instruction manuals for present-day activism. For this reason, I have specifically excluded from my analysis popular culture narratives dealing with present-day environmental and animal activists, given the potential for distraction in the illusion of realism.[47] My reaction to any such tendencies would be to note, as have others far more experienced than me, that narrative is a truth of meaning rather than of fact.[48] My objective is to look not for the truth of activism in artefacts of popular culture, but rather for the representation and implications of common narratives of resistance, commodification, and alternity that we find in works of popular culture, and in the narrative identity formation of our narrative/*nomos* obligational selves.

Given that the narrative/*nomos* obligational self is an elaboration of the jurisgenerative legal subject of critical legal pluralism, this is also an explicit recognition of discursive plurality and inter- and intra-subjectivity. Arguably, however, recognition of plurality involves recognizing one's own analysis as part of this plurality. If the strength of literature is not the finality of truth but the openness of interpretation that inaugurates dialogue with others,[49] then arguably analytical reflections are included in the scope of the conversation. As Bal argues, reflecting on cultural expression is part of the cultural expression being reflected upon.[50]

Normative orientation

As discussed in the introduction, Bal refers to characters as "character effects" to emphasize that their narrative function cannot (or at least should not) be reduced to flat realism. Characters are one of the most significant aspects of narrative, and for this reason we should avoid projecting onto them anthropomorphic examinations or evaluations. We identify with character effects both emotionally and intellectually, which is why I am able to link collective narratives and alternity characters with McAdams's concept of the imago and its role in our self-narrated identity formations. Recall that the focus of narratology is on how narrative comes across to the reader or viewer, not the substance of what is communicated. Accordingly, for Bal the appropriate analysis of character effects is not to determine who they are, but rather what they are, in terms of their narrative function, and how we might acquire this information.[51]

Her framework for identifying and explaining character effects involves a number of different textual and extra-contextual considerations. The most relevant consideration for this project, given Macdonald's account of law as a function of personal narration and interaction, is a character's relations with others, including its relation to itself in the past. Bal suggests analyzing these relations with reference to semantic axes, being pairs of relevant and contrary meanings. While Bal acknowledges the difficulties this type of categorization typically involves, she also argues that oppositional meanings reflect the way many people process semantic categorization.[52] While polarity would be an oversimplification, we can focus on the extent of qualitative and quantitative differences along each semantic axis.[53]

As Bal notes, a semantic axis is populated according to the interests and ideological perspectives of the person who is conducting the analysis. As discussed above, McAdams uses the themes of agency and communion to construct a typology of representative imagoes, based on his empirical analysis of people's accounts of their life stories. Semantic pairings organized with reference to these concepts, while arguably validated by empirical evidence, are not particularly informative when applied to identify and analyze alternity characters in critical dystopia. Instead, I locate empirical validity in the online, crowd-sourced folksonomy known as TV Tropes.[54] Relying on the concept of character alignment, I identify an alternity character as one oriented toward neutral good on the semantic axes of normativity and regulation.

A brief explanation is perhaps in order before proceeding to discuss the relevance of the alignment of neutral good to identify alternity characters (should they exist) in any particular work of bio-punk critical dystopia. TV Tropes is a wiki-based collection of common fictional tropes and conventions, or to use classification terms, as "limited, fixed sets of co-occurring properties."[55] Although initially based in television, the wiki has grown exponentially. A wiki is a website in which the users provide content and editing, the most well-known example being Wikipedia. Wiki sites have editors, who exercise greater or lesser control over the contribution process, including content rules such Wikipedia's notability requirement. Subject to the manner and extent of editorial control, the content, organization, and most significantly the validity of a wiki is a function of user contributions. Crowd-sourced validity is particularly evident in TV Tropes, given the explicit lack of a notability requirement. The knowledge domain of fictional tropes and conventions is constituted by consensus (or lack of objection) by contributors, not by citation to documented sources, although arguments must be supported by reference to illustrative works of popular culture.

While wiki is the appropriate and familiar term, TV Tropes may also be characterized as a means for classifying and organizing information, specifically as a folksonomy, as noted above. A folksonomy is perhaps best defined by first distinguishing the concept from a taxonomy. As a method of classification, taxonomy identifies the essential characteristics of the entities (or more accurately, information about the entities) to which it applies, and then uses these characteristics to organize the entities into hierarchal and mutually exclusive classes.[56] Relevant entities are organized into terminal classes, meaning classes which cannot be further divided, and which convey highly specific information regarding the essential characteristics. These classes are subsumed along with others within more general classes, in a process that repeats until the highest level of meaningful abstraction is reached. This apex classification will contain every sub-classification below, so to speak, down to the terminal level.

Folksonomies, being a combination of "folk," as in user-generated content, and "taxonomy," as just described, differ from taxonomies in that no authority exists for a single, hierarchal structure of entities with a class, or classes within classes. Folksonomies are self-indexing, in that classes are organized as contributors assign key words to entities, and the key words are not necessarily derived from a pre-defined vocabulary. Folksonomies are also multi-indexing, which may result in a flexible and more horizontal organization rather than the strict hierarchy of classes within a taxonomy. If key words are organized hierarchically, and contributors may assign different key words to the same entity, the entity may exist in both subordinate and superior classes.[57] If key words are not organized hierarchically, the entities will be related to each other by virtue of the key word but will not be organized into subordinate and superior classes.

Lack of pre-defined vocabulary or a predictable hierarchal structure is not a deficiency but an acknowledgment that user-generated content provides the folksonomy's utility and value. Van der Wal has described the process of creating online folksonomies as "tagging that works," in that people in relevant social environments create connections between entities that are derived from, and contribute to, their own meanings and knowledge. The result is a sophisticated understanding of the entity being tagged, with a minimum of disambiguation.[58] In other words, the wisdom of a folksonomy is a function of its openness to a plurality of meaning, wherein the meanings that attract the most affirmation prevail.

This recalls the discussion in Chapter 4, where I argued that the jurisgenerative capacity of narrative/*nomos* obligational selves does not regress into a multitude of legal meanings that contradict the integrated functions of law as social meaning and social control. I noted that Melissaris, Macdonald, and Manderson all reject the presumptive authority of legal experts to interpret legal meaning. I noted as well that all three locate law's legitimacy in social relations, whether in shared normative experiences (Melissaris), the requirement of reciprocity (Macdonald), or participation in legal discourse (Manderson). The crowd-sourced nature of a folksonomy provides its own demonstrable, evidence-based validity,[59] not to mention a working model of crowd-sourced normative consensus. Nonetheless, should more traditional evidence be required, I note that academic authors have also confirmed the relevance and efficacy of TV Tropes as a repository of crowd-sourced knowledge of popular culture.[60]

As a fictional trope or convention, character alignment is a succinct way to refer to a character's normative orientation, the most familiar instantiation being in Dungeons and Dragons, a tabletop role-playing game. The system of character alignment is incorporated directly into the game design as a role-playing tool. Character alignments in these types of games are also subject to the canonical interpretation, that is to say, an authoritative interpretation of characteristics and behaviors provided by those who create, produce, or distribute the work as part of its storyline or backstory. For other works of popular culture, character alignment is a subject of discussion among those who engage with the work, rather than an aspect of the work itself.

As noted on the TV Tropes topic page, the alignment system was not designed to be a comprehensive and generally applicable classification system for characters in works of popular culture.[61] For works of popular culture that do not involve game mechanics, the semantic axes of morality and ethics may be irrelevant, the information regarding a character's attributes may be insufficient to make a determination, or conversely, the characters' attributes may be too complicated or contradictory to assign to a specific orientation. This is illustrated by reference to a graphic illustration of Batman, posed in each of the nine specific character alignments, all of which are plausibly defended with information taken from the source materials.[62]

With these caveats in mind, the conventional character alignment developed for role-playing tabletop games can be adapted to populate the semantic axes proposed by Bal. First, recall that for Bal, semantic axes are purposive in nature, in that they reflect the interests and ideological orientation of the person who is conducting the analysis. The objective is to identify character attributes that are relevant to the purpose of the analysis and to provide a means by which the results of analysis can be readily conveyed to others for discussion and debate. Second, recall my assessment of the validity of character alignment as a crowd-sourced contribution to the TV Tropes folksonomy (wiki). These two factors are more than sufficient to demonstrate the efficacy using character alignment as the semantic axes for examining alternity characters in works of bio-punk critical dystopia.

Character alignment specifies both a moral axis, which refers to a character's sense of obligation toward others, and an ethical axis, which refers to a character's attitude toward the necessity and/or value of law. I have adapted these to be a normative semantic axis and regulatory semantic axis, respectively. To some extent, character alignment addresses Bal's concerns regarding semantic polarity, in that each axis has three possible alignments, resulting in nine distinct combinations. Only one of these alignments, neutral good, appears suitable for identifying those attributes that most facilitate an alternity character, although the choice between the regulatory orientations of neutral and chaotic demonstrates the permeable nature of the boundaries between these classifications.

Along the ethical (regulatory) axis, the alignments of lawful, neutral, and chaotic represent a character's attitude toward law. A lawful alignment represents a character who believes in the importance of social order, which is best accomplished through legal rules. Faced with an unjust law, a lawful character might still think that obedience causes less damage than transgression, or that law reform is the appropriate response. A chaotic alignment represents a character who believes first and foremost in individual freedom and may even oppose the idea of law in the abstract as necessarily antithetical to personal freedom. Faced with an unjust law, a chaotic person will simply disregard its authority. A neutral alignment represents a character whose orientation toward law is more situational than dispositional. Faced with an unjust law, a person oriented toward neutral might agree that disobedience is problematic, but if law reform does not achieve the desired result, this person will disregard its authority, albeit not with the same easy sense of indifference as the person oriented toward chaotic.

Along the moral (normative) axis, the alignments of good, neutral, and evil represent a character's attitude regarding obligations owed to others. A good alignment represents a character who believes she has an obligation to help achieve justice for others whenever possible. A neutral alignment represents a character whose sense of obligation is limited to herself and those close to her. This is not to say that a neutral alignment disregards law, which is a function of the regulatory axis, not the normative axis. The alignment refers to the scope of the character's sense of obligation. A good person feels obliged to help everyone, while a neutral person feels obliged to help only family and friends. An evil person's only sense of obligation is toward herself.

Reviewing the various combinations, the most relevant character alignment on the regulatory semantic axis is neutral, although some attributes of the chaotic orientation are also compelling. To begin by ruling out the inapplicable, the lawful orientation is not consistent with the narrative function of alternity characters. I conceive of alternity characters in bio-punk critical dystopia as being those characters whose beliefs and behaviors help transform the fictional world-that-is to the world-that-ought-to-be. This typically involves resistance, either alone or as part of a group, against those in positions of authority who are considered responsible for the current dystopian conditions. A regulatory orientation of lawful contradicts both the alternity function of resisting authority, as well as the perceptions of the characters themselves as engaged in justified resistance against illegitimate authorities.

The choice between the orientations of neutral and chaotic is more complicated. A regulatory orientation to chaotic may, depending on the paired normative orientation, describe a character who will readily break unjust laws in pursuit of justice. Another possibility, however, is a character who opposes the concept of law generally, on the basis that laws limit personal freedom. In both instances, the characters demonstrate normative aspiration, in that they are seeking to achieve justice in circumstances of injustice. The latter orientation, however, is an uneasy fit with Moylan's articulation of the definitive characteristics of the genre of critical dystopia.[63] The analysis is causal rather than symptomatic, providing an explanation not just of how the dystopia world came to be, but also of what should be done to move toward a utopian alternative. Significantly, the transformation from real to ideal, to use the terms of alternity here, requires collective resistance.

The objective is to recreate the world of social relations, which assumes a character's regulatory orientation involves opposition to abuse of legal authority, rather than legal authority itself. This distinguishes critical dystopia from similar narratives that focus on solitary protagonists, such as the prototypical hackers, whose actions liberate them but lack a broader transformative effect. In terms of a chaotic regulatory orientation, a character who is a solitary rebel is not necessarily an alternity character engaged in resistance, even though her actions may help others around her at the time. Her objective is to oppose rather than transform society, which will lead to temporary alliances with resistance movements, but alliance is not the same as membership.

The most appropriate regulatory orientation is neutral, which indicates a character with a situational rather than dispositional approach to law. A regulatory orientation of neutral indicates an alternity character who would pursue lawful means if possible, but otherwise, an unjust law need not be obeyed. The decision would not be taken so lightly as a person oriented toward chaotic, but the decision would be taken just the same. A neutral orientation indicates a character most similar to a protagonist in a critical dystopia, who resists the abuse of law rather than law itself, and who is focused on social transformation rather than simply individual liberation. If individual liberation were all that mattered, a character oriented toward neutral would not first attempt to pursue reform from within a system, as a necessary precursor to resistance and revolution from without.

Turning to the normative semantic axis, the most relevant alignment is good, which creates the semantic alignment of alternity characters as oriented toward neutral good. Referring once again to the conventions of critical dystopia, we can be fairly certain that alternity characters are not oriented toward evil, even if those in authority might perceive them as acting either solely for their own benefit or with selfish disregard for the needs of others in society. Similarly, a neutral orientation, being a sense of obligation limited to self, friends, and family, is inconsistent with the narrative function of alternity characters and the conventions of critical dystopia. Alternity characters and protagonists of critical dystopia are those whose beliefs and behaviors provide a means of collective resistance and social transformation. Arguably, a character oriented toward neutral is similar to the solitary protagonist who characterizes a dystopian narrative. The character might liberate herself, and have a sense of obligation to those closest to her, such as friends and family, but "greedy families" arguably do not organize themselves into collective resistance. Such an inwardly focused circle of normative concern may be sufficient to constitute a legal community in other circumstances, but not a resistance movement in the context of critical dystopia.

Character and focalization

The significance of popular culture narratives for our narrative/*nomos* obligational selves is that in the process of telling stories of ourselves, we become the people in the stories we tell. Narrative identity formation draws upon collective cultural narratives, a point made by both Bruner[64] and McAdams.[65] Hence the relevance of examining the normative dimensions of what I have termed alternity characters in works of bio-punk critical dystopia, meaning those characters whose beliefs and behaviors facilitate a community's transition from the dystopian real to a utopian ideal. The objective is to determine whether common patterns of representation exist between the normative aspects of alternity characters and the normative beliefs and behaviors of eco/animal activists.

In hypothesizing law and popular culture as mutually constitutive discourse, I am not claiming a cause and effect relationship. Not only would this be an unduly simplistic account of the complexities of discourse, but also to speak of cause and effect is to return once more to an understanding of law as an entity distinct from culture. Also note that as with any hypothesis of law, the concept of narrative/*nomos* obligational selves is not a truth claim,[66] but rather a means by which we can explore different possibilities for how we make sense of our normative behavior. If we accept McAdams's account of imagoes and identity formation, a circulation of legal meaning among popular culture narratives of alternity and resistance and our narrative/*nomos* obligational selves (which do not constitute the whole of our identities) is a plausible response to the question of how we might conceive of popular culture as legal authority. In creating the imagoes who populate our life stories as idealizations of different aspects of ourselves, we draw upon the examples of those we see as exemplars, or role models, of the aspects being idealized. These examples may be people, but they may also be alternity characters from popular culture narratives.

My claim is that normative attributes of alternity characters, which I characterize with reference to the semantic orientation of neutral good, can inform the imagoes we create in the ongoing process of telling our life stories of ourselves as eco/animal activists. Identity is obligation, not in the sense that identity precedes and obligation follows, but in the sense that obligation cannot be disaggregated from identity, no more than law can be isolated and abstracted from culture.

I cannot tell myself the ongoing story of the person I think I am without referring to what I consider myself obliged to do and without wondering if I am living up to my normative aspirations.

Recall that I propose four normative orientation questions to examine both the normative attributes of alternity characters and the normative beliefs and behaviors of eco/animal activists. The first two questions determine whether a character effect may be considered an alternity character, with reference to the semantic character alignment of neutral good. On the normative semantic axis, an alternity character has a personal sense of obligation to pursue justice on behalf of others, as opposed to a more narrow self-interest in one's own welfare and that of family and friends. Consistent with the definitional requirements of critical dystopia, an orientation of good requires an alternity character to fight against dystopian forces for the benefit of a collective normative community. Stories about a character's own escape from dystopia, even if this involves her family and friends, are not sufficient. This would be an individual rather than collective liberation, and the dystopia persists for those who have not managed to escape.

On the regulatory semantic axis, an alternity character's attributes indicate a situational rather than dispositional attitude to law. A semantic regulatory orientation of neutral indicates alternity characters who are willing to pursue meaningful change through legal means, but otherwise, they will consider themselves obliged to disobey unjust law in pursuit of justice. Note that I characterize defiance of unjust law as an obligation, in order to reflect normative parity with the obligation to pursue justice on behalf of others. Many of us might share the same views as eco/animal activists on many issues, but we do not feel obligated to engage in unlawful acts, including acts of economic sabotage in the form of property damage. For alternity characters and eco/animal activists oriented toward neutral good, the consequences of unlawful behavior do not provide relief from performance.

A difficulty with this orientation is that in critical dystopia narratives, the timeline tends to begin (even if out of sequence in the story) at a point when law has been rendered fully illegitimate by dystopian forces. Alternity characters in this dystopian world have no opportunity for attempts at law reform. Since the alternity character is already engaged in resistance, we may have difficulty determining whether an alternity character is opposed to an unjust law (situational), or hostile or merely indifferent to the concept of law in general (dispositional).

Both the normative and regulatory semantic axes are relevant to the third question, which examines the rules of resistance, specifically the extent to which violence is permitted, and under what circumstances. The fourth question involves the requirement of reciprocity, which ensures that the normative aspects of alternity characters, being consistent with those of the relevant community, can be re-imagined as legal claims.

In this section, I explain in more detail how I apply Bal's theory of narratology to respond to these four normative orientation questions, using two elements at the story level of analysis, character and focalization. Adopting only two elements from a comprehensive theory of narratology may appear a bit too abbreviated to provide useful information, but a selective approach is consistent with Bal's emphasis on choice and subjectivity as inescapable aspects of both narrative and narrative analysis.[67] In addition, character and focalization are two of the most important narrative techniques at the level of the story. Bal refers to character as "intuitively the most crucial category of narrative,"[68] and underscores the significance of focalization as a means to identify what, in the game of narrative make-believe, we are being asked to believe.[69]

The narrative technique of character is relevant to the first three questions. As for how to acquire this information, Bal notes that character attributes are provided either explicitly by the character or by the deductions we make based upon a character's actions. Explicit references would include self-analysis, which occurs when an alternity character talks about itself, either to itself (internal monologue) or to others. Explicit references also occur when other characters talk to themselves (internal monologue) or each other about the alternity character. Explicit references also occur when the narrator conveys information about the attributes of the alternity character. Just as in our everyday lives, we cannot assume that others will share an alternity character's self-perception. The narrator may convey information, and other characters may respond to the alternity character and to each other, in ways that affirm or deny the self-analysis communicated by the alternity character or the other-analysis of the alternity character by other characters. Characters may also affirm or deny information about the alternity character conveyed by the narrator. Again, just as in everyday life, we cannot be certain that the perceptions of others regarding the alternity character, including the narrator's, are objectively correct or free of bias.[70]

The attributes we deduce from a character's actions depend to a large extent on our frames of reference, some of which may be common to many readers and some of which may be highly idiosyncratic.[71] We may assume, for example, that most people reading a murder mystery will deduce that a character who commits an act of murder, or who is revealed by another character as a character who commits an act of murder, is a murderer. We might not have such a high degree of consensus as to whether Walter White is simply a man trying to provide for his family in a country that does not offer universal health care. Another consideration is the frequency of an action. If a character repeatedly engages in certain types of actions, we may more likely deduce that these are representative attributes.[72] For example, if an alternity character frequently engages in acts such as interrupting other characters, we may deduce that the alternity character demonstrates some degree of impatience and disrespect for others' opinions. As this example indicates, however, even a presumptively objective metric such as frequency is nonetheless affected by our frames of reference.

The narrative technique of focalization is ideally suited to responding to the fourth question, which examines the requirement of reciprocity between the normative understandings of alternity characters and members of the relevant normative community. For Bal, focalization's organizing function at the analytical level of the story simply cannot be accounted for by reference to narration or perspective. The difficulty with approaches that refer, for example, to a narrative point of view, is that they fail to distinguish between who speaks and who sees.

As Bal notes, we often talk to each other about what others have seen. A narrator who speaks may be expressing the vision of a character who sees, in which case referring to this exclusively as narrative perspective is inaccurate.[73]

Conflating narration with vision is also misleading.[74] When actors and events from the fabula are presented in a story, they are necessarily conveyed from a particular perspective. No disrespect intended to Nagel,[75] but a view from nowhere is simply not possible. Storytelling is inescapably subjective, a point made by Verstraten in describing the narrative technique of focalization as "subjectified content."[76] Jahn also emphasizes the subjective nature of storytelling as a matter of limits on perspective. We can never tell the whole of the story, only what we know of the story in terms of what we have perceived. Accounting for the bounded nature of perspective, he describes focalization as "the submission of (potentially limitless) narrative information to a perspectival filter."[77]

When we take note of the inescapable subjectivity of both voice and vision, we can appreciate why Bal emphasizes the importance of distinguishing between who speaks and who sees at the level of the story. Focalization is "the most important, the most penetrating, and the most subtle means of manipulation."[78] All aspects of a story are focalized by either an external or character focalizer, which means that every story presents a "certain, far from innocent, interpretation of the elements."[79] Focalization, in other words, may be conceived as a narrative counterpart to legal subjectivity and narrative/*nomos* obligational selves. Subjective storytelling involves a process of evaluation, in that the focalizer provides a version of events she has judged to be accurate, even though competing visions exist, which also claim to be accurate accounts. We need to acknowledge the presumptively objective narrator's perspective as misdirection. We need to ask, what is the vision, and from where does it come?[80]

Once we set aside the confusion created by terms such as narrative perspective, the narrative technique of focalization is a fairly accessible concept. Focalization takes the form of a relationship between the narrative elements that are presented, and the vision through which they are presented.[81] The relationship between narration and focalization can be summarized as: A says that B sees what C is doing.[82] Since focalization is a relationship between the subject who focalizes and the object who/that is focalized, analysis must account for both of these aspects.[83] The focalizer determines the image of the object presented in the story, so while identifying this object may be fairly straightforward, we also need to identify with certainty the focalizing subject.

First, we can distinguish between external and internal focalizers. Internal focalizers are characters in the story, what Bal refers to as character-bound focalizers, while external focalizers exist outside the story, typically in the form of a narrator. Second, we can distinguish between levels of focalization. The first level involves an external focalizer, such as an external narrator, providing an all-encompassing vision. Internal character-bound focalizers are embedded within this vision, as the external focalizer yields to one or more internal focalizers. The relationship between the two levels is an external focalizer's vision of an internal character-bound focalizer. This is a question of who allows whom to watch whom or what, which nicely demonstrates why narrative perspective is an insufficient account of who is seeing and what is being seen. Sometimes the levels of focalization may overlap such that distinguishing between external and character-bound focalization is not possible. Just as narration can take the form of free indirect discourse, where we are not entirely sure if the voice of the narrator has yielded to the voice of the character, so too can there be free indirect focalization, where we are not entirely sure if the vision of the external focalizer has yielded to the vision of a character.

As for the object that is focalized, this may be classified as perceptible or non-perceptible. A perceptible object can be observed. This includes indications of location and time, the presence of characters, the actions in which characters engage, the objects that characters handle, and the words and other forms of expression characters communicate. A non-perceptible object can be perceived but not observed, such as character's mental activity, including dreams or other states of consciousness. An external focalizer can perceive the internal mental activity of characters, whereas a character-bound focalizer can perceive its own internal mental activity but not that of other characters. Such mental activity may be deduced, however, from perceptible actions. For example, perceptible objects such as facial expressions may accompany internal mental activity and emotional states.[84]

As is evident from this discussion of the narrative techniques of character and focalization, a narratological analysis of a work of popular culture is not concerned with interpretation per se, particularly not as a matter of truthful proposition, but rather with how the narrative is structured. Focalization cannot predict reader response but does indeed affect reader response. Abbot, for example, notes that focalization can affect how we think and feel about the characters and events presented in the story, by conveying various intensities of thought and feeling on the part of the narrator(s) and character(s).[85] Miller argues that narrative techniques can encourage our sympathy for characters who engage in actions we might consider morally ambiguous at best. If a morally ambiguous character's point of view predominates, she will tend to receive our support not because she is good, but because she is familiar.[86] Again, we might consider Walter White a particularly illustrative example.

When we read or watch through the character's eyes, we are more likely to identify with and accept the vision of events they present. This is the case even if character-bound focalization shifts between characters, another circumstance that provides compelling support for Bal's rejection of the concept of narrative perspective. The narrator's vision is likely to remain constant even as the character-bound focalizers change. If we conflate narration with vision, we will overlook how different focalizers convey different information about objects as well as any differences in character attributes that could have implications for persuading us of the validity of their version of events. Even if a story provides all character-bound focalizers with equal time, so to speak, we are typically given an indication of whose vision should attract our sympathetic attention.[87]

Our sympathies can also be affected by what is focalized. Readers will have greater insight into a character who can focalize both perceptible and non-perceptible events, such as its internal mental states, than characters who focalize only perceptible events.[88] Greater insight into a character does not necessarily mean we will affirm the character's beliefs and behaviors over the course of the story. Just as in everyday life, however, the more we understand about a character's motivations, the more we have an opportunity for a more informed (and perhaps less judgmental) opinion. Depending upon how skillfully the story is presented and how skillfully the text is written, we may not be aware of how characters who focalize only perceptive events know much less about what is taking place than we do.[89] In this case, we may be inclined to judge them more harshly, since we are holding them to the standards expected of a person who is fully informed.

In addition to encouraging our sympathy for particular characters, focalization can also encourage us to respond to a particular vision of events as being more objective and thus more authoritative. For example, if the story is exclusively focalized by an external narrator, we may be inclined to treat the narrator's vision as an objective account of what really happened in the story.[90] This presumption may persist even in stories where the external narrator hands off focalization to different character-bound focalizers. If the character-bound focalizers present conflicting or inconsistent visions, we may think of the external narrator's vision as an objectively neutral arbitration between different accounts of what really happened. We may overlook the logic of the point made by Bal, that even an external narrator focalizes with a particular, subjective vision.[91]

With these considerations of objectivity and sympathy in mind, I use focalization to respond to the fourth question, which is whether an alternity character's normative understandings are shared by members of the relevant community, such as other participants in a resistance movement. A number of different configurations of focalization are possible, involving factors such as whether focalization is external or character-bound, the distribution of vision between external and character-bound focalizers as well as among character-bound focalizers, whether focalizers are members of the same normative community, whether we are presented with an illusion of objectivity in either an external or character-bound focalizer, or whether we are encouraged to align our sympathies with one or more characters. Regardless of which configuration applies, does the vision of events presented to us affirm the legitimacy of the alternity character's orientation of neutral good as well as the character's attitude toward the use of violence?

If a story relies exclusively on an external focalizer, and the external focalizer presents a vision of events affirming relevant attributes of the alternity character, we may be influenced by the illusion of objectivity to accept this vision. If a story makes predominate use of a character-bound focalizer who is a member of the same normative community, and we are given an indication that this character should attract our sympathies, then if the character affirms the relevant attributes, we may be influenced by our sympathies to accept this vision. Most effectively, if the predominant character-bound focalizer is also the alternity character, and we are given an indication that this character should attract our sympathies, then in the absence of information to the contrary, we may be inclined to accept the character's self-analysis.

Instead of an exclusive external focalizer or a predominant character-bound focalizer, a story may involve a number of different character-bound focalizers, which presents different possibilities for accepting their vision on the basis of either an illusion of objectivity or an encouragement of our sympathies. If a series of character-bound focalizers present an affirmative vision of the alternity character, if all or most of them are members of the same normative community, and if we are given no indication that any particular character should attract more or less sympathy than any other, we may be influenced by an illusion of objectivity to accept their assessment. On the other hand, if a series of character-bound focalizers, again all or most of them members of the same normative community, present conflicting visions that both affirm and deny the legitimacy of the alternity character, we are not presented with an illusion of objectivity. In these circumstances, we will be inclined to accept the assessment of the characters with whom we have been encouraged to sympathize. The requirement of reciprocity will be met only if the character-bound focalizers who attract our sympathy provide an affirmative vision of events involving the alternity character.

To answer the fourth question, the simplest way to proceed is to organize the information provided based on the alternity character's status, which may shift in the course of a story, as a character-bound focalizer, or as an object focalized by either an external focalizer or one or more character-bound focalizers.

When the alternity character functions as a character-bound focalizer, whether predominate or in combination with an external focalizer and/or one or more character-bound focalizers, the relevant questions to ask are: (a) what does the alternity character focalize relevant to its normative understanding of violence, taking into account that what is overlooked can be as important as what is noticed; and (b) are we inclined to accept this vision as one that attracts our sympathies? We can assume that an alternity character affirms itself, notwithstanding that a conflicted alternity character makes for an interesting story.

When the alternity character functions as the object focalized, whether by an external focalizer and/or one or more character-bound focalizers, the relevant questions to ask are: (a) who focalizes the alternity character; (b) are we inclined to accept this vision as based on either illusory objectivity or as one that attracts our sympathies; (c) does this vision affirm or deny the alternity character's normative understanding of violence; and (d) is the focalizer a member of or distinct from the relevant normative community?

Analysis of focalization will not provide an objective truth about alternity characters, nor should this be the purpose. Much of the pleasure derived from works of popular culture comes from arguing with others about characters. The realism of character effects can lead to us think of them as people we actually know. The value of a narratology as a methodology is the ability, as Bal notes, to make our arguments discussable.[92] When we discuss fictional characters in popular culture, we do not refer to a definitive interpretive source, but on the other hand, the number of contradictory perspectives tends to be manageable, because not all interpretations are equally plausible. I do not claim that any percentage of readers will agree with my analysis of alternity characters. I do claim to provide persuasive supporting argument that my analysis is plausible.

Critical dystopia in Atwood's **MaddAddam** *trilogy*

Having suggested above that critical dystopia might be characterized as the narrative counterpart to Cover's understanding of law as alternity, I develop this argument in more detail in this section. I also explain my choice of Margaret Atwood's *MaddAddam* trilogy, consisting of *Oryx and Crake*,[93] *The Year of the Flood*,[94] and *MaddAddam*,[95] as an ideal popular culture narrative for this case study.[96] The biopunk subject matter, primarily genetic modification, has near-future implications that are relevant to present-day concerns of eco/animal activists regarding environmental damage and animal exploitation. The character I identify as an alternity character, Zeb, is engaged in acts of resistance that include the use of violence, and as a member of a resistance movement, his normative understandings can be assessed with reference to the requirement of reciprocity.

Narratives of critical dystopia are particularly relevant for conceiving of popular culture and law as mutually constitutive discourse. First, critical dystopia is contemporaneous with our present circumstances. As Moylan notes, critical dystopia is a creative continuation of dystopian tradition that emerged in relation to the social, economic, and political circumstances of the late 1980s through to present day. After a brief revival of utopian narrative in the 1970s, writers increasingly adopted dystopian strategies to address changing economic and cultural conditions. Critical dystopia was not simply a dystopian revival, but also a purposive interrogation of prevailing economic, political, and cultural conditions.[97]

Second, critical dystopia presents compelling narratives of alternity. Critical dystopias construct a dystopian world that references our own world-that-is, but they also demonstrate strategies of collective social behavior for achieving worlds-that-might-be. What distinguishes critical dystopia from both dystopia and utopia is that causal explanations predominate. Both utopia and dystopia are characterized by symptomatic analysis, a detailed account of what constitutes a utopian or dystopian society. A critical dystopia, in contrast, is characterized by a causal analysis. A critical dystopia will explain the circumstances of how a dystopian society comes to be and what can be done to bring about a better world.[98] The distinction is demonstrated in Sargent's definition of a critical dystopia, which focuses on the characteristics of the fictional society: (a) the society is described in detail; (b) the description indicates the author intends the reader to view the fictional society as worse than contemporary society; and (c) at least one utopian place exists within the larger dystopian territory, or the story conveys hope that the dystopia will be replaced with a utopia.[99]

In contrast, the definition of a dystopian society includes (a) and (b), but not[100] (c). Fitting, for example, differentiates the dystopian *Dark City* from the critical dystopia of *Pleasantville*. *Dark City* presents social critique, but collective resistance is absent. In *Dark City*, the protagonist may end up on a sunny beach with his girlfriend, but he has created nothing more than "his own solipsistic utopia."[101] In contrast, *Pleasantville* provides not only a causal analysis our own immediate dystopian circumstances, through the illusory dystopia of the film, but also demonstrates a collective mode of resistance, one that is meant to be applicable to our own experiences as well. As a critical dystopia, *Pleasantville* challenges our perception that things just are the way they are, and that there's nothing anyone can do about it.[102]

Works of critical dystopia thus provide an excellent opportunity to explore "possible worlds and possible selves."[103] They also provide unparalleled narratives of alternity, the "bridge in normative space" between the world-that-is and the worlds-that-might-be.[104] Perhaps more explicitly than any other popular fiction genre, critical dystopia provides narratives of movement from real to ideal, from "is" to "ought." If we are to radically reimagine law, the textual strategies of critical dystopia facilitate this process. Critical dystopia narratives generate alternative worlds that stand in critical relationship to our own reality.[105] We are encouraged to question narratives of the inevitability of the way things are, whatever the source, and explore ways in which to narrate ourselves with reference to the way things might be.

Proposing a genre classification for any work of popular culture inevitably invites fierce debate, but nonetheless, for the purposes of this analysis at least, I classify Atwood's *MaddAddam* trilogy as coming within the genre of bio-punk critical dystopia. First, I acknowledge that the bio-punk classification is both more specific and somewhat more obscure than more familiar speculative fiction categories such as space opera and space western. Briefly stated, the central interests of bio-punk narrative fiction are genetic engineering and biotechnology. The common theme is genetic modification and enhancement.[106] For example, humans may be genetically modified to enhance abilities or remove what are considered as imperfections. Chimeras also figure prominently, producing humans with genetic material from animals, and animals with genetic material from other animals and humans. Assuming we accept that bio-punk is a legitimate sub-category of speculative fiction, Atwood's *MaddAddam* trilogy is readily classified as such.[107] As for classifying the trilogy as a critical dystopia narrative, a synopsis is required, which given the density of the material, I limit to the relevant story elements of the first two books, *Oryx and Crake* and *The Year of the Flood*, and the conclusion of the third book, *MaddAddam*. Note that no single book conveys to the reader the indication or hope that the dystopia will be replaced with a more utopian alternative. This is accomplished over the course of all three books in the trilogy.

Information conveyed in the first book, *Oryx and Crake*, is provided here in order to better understand the choice of Zeb as an alternity character. The most relevant book for this case study, however, is *The Year of the Flood*. In this book, we are told the story of Adam and Zeb's disagreement over how best to engage in resistance against the corporations and their collective enforcement mechanism, CorpSeCorps. Adam is the leader of a religious group, God's Gardeners, and is committed to non-violent resistance. His brother, Zeb, is also a member, although he joins some years after the group is founded. We are told that Zeb eventually breaks away to lead his own resistance group, MaddAddam. The rift between Adam and Zeb has a present-day organizational counterpart in the distinction between mainstream advocacy organizations and more radical resistance groups, such as The Earth Liberation Front and The Animal Liberation Front. I discuss these two groups in the next section, where I examine eco/animal activists' accounts of their beliefs and behaviors.

Oryx and Crake begins with Snowman, a mentally unstable man in poor physical condition, who has survived a global pandemic. Snowman is a caretaker of sorts for the Children of Crake, or Crakers, a childlike, humanoid species well adapted to thrive in a post-apocalyptic world. They have thick, protective skin in a variety of hues and obtain all the nourishment they need from eating leaves. Their sexual activity is an efficient, purely physical process, carried out for reproductive purposes only. Snowman tells them stories to explain their origin and the world around them. They are the Children of Crake, while the animals are the Children of Oryx. The world was full of chaos, with people killing animals and each other, so Crake cleared away the chaos to make room for the Children of Crake and to save the Children of Oryx.

We soon learn that Snowman's name is Jimmy, and that prior to the apocalypse, he lived in a world divided by corporate control of technology and capital. The technologically elite, being those who worked for global technology corporations and their families, lived economically and physically secure lives inside corporate compounds. Others lived economically and physically insecure lives in the pleeblands. The CorpSeCorps, the corporations' collective security force, maintained corporate control of society.

Jimmy grew up in a corporate compound along with his friend, Glenn. Whereas Jimmy was friendly but intellectually unexceptional, Glenn was an aloof genius. They often played an online game, Extinctathon, where the object was to identify extinct species. Someone known only as MaddAddam runs the game. While Adam named all the living animals at earth's creation, now MaddAddam names the dead. People played with the names of dead animals as codenames. Glenn, playing as Crake, advanced to the level of Grandmaster, and showed Jimmy how to access a secret chat room hidden within the game. After high school, Jimmy went to a nondescript university and ended up with an equally nondescript job in advertising. Glenn (whom Jimmy refers to as "Crake" when he functions as the narrator), on the other hand, studied bioengineering at an elite scientific university, and was hired by the RejoovenEsense Corporation, where he quickly advanced.

Jimmy and Crake maintained only an occasional friendship over the years, until Crake, who by now was in a very senior position at RejoovenEsense, invited Jimmy to work for him. Crake worked in secrecy on a large-scale bioengineering project, the Paradice Project. The newly engineered humanoid species lived in the Paradice dome and had limited cognitive abilities, no real understanding of their origins, and no knowledge of the outside world. To Jimmy, Crake described the people he created as floor models, so to speak, designed to show prospective parents the range of options for fully customizable children.

Jimmy didn't know that Crake had created them as a replacement for the human species, which he regarded as fundamentally dysfunctional on a genetic level. The only way to end their misery, not to mention the environmental degradation they caused, was to replace them with a humanoid species engineered to correct for humanity's genetic flaws. His captive and brilliant researchers were former Extinctathon players. The game was in reality a forum for secure communications between members of a bioterrorism resistance movement. For a number of years, they had been bioengineering life forms to attack CorpSeCorps infrastructure, hoping to show people the true nature of the relationship between the corporations, CorpSeCorps, and the miserable conditions in which they live, and that the world could indeed be made into a better place.

The requisite love triangle was also present in the form of Oryx, another Extinctathon codename for a woman Jimmy became infatuated with while watching porn as a teenager. Oryx now works with Crake, teaching the names of plants and animals to the people living inside the Paradice dome. Oryx is in a relationship with Crake but soon becomes involved with Jimmy as well, telling Jimmy that Crake does not feel romantic jealousy. While not the smartest character in the story (for example, he believed the floor models explanation), Jimmy may have been sufficiently distracted by Oryx that he did not take much notice of what was really happening with the Paradice Project. Crake assigns Oryx a new project: ensuring the worldwide and rapid distribution of BlyssPluss pills. The pills are advertised as protecting people from all known sexually transmitted diseases, prolonging youth, and the one quality that did work as advertised, providing enhanced libido, sexual performance, and a sense of euphoria.

Given the rapid distribution and rapid effect of the BlyssPluss pills, the spread of the virus and the resulting end of humanity, save for a few survivors, takes place rather quickly. Crake's behavior by this point has become somewhat erratic, and earlier he made Jimmy promise that if anything should to him and Oryx, Jimmy would take care of the Crakers. One night while Jimmy is waiting for Oryx, she calls to tell him that a global pandemic has started, that Crake used the BlyssPluss pills to spread a deadly, untreatable virus, and that she didn't know. All three end up at the Paradice Dome, Jimmy inside the airlock, and Crake outside, holding Oryx. He tells Jimmy that only the three of them are immune to the virus, kills Oryx, and then kills himself.

The book ends with Snowman, who has injured himself while on a supply trip to the Paradice Dome, returning to the Crakers. The Crakers tell Snowman that they saw three humans, like him camping nearby. Snowman arms himself with a gun, and follows footprints to a fire, where he sees two men and a woman, but they don't see him. They are armed as well. Snowman doesn't know whether they are friends or foes, whether to approach and risk being shot, or shoot them now before they see him. He makes up his mind, but the reader doesn't know what he has decided. This is where the story in the first book ends.

The second book, *The Year of the Flood*, takes place during the same time frame as *Oryx and Crake*. The setting is the pleeblands rather than the compounds, and the book tells the story of God's Gardeners, who were occasionally referenced in *Oryx and Crake*. Several so-called greenies activist groups were fighting the corporations and CorpSeCorps by this point. Some were fundamentalist "green" religious groups, while others were secular direct action groups. God's Gardeners are a combination of both. The organization is primarily a religious community, with members adhering to typical "deep ecology" beliefs such as the equality of all of God's creatures and the holiness of the natural world. They avoided using technology, which they identified as having a role in the environmental and social decline, and opposed the corporations and CorpSeCorps. They were also committed to non-violent means of resistance. They live communally in abandoned urban buildings, creating rooftop gardens and apiaries, and otherwise foraging for anything abandoned in the pleeblands that they could put to use. Adam One, whose name really is Adam, founded God's Gardeners. The leaders are referred to as numbered Adams and Eves, with the numbers indicating their function in the group, not their rank. Pilar, for example, or Eve Six, specialized in bees and mushrooms. Adam Seven is Zeb, Adam's brother.

The story begins in Year Twenty-Five, God's Gardeners time, meaning twenty-five years after the founding of the organization. Year Twenty-Five is the year of the Waterless Flood, which is how God's Gardener's referred to the Blyss-Pluss global virus pandemic. God's Gardeners had been predicting the coming of a waterless flood from the beginning, although the means by which this would take place was never made clear. In the third book, *MaddAddam*, we learn that Adam is not necessarily as non-violent as he appears, and his life before founding God's Gardeners did not lack for intrigue. For now, though, all we know is that in anticipation of oncoming destruction on a global scale, Gardeners have been stockpiling supplies in safe locations, called Ararats. The two central characters are Toby and Ren, but I limit my discussion to Toby, since she is the more relevant source of character information and focalization for Zeb.

Toby is somewhat of an accidental convert to the God's Gardeners religion. When Toby was younger, the Gardeners rescued her from Blanco, her abusive boss at SecretBurgers. She had physically attacked Blanco, and had she not been rescued, his usual reprisal of torture and death would no doubt have soon followed. This was Year Five in Gardeners time, and Toby at first stayed with the Gardeners out of fear of Blanco, not because she shared the Gardeners' religious beliefs. As the years passed, however, she increasingly thought of herself as one of them, and eventually assumed a leadership role as Eve Six after Pilar died. She also developed an attraction to Zeb, although for most of her time there he was involved with someone else. The attraction was mutual though, and by the time of the third book, *MaddAddam*, they are in a relationship.

In the present-day setting of Year Twenty-Five, Toby has survived the global pandemic by barricading herself in the AnooYoo Spa-in-the-Park, where she was relocated as an employee with a new identity following a CorpSeCorps raid on the Gardeners. Not knowing if any other Gardeners have survived, and not knowing whom else might be out there, she waits and watches. She tries to maintain basic functions such as a water supply, and also to preserve her food stores. This includes protecting her outdoor garden from pigoons, bioengineered pigs used for xenotransplantation of human organs, whose cognitive abilities have been enhanced with human brain tissue. A global pandemic can challenge even a Gardener's religious beliefs on the equality of all of God's creatures and the importance of non-violence. Armed with a gun, Toby shoots one of the pigoons.

The most relevant story elements for examining Zeb as an alternity character take place prior to the pandemic, and concern the tension between Adam and Zeb over appropriate tactics. The Gardeners are not simply a religious community, seeking to isolate themselves from what they refer to as The Exfernal World. The Gardeners are pacifists, but they have grown over the years into a fairly extensive network of cells, spread across several locations, and engaged in an organized, non-violent resistance movement against the CorpSeCorps. The religious nature of the group is not a facade, and Adam and the other Gardeners are sincere in their beliefs. The Adams and Eves, however, have dual roles, as both leaders of a religious community and organizers of a resistance movement. For example, while Gardeners are opposed to technology, when Toby becomes Eve Six, she is surprised to find that the locked meeting room where the Adams and Eves met twice a week has a laptop with Internet access. The Gardeners have a network of undercover contacts in the corporation compounds, and help with escape routes and new identities for people who wanted to escape the corporations. Many of the Adams and Eves are fugitive scientists from the compounds as well.

While Adam founded the Gardeners, Zeb did not join until Year Seven, although he and Adam had been working together during this time. Adam is the undisputed leader of the Gardeners and is committed to non-violence. Zeb otherwise follows Adam's leadership but believes that violence is often the best or only option. Over the course of the story, Adam and Zeb have several disagreements about this issue. As Zeb says of himself, foot soldiers use their feet, and that's why he wears boots. Adam's concerns are both religious and pragmatic. As a pacifist, he is against violence on principle, and he is also concerned that violent actions attract too much attention, making them more of a target to the CorpSeCorps.

A pivotal event characterizes the differences in approach. Zeb contacts Toby at AnooYoo Spa-in-the-Park and tells her that he has left the Gardeners. He now leads a splinter group called MaddAddam. Mad Adam had been Zeb's nickname among the Gardener children, while MaddAddam was the code name for the secret chat room in Extinctathon. Now the name refers more generally to Zeb's splinter group, composed of former Gardeners, renegade scientists from the compounds, and other activists. They use the MaddAddam chat room for secure communications. Zeb is now Spirit Bear, while Toby is Inaccessible Rail. Crake, who had been an inside informer and operative for the Gardeners since he was a boy, is involved as well. The group's primary activity is bioengineering diseases and infestations, such as a weevil that destroyed a corporation's coffee plantations, and a microbe that destroyed highways by consuming asphalt. The level of violence is less than that of other activist groups, given an explicit reference to another groups' lethal bomb attacks on a restaurant chain where people were killed.

The Year of the Flood begins to orient the trilogy toward critical utopia. In both *Oryx and Crake* and *The Year of the Flood*, a causal explanation is provided for the current dystopian conditions. The explanation is not a simplistic condemnation of science, genetic engineering, or biotechnology. The world is not divided by technology per se, but rather by the concentration of both technology and capital under corporate control. Humanity has hope for a better world in the form of two resistance movements, one non-violent and one violent (although not lethal), which means that both Adam and Zeb could be viewed as alternity characters.

I focus on Zeb precisely because he does engage in violent actions, as these are the rules of resistance relevant to the corresponding examination of direct action carried out by eco/animal activists. The Gardeners are destroyed, forced into hiding by the CorpSeCorps, and while they evade the virus for a time, it finally catches up to them. On the other hand, former Gardeners and many of the members of MaddAddam survive, including Zeb. They have a fairly secure place to live, or at least a place that can be defended, access to food and water, and rudimentary agriculture, and are planning for the future.

Arguably, however, their rate of reproduction is not nearly enough to sustain the human race, which is why the necessary utopian vision is found in a shared future between Crakers and humans in the third book, *MaddAddam*. The Crakers and the remaining humans coexist in close relation, and three human women have babies with Craker fathers. Zeb, Toby, and the former MaddAddam members find that Adam is still alive, captured by Painballers who have also survived the virus. In the final showdown, the MaddAddam community, aided by Crakers and pigoons, defeats the Painballers, but Adam and Jimmy are both killed in the fight.

Toby has taken over from Jimmy as the storyteller for the Crakers, and she teaches a young Craker boy, Blackbeard, how to write. Blackbeard teaches other Crakers how to write in turn, and overall they are gradually becoming more proficient at symbolic thought. Zeb lives on for a time, continuing his role as defender of the community, both humans and Crakers. Toby does as well, telling stories to the Crakers, teaching Blackbeard to read and write, and working once again with bees and mushrooms. The story ends with Blackbeard as the storyteller. He tells the story of Zeb, who one day did not come back from a fight; the story of Toby, who died soon afterward; and the story of another baby soon to be born to a human mother with a Craker father.

As for the causal explanation of how the dystopia came to be, we can follow a trajectory from current concerns to future dystopia, whereby distortions in the functioning of globalized market economies result in an intense culture of commodification as a near-future threat to humanity. The near-future dystopian trajectory of bio-punk technology is extrapolated from current circumstances of increasing and unregulated consolidation of technology, science, and capital. Atwood's trilogy explores the consequences of exposing transgenic technologies to the market forces of global neoliberalism (i.e. decreased regulation of financial institutions, capital markets, and corporate conduct). The abuse of technology represented in the trilogy is arguably a matter of symptom, not cause. Commodification and ownership, more so than the ethics of biotechnology in the abstract, are the overarching normative issues.

If bio-punk critical dystopia narratives such as Atwood's trilogy caution against the tyranny of economic power, this may reflect concerns that a perfect storm of commodification is heading in our direction. An increasing alliance of technology, science, and capital is taking place under conditions of neoliberalism. Technological development is tracked by an expansive intellectual property trajectory, an inverse deregulation of corporate conduct, financial institutions, and capital markets, as well as the dismantling of social welfare and environmental standards as impermissible non-tariff barriers to international trade. In other words, conditions are ideal for considering the limits of our legal imaginations as we re-imagine law with reference to a narrative/*nomos* obligational self.

As I discuss in the next section, the focus of present-day eco/animal activists on acts of economic sabotage, particularly animal activists, reflects their perception that widespread and devastating exploitation of non-human animals and the environment reflect illegitimate hierarchal distinctions between humans and non-humans, and humans and nature. The institutions that maintain this illegitimate hierarchy of dominance and abuse include not only law, but also global economic relations. By commodifying animals and other aspects of nature, by treating them as objects of exchange, we have ensured their vulnerability to exploitation and abuse. The question I consider in Chapter 6 is whether rejecting hierarchal relations and excluding animals from commodification will be sufficient. In other word, if we reconceive of the rules of resistance as legal claims, should our re-imagined narrative/*nomos* legality have a place for animals?

Obligation and the rules of resistance

Atwood's trilogy presents at least two possible alternity characters, Adam and Zeb, and two different approaches for law as alternity, Adam's non-violent resistance and Zeb's (mostly non-lethal) violent resistance as they both seek to transform the dystopian present into the imagined utopian future. I examine Zeb rather than Adam because a non-violent approach is not relevant to this case study. As I discuss below, radical eco/animal activists who engage in direct action, typically in the form of unlawful property damage, do not consider these to be violent acts. Nonetheless, the distinction is a matter of definition, not the nature of the acts themselves. Adam's approach to non-violence would exclude many of the direct actions involved in eco/animal activism. After repeated readings, I am still not entirely sure that Adam is as non-violent as his presentation to others indicates, but that's a discussion for another time.

I use the four normative orientation questions to organize my examination of Zeb as an alternity character oriented toward neutral good. As discussed above, the narrative technique of character applies to answer the first three questions concerning character attributes. With reference to the normative semantic axis, does the character act out of a sense of obligation to achieve justice on behalf of others, or is the character motivated instead by a desire for self-preservation that may include family and friends? With reference to the regulatory semantic axis, are the character's unlawful acts a consequence of moral imperatives that trump illegitimate law, and does the character feel an obligation to pursue these moral imperatives, notwithstanding the likely consequences of unlawful action? An affirmative answer to both of these questions demonstrates a normative orientation toward neutral good. The third question regarding the character's normative understanding of violence establishes the relevant rules of resistance. The narrative technique of focalization applies to answer the fourth question, whether members of the relevant normative community share the character's normative understanding. This requirement of reciprocity is necessary for claims of moral imperatives to be re-imagined as legal claims, rather than merely an assertion of power. In a narrative of resistance, re-imagined legal claims are unlikely to be accepted by those in power, but so long as the claims are legally valid among the participants, the result is a not unfamiliar conflict of law scenario.

Question One: With reference to the normative semantic axis, is the character's attitude oriented toward good in a way that involves a sense of personal responsibility or obligation for the welfare of others?

As Bal notes, we acquire information about a character's attributes both explicitly and implicitly. Alternity characters may make explicit statements about themselves, for example in the form of an interior monologue, or in describing themselves to others. Other characters, as well as the narrator, may make explicit statements about the alternity characters. Implicitly, we deduce alternity characters' attributes based on their statements and actions. Neither Zeb, nor other characters, nor the narrator, provide explicit references to attributes that indicate, except indirectly, Zeb's sense of obligation to achieve justice for others. Many explicit references are made to Zeb's concern for members of God's Gardeners. As discussed above, however, on the normative semantic axis this would result in an orientation toward neutral, which involves an obligation to achieve justice for self, friends, and family. That an alternity character would feel an obligation toward friends and family is not inconsistent with a broader obligation toward the welfare of others more generally, but this must still be established.

This can be demonstrated implicitly, by making deductions based on Zeb's statements and actions. Zeb has a strong sense of obligation to others, which in this case includes everyone who opposes the environmental damage and species extinction caused by corporate control of science, technology, and capital. As discussed above, the attributes we deduce from an alternity character's statements and actions depend to a large extent on our frame of reference, which may be widely or narrowly shared by others. Deductions regarding Zeb's sense of obligation are relatively straightforward, although as always we need to be aware of how our own presuppositions influence our assessments. Deduction in this case does not require agreement on a normative frame of reference. We need only identify that Zeb has a sense of obligation to address the injustice experienced by others, and that this obligation extends beyond his own self-interest and his interest in the well-being of his family and friends. We do not need to agree with his assessment of whether an injustice exists or how injustice should be addressed.

Taking the example of a representative statement, in fighting with Adam about tactics, Zeb is unequivocal in stating his concerns regarding the environment and animal species. Referring to the rapid pace of a hundred new extinct species every month, he says he needs to act immediately, that he can't just wait and watch it happen.[108] With respect to deductions based on Zeb's actions, Zeb's break with Adam and the Gardeners to lead his own organization, MaddAddam, is a significant event. Members of the group do not engage in bioform resistance against

CorpSeCorps merely to liberate themselves and those they love from the current dystopia, but rather to save all humans, animals, and the environment.[109] No single group, not even MaddAddam, could accomplish this alone, but as Zeb said, they had to start somewhere.

All of the information about Zeb's character attributes relevant to the normative regulatory axis is obtained by implicit deduction. While acknowledging the limits of my own frame of reference, none of the information is contradictory. Others may disagree with my deductions, but at this point, I do not need to adjudicate between conflicting statements and actions by the narrator and other characters. I conclude that Zeb's character attributes are consistent with the orientation toward good on the normative semantic axis.

Question Two: With reference to the regulatory semantic axis, is the character's attitude toward law and illegal activity oriented toward neutral, wherein a moral imperative takes precedence over an unjust law, and furthermore, that the expected consequences of unlawful activity do not provide relief from performance, as would be the case for many of us?

The regulatory semantic axes of neutral is typically articulated as a willingness to pursue meaningful change through legal means, but in the face of a conflicting moral imperative, an unjust law need not be obeyed. The difficulty with the formulation, as noted above in the discussion of critical dystopia, is that in the near-future timeline the conditions of dystopia are already established. This means the opportunity to pursue lawful means of reform has passed. Accordingly, unless a character demonstrates an objection to law in principle, I will assume that a typical resistance scenario involving moral imperatives that conflict with illegitimate laws satisfies the orientation of neutral. The relevant question, then, is whether a character feels obligated to act notwithstanding the likely consequences if apprehended by official authorities. As I discussed above, many people may share the same normative understandings of eco/animal activists, but for most of us, the necessity of acting lawfully, whether as an affirmation of the importance of law or fear of its consequences, relieves us from performance of our moral obligations.

Once again, Zeb does not provide explicit information about attributes that would indicate his willingness to act on the basis of a moral imperative, regardless of the consequences of illegal activity. Nor does the narrator provide any relevant information. Explicit statements by other characters, however, affirm that on the regulatory semantic axis, Zeb is oriented toward neutral. Most of the statements are indirect, in the sense that characters are conveying information about participation in MaddAddam, and the resulting consequences.[110] Nonetheless, they are sufficient to confirm Zeb's sense of an obligation to take action against CorpSeCorps, even though he is aware of what happens when people are caught.[111]

Implicit information concerning these attributes can also be deduced from Zeb's statements and actions. This is particularly well demonstrated in the many disagreements between Adam and Zeb regarding tactics. Adam repeatedly admonishes Zeb that his actions risk drawing CorpSeCorps attention to the Gardeners, and that provoking them will result in retaliation. Zeb in response argues that they need to stand up for themselves and take action against the CorpSeCorps. If they don't, action will be taken against them, and they will be destroyed.[112]

In this case, information regarding Zeb's character attributes is provided both explicitly and implicitly by deduction. None of the information conveyed is contradictory. Bracketing for now the fallibility of my own deductions, the implicit information provided by Adam's disagreement with Zeb regarding tactics does not conflict with the explicit information conveyed by other characters regarding Zeb's sense of obligation to act in pursuit of a moral imperative, regardless of the unlawful nature of the activity and the expected consequences. Adam does not dispute that Zeb's actions are a consequence of unjust laws. While Zeb may not share Adam's religious sensibility, they share the same moral imperative regarding the environment and animal life. Zeb's willingness to engage openly in unlawful activity is precisely Adam's concern.

Question Three: What is the character's normative understanding of violence, in terms of prescriptive limits placed on the nature and extent of violent behavior as part of the rules of resistance?

Numerous explicit references characterize Zeb as a person willing to engage in violence. The defining tension between Adam and Zeb, which leads Zeb to break off to start his own group, is Adam's insistence on a non-violent approach. Nonetheless, resistance has rules, as reflected in the relevant character attributes. As an alternity character, Zeb's normative understanding of the rules of resistance is that he is willing, as the leader of MaddAddam, to engage in violent means in order to transform the world-that-is to the world-that-ought-to-be. Violence, however, is limited to bioform attacks against CorpSeCorps infrastructure, rather than physical attacks against the CorpSeCorps members themselves.

As for Zeb's more individualized acts of violence, for example his attack against Blanco, his normative understanding is that violence is justified against those who initiate or engage in violence themselves. This can be deduced, for example, from Zeb's defending his decision to attack first. Zeb's assessment was that Blanco got what he deserved, and they should be praised for their initiative.[113] Individual acts of violence in this context, however, are not as relevant to Zeb's role as an alternity character, and thus will not be explored further. Otherwise, different accounts do not provide conflicting information. Adam rejects Zeb's reasoning, but nothing indicates Zeb is disingenuous in his explanations, for example, that resistance against the CorpSeCorps is simply a convenient opportunity for him to express a violent nature.

Regarding his own propensity for violence, Zeb does provide explicit information. Note that the lack of explicit information relevant to the questions so far is not unexpected. Zeb does not have interior monologues and rarely explicitly describes himself to others. An exchange with Adam, however, provides a representative example of how he describes violence as one of his relevant attributes. Responding once again to Adam's disapproval of his methods, Zeb refers to himself as a foot soldier, and that foot soldiers use their feet, which is why he always wears boots.[114] When Adam tells Zeb that by breaking the law, he is giving the CorpSeCorps an excuse to attack them, Zeb argues that the alternative, to not fight back, would be worse.[115]

Other characters talking to each other about Zeb and their involvement in MaddAddam provide more detailed information about violence and the rules of resistance. The most significant conversational exchange, particularly for comparison with the normative understandings of eco/animal activists in the next section, takes place between four young former Gardeners, Shackleton, Oates, Amanda, and Ren. Shackleton and Oakes left the Gardeners and followed Zeb to MaddAddam. From their conversation, we learn that Zeb does not believe in taking human life, if this can be avoided, which is why he focused their resistance efforts on bioform attacks against CorpSeCorps infrastructure, rather than attacking people directly. The rules of resistance thus limit violence to property damage. There is only a passing reference to collateral damage in the form of foot injuries when some microbes designed to attack asphalt attacked shoes instead.[116]

No information either explicitly conveyed or implicitly deduced contradicts Zeb's self-assessment of his willingness to engage in violence. As for the information implicitly deduced from the young members of MaddAddam, while I again bracket the necessary contingency of my own frame of reference, the narrator confirms this information. After Zeb informs Toby that he has left the Gardeners to lead his own group, the narrator tells us that Toby follows their progress online in the secret MaddAddam chat room. The narrator then tells us that Toby sees the news about the bombing attacks that destroyed a chain of restaurants, and that killed people in the process. Toby reads a more detailed account in the MaddAddam chat room, confirming that another group was responsible, along with their motivation for doing so.[117]

Question Four: Is the character's normative understanding of violence consistent with the shared normative understandings of the relevant community?

As discussed above, while the narrative technique of character applies to determine the first three questions, the narrative technique of focalization is used to determine the fourth. The task is to determine if reciprocity exits between Zeb's normative understanding of violence and that of the relevant normative community. Focalization is a subjective vision of a story, that is to say one version of the story, in the same way that many of us might witness the same event and yet diverge in our accounts after the fact. Focalization involves evaluation and assessment; what really happened, and what does it mean? For the requirement of reciprocity to be met, focalizers of Zeb's actions as the leader of the MaddAddam resistance movement must share or at least accept the legitimacy of bioform resistance that results in extensive property damage.

In MaddAddam, the external narrator provides the all-encompassing vision. The narrator yields to an internal character narrator, Ren, and to a number of internal character focalizers. Since the external narrator exists outside the story, the external narrator cannot be a member of the relevant normative community, and thus external focalization is not discussed. Also, while internal focalization is at times yielded to Zeb, the question of reciprocity involves the evaluation of others. Accordingly, I do not discuss Zeb as the subject of focalization, but rather as the object. The relevant questions are: (a) Who focalizes Zeb? (b) Are we inclined to accept this vision as credible, based on either the focalizer's assumed objectivity or because the focalizer is intended to attract our sympathy? (c) Does the focalizer's vision of Zeb affirm or deny his normative understanding of violence? and (d) Is the focalizer a member of the relevant normative community?

The most informative internal character-bound focalizers are Adam, Toby, and Shackleton and Crozier, two young members of the MaddAddam group. As participants in MaddAddam, Shackleton and Crozier are members of the relevant normative community. Toby's position is somewhat more ambiguous. Toby was Eve Six, a position of leadership in the Gardeners, but was forced to leave and assume a new identity at the AnooYoo Spa-in-the-Park when Blanco was released from Painball. We do not know whether, had she stayed with the Gardeners, she would have followed Zeb when he started MaddAddam, although a number of other Gardeners did. We can assume members of MaddAddam share Zeb's normative understanding of violence. Toby's perspective, however, is not determined by membership in the group itself, which in turn raises the interesting question of whether the relevant normative community includes only members of a particular resistance group, or extends more broadly to a resistance movement. Would the relevant normative community, for example, include Adam?

I begin with how Zeb is focalized by Shackleton and Crozier. The characters' conversation is quite brief, but they provide the books' most explicit information regarding MaddAddam's rules of resistance, established by Zeb, with respect to violence. The rules are remarkably similar to those maintained by direct action groups such as The Earth Liberation Front and The Animal Liberation Front, discussed in the next section. MaddAddam's bioform resistance was limited to property damage and did not extend to direct attacks on people themselves.

Recall the operation of narration and focalization: A says that B sees what C is doing. In the account of Zeb and MaddAddam provided by Shackleton and Crozier, Ren is an internal character narrator. Ren tells us that Shackleton and Crozier have seen what the members of MaddAddam under Zeb's leadership have done. We are inclined to accept this vision as credible because Shackleton and Crozier are members of MaddAddam, which also establishes them as members of the relevant normative community. Note that this does not mean we have to accept the legitimacy of the group's methods, only that we have no reason to doubt Shackleton and Crozier's subjective vision. If anything, in the past they have been inclined to exaggerate Zeb's propensity for violence.[118] Through their approval, they affirm Zeb's normative understanding of violence, and thus the requirement of reciprocity is established.[119]

With respect to Toby, the external narrator says that Toby sees what Zeb is doing. Again, the relevant section is when Zeb reveals to Toby that he has left the Gardeners to establish MaddAddam. Toby's vision of Zeb affirms his normative understanding of violence. When Zeb tells Toby he has left the Gardeners to start his own group, Zeb uses the word "schism," and given Toby's awareness of their disagreement on the use of violence, we can assume Toby understands that Zeb's new group is not pacifist in nature. She does not protest and merely asks who else from the Gardeners has joined. After Zeb shows her how to communicate with the group through the Extinctathon chat room, she follows their progress regularly. She does not participate, but she feels happy to be included.[120]

We are inclined to accept Toby's vision. *The Year of the Flood* follows the events as they happen to Toby and Ren, and as a result, they are character-bound focalizers for much of the story. As discussed above, when we see a story through the eyes of character-bound focalizers, we are more likely to identify with them and accept the vision of events they present. We also have greater insight into Toby, because she focalizes not only perceptible events, but also her non-perceptible internal mental states. In other words, Toby is a character intended to attract our sympathy. As to her membership in the relevant normative community, this depends on whether the community extends beyond membership in the resistance group to include those who support but do not directly participate in the group. If Toby is a member of the relevant normative community, then reciprocity is established.

The same cannot be said with respect to Adam, who as expected does not affirm Zeb's normative understanding of violence. In Adam's case, the narrator begins each chapter with a speech by Adam at the start of a Gardener celebration day. The speech is conveyed in uninterrupted direct discourse that continues for sometimes several pages. Adam conveys information about the celebration day and the Gardeners' beliefs, recounts events that have taken place, responds to them with his assessment of their importance and meaning, and provides advice and guidance to members of the group. After Zeb leaves the Gardeners, Adam's speeches contain expressions of disapproval of Zeb's violent means of resistance, even though Adam knows that the violence is limited to property damage against CorpSeCorps infrastructure.[121]

Recall that focalization is subjective content. Whereas Shackleton and Crozier tell a story of Zeb leading a successful resistance group, Adam tells a story of Zeb and other former Gardeners who have abandoned their principles, and in the process, give the CorpSeCorps the excuse they needed to eradicate all "greenie" groups, including the non-violent ones. We may well be inclined to accept Adam's vision, in which case we have a conflicting assessment of Zeb's rules of resistance. As is the case with Toby, Adam is a character intended to attract our sympathy, although perhaps to a lesser extent. We see the story through Adam's eyes, and as a result, are more likely to identify with him and accept the vision of events he presents. On the other hand, unlike Toby, Adam focalizes only perceptible events, and thus we do not have as much insight into his character. Whether Adam is a member of the relevant normative community depends on whether the community extends to all those who have common cause, or includes only members in a specific group and their supporters. If Adam and Zeb are in the same normative community, Adam does not affirm Zeb's understanding of violence.

In summary, I conclude that Zeb's attributes are consistent with an alternity character's overall normative orientation of neutral good. On the normative semantic axis, Zeb's sense of obligation to address injustice on behalf of others is not limited to his own interests, and those of his family and friends, but extends to everyone subject to the dystopian forces of the corporations and CorpSeCorps. On the regulatory semantic axis, he has a sense of obligation to pursue a moral imperative by fighting against an unjust legal authority, fully aware of the severity of the consequences should he be apprehended. His normative understanding of violence, which I limit to the rules of resistance of MaddAddam and exclude his individual acts of violence, is that property damage is legitimate, but direct attacks against people are not. Finally, his normative understanding of violence is reciprocated by members of the relevant normative community, when deduced in narrow terms as members of MaddAddam and its supporters. As I discuss in the next section, eco/animal activist groups also disagree and divide on the issue of violence and direct action. On the requirement of reciprocity, once we move beyond inferences based on specific group membership, this is arguably a question that can only be answered by participants themselves.

Acts of obligation

In this section, I examine accounts provided by eco/animal activists of their normative understandings as participants in what Fritsvold characterizes as revolutionary resistance movements.[122] Given the prevailing image of state law as exclusive legal authority, eco/animal activists typically explain their beliefs and behaviors as moral obligations that take precedence over unjust state law. As discussed in Chapter 2, the endless oscillation between law and justice that we find in legal theory is also a recurrent theme in works of popular culture. In this section, we see this oscillation is also a common frame of reference for the normative understandings of eco/animal activists. Activists do not refer to themselves as jurisgenerative legal subjects, who could if they so desired reconceive of their moral imperatives as legal claims. They most certainly do not refer to themselves as narrative/*nomos* obligational selves. In reflecting upon their history of activism, they may incidentally convey information in the form of a life story. Outside of research or clinical settings, however, activists are unlikely to refer to imagoes and alternity characters.

This is to be expected. It does not affect the utility of searching for common normative understandings in the attributes of alternity characters in popular culture narratives and accounts of belief and behavior provided by eco/animal activists. A theoretical project of re-imagining law begins with our existing beliefs and behaviors, and similar to the turn of a kaleidoscope, considers the implications of how we might conceive of these same beliefs and behaviors from a different perspective. As noted above, I apply the metrics of character alignment not only to alternity characters, but also to the accounts provided by eco/animal activists. The same metrics are required to demonstrate consistent normative understandings, but the additional value of this approach is that by referring to normative and regulatory orientations, analysis can proceed independently of an activist's conception of law.

Assessment of semantic orientation allows for consideration of any information relevant to the question of whether an activist's orientation on the normative axis indicates a sense of personal obligation to achieve justice for others, and whether an activist's orientation of the regulatory axis indicates an obligation to pursue moral imperatives, such that the adverse consequences of engaging in illegal activity does not provide relief from performance. The remaining normative orientation questions address the rules of resistance. What prescriptive limits on the nature and extent of violence does the activist acknowledge, and is this normative understanding of violence in pursuit of moral imperative consistent with the understandings of other members of the relevant normative community?

In this section, I first provide a brief overview of the objectives, principles, and strategies of two radical organizations. For radical animal activism, I examine the normative understandings of members of The Animal Liberation Front, a choice determined by looking to visual media for source material to reflect this project's engagement with popular culture. *Behind the Mask*,[123] a documentary film about The Animal Liberation Front, provides the most suitable representative example. For environmental activism, I focus on The Earth Liberation Front, which is one of three groups characterized by Fritsvold as having a legal consciousness of "under the law." While Fritsvold's conclusions apply to all three groups, The Earth Liberation Front was intentionally modeled after The Animal Liberation Front. This allows me, at an appropriate level of analytical abstraction, to consolidate these two groups into an example of eco/animal activism to use in this case study. For both organizations, direct action is the preferred strategy for achieving meaningful change. Direct action, or as characterized by The Animal Liberation Front, economic sabotage, involves damaging the property and thus the economic interests of those involved. This reflects radical eco/animal activists' identification of corporate consolidation of technology, science, and capital as a systemic explanation of exploitation and abuse, for example, the technology of agribusiness, and the science of animal testing in pharmaceuticals. Note that state law responds to these acts of property damage with not only criminal charges, which is to be expected, by also prosecution as terrorism offences.

Substantial discussion has taken place among activists, scholars, and other commentators as to whether admittedly criminal activity should be labeled as terrorism. The question, while crucially important, is nonetheless not relevant to my analysis. My objective is to consider the emancipatory potential of re-imagining law and popular culture as mutually constitutive discourse. Whether eco/animal activists choose to understand their normative beliefs and behaviors as moral imperatives or re-imagined legal claims is a matter for them to decide. I have consistently emphasized that my project is not programmatic in nature. I am not engaging here in disingenuous evasion, motivated by a concern that I might be perceived as supporting criminal activity. Instead, I take seriously how both Macdonald and Melissaris emphasize that the emancipatory potential of their theoretical approaches is a function of the agency (however constrained) and constructive capacities of legal subjects themselves.

Melissaris rejects the presumptive superiority of expert legal culture and insists on an inter-perspectival dialogue involving members of plural legal communities.

Macdonald insists that both law and inter-legality are noumenal, not phenomenal, in nature, and that only legal subjects themselves can answer the question of what is law, in the circumstances of normative heterogeneity in which the question arises. In addition to these considerations, I also identify the emancipatory potential of a narrative/*nomos* obligational self with reference to capacity, not outcome. As I argued in Chapter 4, I do not claim that the existing beliefs of eco/animal activists are false consciousness. Eco/animal activists may choose to conceive of themselves as acting with reference to a reimagined legality. They may also choose to maintain their current normative understandings of resistance based on direct action.

Following a brief overview of The Earth Liberation Front and The Animal Liberation Front, I explain the methodology used to examine eco/animal activists' accounts of their normative understandings. To examine the normative beliefs and behaviors of The Earth Liberation Front, I engage in what might aptly be described as a translation of analytical perspectives. Recall Fritsvold's characterization of the legal consciousness of radical environmental activists as "under the law." I consider whether this legal consciousness, when considered with reference to the four normative orientation questions, can be equated with an orientation toward neutral good. I then examine the rules of resistance with respect to legitimate uses of violence, and whether the requirement of reciprocity is met in that members of the relevant normative community share this understanding. Following this, I examine the normative understandings of radical animal activists. I rely on the validation provided by Fritsvold's example of content analysis to examine activists' discussion of their participation in The Animal Liberation Front in *Behind the Mask*.

As with the selection of Atwood's *MaddAddam* trilogy, coverage of materials is necessarily limited to representative examples. As noted, this case study is meant as proof of concept only, not proof of result, but nonetheless the examples chosen are sufficiently illustrative. Examining the beliefs and behaviors of eco/animal activists allows us to think of the implications of understanding presumptively transgressive behavior with reference to a re-imagined narrative/*nomos* obligational self. This should not be interpreted as a causal analysis, which would involve complex factors of culture, identity, and socialization in seeking to explain how and why a person becomes an eco/animal activist. My hypothesis of law and popular culture as mutually constitutive discourse, and the analytical framework I use to develop the narrative/*nomos* obligational self, is not a claim of truth but rather an invitation to participate in an ongoing process of re-imagining law.

Economic sabotage

Eco/animal activism involves coordinated action, and the environmental and animal movements are not monolithic. While they may share the same overarching objective, activist groups have different motivations and justifications. For the purpose of this project, the most relevant distinction is between mainstream organizations that focus on advocacy and law reform, and more radical groups that engage in direct action. Some of these activities fall within the scope of civil disobedience, but direct action is more likely to involve property damage, the objective being to disrupt profits made by people and corporations viewed by the activists as illegitimately exploiting animals and the environment. Since this is a project of re-imagining law, I examine radical groups who engage in unlawful activity rather than mainstream organizations. The emancipatory potential of re-imaging law is not limited to those who engage in unlawful acts, but they do provide an apt illustrative example for the case study.

To examine the beliefs and behaviors of radical environmental activists, I rely upon the information collected and analyzed by Fritsvold, first referenced in Chapter 4 in discussing legal consciousness, and explored in more detail below. For radical animal activists, I examine accounts provided by members of The Animal Liberation Front. In choosing representative groups, the first consideration was relevance. While radical eco/animal activism is of fairly recent origin, The Earth Liberation Front (one of three groups included in Fritsvold's study) and The Animal Liberation Front each have an ongoing, international presence, although activity levels do vary over the years.

A second consideration is normative orientation. As discussed above, the most appropriate normative orientation for re-imagining moral imperatives as legal claims is neutral good. On the normative semantic axis, an orientation of good arguably applies to all eco/animal activists, both mainstream and radical, since we can assume they are motivated by a sense of obligation to address injustice experienced by others. I include concern for the environment in this category. Environmental activism could be construed as motivated by self-interest, in that environmental degradation has an adverse impact on the activists themselves. As explained below, however, radical environmental activists tend to adopt more of a deep ecology approach. Nature has inherent value, which means that damage to the environment is a harm suffered by nature as well as by humans.

What distinguishes radical eco/animal activists from mainstream organizations is the regulatory semantic axis. Mainstream organizations engage in lawful activities such as protest, advocacy, and law reform, but avoid illegal activity. This results in an orientation of lawful, which excludes them from consideration. For radical groups such as The Earth Liberation Front and The Animal Liberation Front, the question is whether they are oriented toward chaotic, which involves antipathy or opposition to law generally, a dispositional attitude so to speak, or whether they have a more situational orientation of neutral, which involves rejecting only those laws that conflict with moral imperatives. I classify both groups as oriented toward neutral and explain this decision in more detail below.

Background information for each group helps to place this analysis in context. The direct action movement of hunt saboteurs in England led to the establishment of The Animal Liberation Front in 1976. In the early 1990s, radical environmental activists from Earth First!, inspired in part by The Animal Liberation Front's strategy of liberating animals and economic sabotage, established The Earth Liberation Front.[124] The groups share the same organizational structure of independent, self-organizing cells rather than top-down leadership, a tactic intended to frustrate law enforcement efforts. Membership is a matter of like-minded individuals who cooperate to take direct action against animal or environmental exploitation, follow the guidelines established by each group in doing so, and subsequently state this action has been taken in the name of the organization.[125]

At the risk of oversimplification, the groups also share similar philosophical foundations. Members of The Animal Liberation Front reject the anthropocentric hierarchal distinctions between human and non-human animal species that have allowed humans to exploit animals in ways that institutionalize and inflict utterly horrific pain and death.[126] Members of The Earth Liberation reject the anthropocentric hierarchical distinctions between humans and other constituent elements of nature that have allowed humans to exploit nature, including other life forms, in ways that institutionalize and inflict irreversible damage and destruction.[127]

Finally, both groups share similar strategies of direct action for interfering with and inflicting damage upon anyone engaged in acts of exploitation. Both groups define the purpose of these actions as economic sabotage, the objective being to inflict maximum economic costs on those who profit from exploiting animals and nature.[128] Both justify illegal activity on the basis that moral imperatives take precedence over unjust laws.[129] Many actions are carried out by relatively few individuals, and cause limited economic damage, such as putting glue in the locks of a retail clothing store that sells coats made from animal fur, or disabling a bulldozer at the site of a housing development. Other actions are large-scale, coordinated attacks that result in significant damage. In November 1996, The Animal Liberation Front claimed responsibility for the arson fire that destroyed a fur company in Bloomington, Minnesota. Damages were estimated at $2,000,000 for the fur coats, and $250,000 for the building.[130] In October 1998, The Earth Liberation Front claimed responsibility for setting the explosives that destroyed five buildings and four ski lifts at a ski resort in Vail, Colorado. Damage was estimated at $14,000,000.[131]

Note that both groups characterize economic sabotage, being the property damage inflicted and associated economic losses, as non-violent direct action. This is a logical consequence of justifying these actions by reference to moral imperatives. I cannot do justice here to the complexity of the philosophies and moral reasoning conveyed by members across a broad range of media over a lengthy period of time.[132] As a generally applicable statement, however, direct action is an intentional act of resistance against illegitimate law. In other words, direct action is not merely a tactic, but also an obligation. As conveyed in a statement by members of The Animal Liberation Front following a raid on a research laboratory, "When darkness falls, their laws enforcing savagery are voided . . ."[133]

The principles that establish whether an action can be claimed in the name of each organization are an important source of information for examining whether radical eco/animal activists are normatively oriented toward neutral good. Accordingly, I produce them here in full. The Animal Liberation Front Guidelines are as follows: (a) to liberate animals from places of abuse (i.e. fur farms, laboratories, factory farms, etc.) and place them in good homes where they may live out their natural lives free from suffering; (b) to inflict economic damage to those who profit from the misery and exploitation of animals; (c) to reveal the horror and atrocities committed against animals behind locked doors by performing non-violent direct actions and liberations; and (d) to take all necessary precautions against hurting any animal, human and non-human.[134] The Earth Liberation Front Guidelines are as follows: (a) to cause as much economic damage as possible to a given entity that is profiting off the destruction of the natural environment and life for selfish greed and profit; (b) to educate the public on the atrocities committed against the environment and life; and (c) to take all necessary precautions against harming life.[135]

As noted, both groups explicitly state that causing damage in a manner consistent with these principles is not a violent act,[136] but rather a form of economic sabotage. For example, in the case of The Animal Liberation Front, exploitation of animals on a global scale is often expressed through individual pathology, but the incentive is economic. Given the extent to which animal exploitation is embedded into our economic relations, the only options for reform are direct action or consumers altering their preferences. In each case, the objective is to remove the potential for profit. The focus on economic sabotage, and the corresponding principle of non-violence, distinguishes these groups from organizations such as The Animal Rights Militia and the Justice Department, both of which advocate physical confrontation and harm to people who exploit animals.[137] Simply damaging their property and economic interests is not enough.

The characterization of property damage as non-violent direct action in the form of economic sabotage does create some difficulties with terminology, given that the four normative orientation questions used to analyze alternity characters and radical eco/animal activists refer specifically to normative understandings of violence. For the sake of consistency, I will continue to refer to violence when examining the accounts of beliefs and behaviors provided by eco/animal activists, while explicitly acknowledging here that violence is not a neutral term. Otherwise, I am not concerned with the question of whether these actions are violent, criminal, or terrorist in nature.[138] I have emphasized throughout that this project re-imagines law as capacity for aspirational belief and committed behaviors. I do not provide a prescriptive outcome for how eco/animal activists might defend themselves against criminal prosecutions. If I take a position on any of these issues, I am simply providing my own external perspective on an internal normative system, an approach thoroughly discredited by Melissaris.[139] The emancipatory potential of the concept of a narrative/*nomos* obligational self is a matter for eco/animal activists themselves to consider and cannot be imposed.

The characterization of non-violent direct action as economic sabotage, particularly by members of The Animal Liberation Front, raises another interesting issue. As I discussed above in examining Atwood's *MaddAddam* trilogy, the threat posed is not so much biotechnology per se, but rather the dystopian forces created by an alliance of science, technology, and capital in circumstances of increasing global neoliberalism. The Animal Liberation Front focuses on economic sabotage because of the understanding of its members that illegitimate hierarchal relations are maintained not only by unjust laws, but also by unjust global neoliberal economic relations.[140] The legal status of animals is purposive, so that we can commodify them as objects of market exchange, thus ensuring their vulnerability to exploitation and abuse. Through their beliefs and behaviors, members of The Animal Liberation Front reconfigure normative discourse in a way that destabilizes the presumptive hierarchy in Western legal traditions between humans and animals.[141] This creates ideal conditions for considering the limits of our legal imaginations as we reconceive of law with reference to a narrative/*nomos* obligational self. In rejecting hierarchal relations, will the absence of commodification be sufficient? In other words if animal activists reconceive of their rules of resistance as legal claims, should their re-imagined narrative/*nomos* have a place for animals? I discuss this issue in Chapter 6.

Examining belief and behavior

Having examined the relevant attributes of Zeb as an alternity character in Atwood's *MaddAddam* trilogy, including whether his normative understanding of violence is consistent with members of the relevant normative community, I now turn to accounts of beliefs and behaviors provided by radical eco/animal activists themselves. Recall that the objective is to identify whether the attributes of alternity characters and the normative understandings of eco/animal activists demonstrate a shared normative orientation toward neutral good, as well as a shared normative understanding of the rules of resistance with respect to violence. Recall that the narrative/*nomos* obligational self is conceived as a nexus for mutually constitutive discourse of law and popular culture, and thus a means to answer with greater specificity the question of how popular culture might function as legal authority. If commonality exists, I can extrapolate from this support for the explanatory force, admittedly and necessarily partial, of the narrative/*nomos* obligational self.

I do not adopt Bal's theory of narratology as the methodology for this section. Although the scope of what is considered narrative in nature continues to expand, I do not want to engage in a debate as to whether the materials examined here can be classified as narrative. Nor do I want to approach these materials as life stories per se. In accounts of belief and behavior provided by activists, individuals may at times organize their telling of events as a contribution to their ongoing life story. McAdams, however, developed the concept of the imago through the course of research in which participants were specifically asked to provide their life stories. I am reluctant, in the absence of this type of direct inquiry, to characterize these accounts more generally as the life stories of the activists involved.[142]

Instead, I use two different methodologies in this section. Recall Fritsvold's characterization of the legal consciousness of radical environmental activists as "under the law." Members of radical environmental groups differ from their mainstream counterparts in that they are intentional lawbreakers. Motivated by a philosophy of deep ecology, participants in radical environmental movements perceive their world as one of illegitimate social relations, maintained by an illegitimate legal system. Direct action, not law reform, is the only viable option.[143] The task is to determine whether a legal consciousness of "under the law" is consistent with the normative understandings and rules of resistance conveyed by Zeb as a representative alternity character in Atwood's *MaddAddam* trilogy. To answer this question, I engage in an exercise of translating analytical perspectives by applying the four normative orientation questions to Fritsvold's conclusions regarding legal consciousness.

To address the normative understandings of radical animal activists, I adapt Fritsvold's methodology of content analysis, although with a certain note of caution. Fritsvold's methodology includes fieldwork in the form of interviews with activists and content analysis. The latter included reviewing material produced by activists such as websites, newsletters, magazines, articles, and books. I readily acknowledge that adopting content analysis in the absence of field interviews is a marked departure from Fritsvold's methodology, which included thousands of pages of content. I emphasize, however, that my primary objective in this section is to provide proof of concept, not proof of result, in the form of an illustrative case study, and to demonstrate the open-source nature of the analytical framework as amenable to different disciplinary perspectives and methodologies.[144]

I also apply content analysis to visual media, specifically *Behind the Mask*,[145] a documentary in which animal activists discuss their participation in The Animal Liberation Front. The choice of visual media is intended to reflect this project's engagement with popular culture, which includes textual, aural, visual, and mixed media. While my source material differs in terms of subject matter and media type, Fritsvold's comment regarding the clarity of activists' accounts of their normative understandings still applies. As Fritsvold notes, activists engage in sophisticated moral reasoning when providing their reasons for action.[146]

Fritsvold organized information obtained from both field interviews and content analysis using successively granular categories, refined over the course of several iterations. This reflects the open-ended nature of his inquiry into radical activists' legal consciousness, which was conceived as being distinct from those involved in moderate environmental groups. The highest level of abstraction specified themes and concepts associated with the research question, such as the relationship between moderate and radical environmental groups. The subcategories explored more specific themes, such as positive and negative relationships between factions, organizational structure, and methods of operation.[147] Given the specificity of the four normative orientation questions I use to examine the case study materials, as well as the restricted scope of these materials, an organized taxonomy is not required. The task is to determine whether accounts of beliefs and behaviors provided by animal activists, when considered with reference to the four normative orientation questions, are consistent with Zeb's orientation toward neutral good as an alternity character, his normative understanding of the rules of resistance with respect to violence, and whether these normative beliefs are reciprocated by members of the relevant normative community.

Translating normative orientation

In this section, I engage in an exercise of translating analytical perspectives. A legal consciousness of "under the law" is revolutionary in nature but remains nonetheless a response to state law rather than a re-imagined legality. Environmental activists are still confined to the binary choice of obey/disobey. The objective in this section is to determine whether legal consciousness can be transposed onto the analytical framework of the narrative/*nomos* obligational self. At issue is whether a legal consciousness of "under the law" can be interpreted as a normative orientation of neutral good, what are the rules of resistance with respect to violence, and whether the requirement of reciprocity is met by a shared understanding of these rules among members of the relevant normative community.

As discussed briefly in Chapter 3, Fritsvold applied the insights of legal consciousness scholarship to investigate civil disobedience and law-breaking activity carried out by radical environmental activists.[148] Relying on fieldwork and content analysis, Fritsvold analyzed radical activists' accounts of their participation in direct action, including their motivations and the justifications they provide for engaging in what state law classifies as criminal and terrorist activity. To the three categories of legal consciousness outlined by Ewick and Silbey, being "before the law," "with the law," and "against the law," Fritsvold adds a fourth, "under the law," to characterize the legal consciousness of participants in resistance movements.

Note that a single classification is not meant to capture the entirety of a radical activist's legal consciousness, nor reflect a static orientation over time. Both "against the law" and "under the law" describe a legal consciousness in which people observe and respond to the failure of law to achieve justice, including through dissent and defiance. The distinction is that for a legal consciousness of "under the law," inadequacy is a result of intentional design rather than corrupting influence. Law's failure to achieve what they would view as justice is actually law's success in maintaining the environmental exploitation so fundamental to industrial capitalism. Since reform by legal means is not possible within an inherently unjust legal system, direct action is a necessary and justified alternative.[149]

Question One: With reference to the normative semantic axis, are members of The Earth Liberation Front oriented toward the good in a way that involves a sense of personal responsibility or obligation for the welfare of others?

Recall that The Earth Liberation Front is organized as independent cells, and that membership is a matter of carrying out direct action consistent with the guidelines and then publicizing this as an act of The Earth Liberation Front. Accordingly, I first consider information obtained from the guidelines before proceeding to Fritsvold's conclusions regarding the legal consciousness of radical environmental groups, including The Earth Liberation Front. Two of the guidelines are consistent with classifying participants on the normative semantic axis as oriented toward good: (a) to cause as much economic damage as possible to a given entity that is profiting off the destruction of the natural environment and life for selfish greed and profit; and (b) to educate the public on the atrocities committed against the environment and life.

I do not characterize participants in The Earth Liberation Front as oriented toward neutral, because their sense of obligation is not limited to acting on behalf of themselves, their family, and friends. Fritsvold argues that "under the law" is a more apt characterization of the radical activists' philosophy of deep ecology. Human beings do not enjoy a privileged, hierarchal status over other living entities. All of the elements that constitute nature exist as part of an egalitarian whole.[150] I understand this perspective as one in which nature has inherent (as opposed to instrumental) value. Humans engaged in actions that damage the environment cause harm not only to other humans, but to nature as well. This is not to say that activists are not concerned for their own interests or the interest of family and friends. The normative orientation of good, however, is a more apt characterization of those engaged in acts of resistance intended, in critical dystopian terms, to achieve collective liberation. Radical environmental activists are the resistance movement counterparts to alternity characters in bio-punk critical dystopia, seeking to transform the world-that-is to the world-that-ought-to-be.

Question Two: With reference to the regulatory semantic axis, are The Earth Liberation Front's members' attitudes toward law and illegal activity oriented toward neutral, wherein a moral imperative takes precedence over an unjust law, and furthermore, that the expected consequences of unlawful activity do not provide relief from performance as would be the case for many of us?

Again, guidelines for establishing membership in The Earth Liberation Front apply. In this case, the relevant guideline is: (a) to cause as much economic damage as possible to a given entity that is profiting off the destruction of the natural environment and life for selfish greed and profit. On the normative semantic axis, the guideline provides information about the extent of an activist's sense of obligation. On the regulatory semantic axis, the same guideline provides information regarding a participant's attitudes toward law and illegal activity. We can deduce from the reference to "as much economic damage as possible" that the moral imperative of resistance to unjust law applies regardless of the anticipated or experienced consequences of illegal activity. Possibility is limited only by the skill and resources of the activists, and is not defined by reference to state law.

Further confirmation is found in Fritsvold's argument that the distinction between a legal consciousness of "against the law" and "under the law" is one of kind, not degree. Participants in The Earth Liberation Front are engaged in resistance, defined by McCann and March as an effort of subordinate groups to either renegotiate the terms of existing power relations or construct an alternative forum for activity.[151] Activity associated with a legal consciousness of "against the law" consists of minor acts of non-cooperation. In contrast, resistance activity associated with a legal consciousness of "under the law" involves routinely and intentionally breaking laws in pursuit of moral imperatives.[152] He also notes the influence of a deep ecology philosophy on the beliefs and behaviors of participants. The premise of deep ecology is that human beings do not enjoy privileged dominion over nature. We are but one constitutive element of an egalitarian whole. Just as deep ecology represents fundamental opposition to the existing social order, the legal consciousness of "under the law" represents fundamental opposition to the existing legal order. Law is not simply a failure of justice, but also an intentional means of injustice.[153]

Based on Fritsvold's conclusions, I conclude that on the regulatory semantic axis, members of The Earth Liberation Front are oriented toward neutral. First, however, I must address the ambiguity of orientation between neutral and chaotic. Fritsvold compares radical environmentalism to similar social movements that have also pursued fundamental social change in a way that challenged the legitimacy of core values and institutions.[154] Radical environmentalists who are "under the law" seek to subvert both unjust law and the unjust social relations of modern industrial capitalism that this law is designed to protect.[155] What remains unclear is whether a just social order, once achieved, would be maintained by a just legal order, or whether law is inherently incompatible with just social relations. The former is a situational regulatory axis orientation and is consistent with an orientation of neutral good. The latter is a dispositional regulatory axis orientation and characterized as chaotic rather than neutral good.

In Chapter 3, I proposed a provisional solution whereby even if we assume that radical environmentalists are opposed to law generally, this opposition is limited to prevailing understandings of state law. The potential for alternative conceptions of law remains unexamined. I would like to suggest another possibility here. If participants' negative attitudes toward law are at least as much dispositional as situational, the more fundamental issue might not be orientation on the regulatory semantic axis, but rather the limits of anthropocentric law more generally. The philosophical foundation of deep ecology may appear to negate the possibility of law, in that a social order of equal relations between all entities in nature cannot be represented in anthropocentric legal systems. I address this issue in more detail in Chapter 6, where I discuss posthumanism and the emancipatory potential of a narrative/*nomos* obligational self with reference to who is being emancipated.

Question Three: What are The Earth Liberation Front's members' understandings of violence, in terms of prescriptive limits placed on the nature and extent of violent behavior as part of the rules of resistance?

The relevant guideline for this question is: (c) to take all necessary precautions against harming life. As discussed above, while members of The Earth Liberation Front characterize their actions as non-violent resistance, I refer to normative understandings of violence for the sake of consistency in terminology. This should not be taken as assessment on my part of the appropriateness of their self-characterization. The necessary implication from this guideline is that actions causing property damage and economic loss are permissible, but actions causing personal injury and death are not.

This is affirmed by Fritsvold's analysis. Fritsvold was interested in radical activists precisely because they deviate from mainstream environmental movements on the question of tactics. Radical activists are willing to engage in direct action, a broad term encompassing a range of strategies and tactics that focus on front line action and confrontation. Many of these actions not only amount to serious breaches of state law, but also were designed specifically for this purpose, given the way in which state law is implicated in broader political, social, and economic patterns of exploitation. Fritsvold's analysis confirms that the rules of resistance limit direct actions to property damage and other means of economic loss.[156]

Question Four: Are The Earth Liberation Front's members' normative understandings of violence consistent with the shared normative understandings of the relevant community?

The relevant guideline for evaluating shared normative understanding is: (c) to take all necessary precautions against harming life. The question is answered by working in reverse order from the discussion in the previous section of Zeb as an alternity character. People who engage in acts of economic sabotage that are inconsistent with this guideline are disqualified from characterizing themselves or their action with reference to The Earth Liberation Front. Assuming that the relevant normative community consists of members of The Earth Liberation Front and their supporters, and bracketing for now the issue of intra-group conflict, I conclude that a potential member's normative understanding of violence is consistent with the shared normative understandings of the relevant community.

A more difficult question is whether the relevant normative community extends beyond members of The Earth Liberation Front and their supporters. Is the relevant normative community more broadly defined by a common cause, or more narrowly defined by common tactics? In discussing Zeb as an alternity character, I noted that if Adam and Zeb are in the same normative community, then Adam does not affirm Zeb's understanding of violence, and the requirement of reciprocity is not met. Within the environmental movement, mainstream and radical groups adopt contrary positions regarding tactics. One of Fritsvold's interview topics was factionalism, with questions such as the tensions between these groups, and how the actions of radical groups affect the efforts of mainstream groups. On the requirement of reciprocity, once we move beyond implicit deductions based on group membership, only activists themselves can answer the question of who constitutes the relevant normative community.

Obligation never ends

The source material selected as a representative example of the normative understandings of radical animal activists is *Behind the Mask*,[157] a documentary about The Animal Liberation Front. The decision did not involve an assessment of production values or audience size, both of which would have favored a source such as *Whale Wars*,[158] a weekly series on Animal Planet. The series documents the activities of Paul Watson, the founder of the Sea Shepherd Conservation Society, as he and his crew use their ships to obstruct Japanese whaling off the coast of Antarctica. While documentary in style, *Whale Wars* is arguably reality television as well, and thus does not provide the same clarity of vision Fritsvold identifies in first person accounts provided by radical environmentalists.

For those oriented toward neutral good, such as the members of The Animal Liberation Front, obligation never ends. While many of us may share the beliefs of radical animal activists, we rely on state law for relief from performance of any moral obligations. We may acknowledge the gap between our normative belief and lack of committed behavior, and this may cause us some discomfort, but we do not associate this discomfort with any normative failure on our part. In the accounts provided by participants in the documentary, obligation is unavoidable; where state law fails, the individual is obliged to act. Direct action, however, is not vengeance or retribution. Animal exploitation is embedded in our economic relations, and thus the rules of resistance focus on economic sabotage. Property damage is legitimate, but no one who claims an act is carried out of behalf of The Animal Liberation Front can cause any harm to a human or non-human animal. Those who engage in direct action that violates this shared normative understanding will never be acknowledged by the community to be members of The Animal Liberation Front.

Question One: With reference to the normative semantic axis, are members of The Animal Liberation Front oriented toward the good in a way that involves a sense of personal responsibility or obligation for the welfare of others?

As with the example of The Earth Liberation Front, information can first be deduced from the relevant guidelines: (a) to liberate animals from places of abuse (i.e. fur farms, laboratories, factory farms, etc.) and place them in good homes where they may live out their natural lives free from suffering; (b) to inflict economic damage to those who profit from the misery and exploitation of animals; and (c) to reveal the horror and atrocities committed against animals behind locked doors by performing non-violent direct actions and liberations. Consistent with the normative semantic orientation of good, members of The Animal Liberation Front have a sense of personal obligation to act on behalf of animals, one which is not motivated by a narrower concern for self, family, and friends.

An argument could be raised that liberating animals serves a human interest in not witnessing or participating in animal suffering. Recall, however, that members of The Animal Liberation Front consider animals to have inherent value and thus a right to their own lives, a point raised in the documentary by several activists. Keith Mann, for example, states that every animal is an individual, with a right to a life, and a right to live their life free of pain and suffering.[159] Mann didn't become involved in The Animal Liberation Front because of his relationship with his companion animals. He was motivated to act when he saw what most of us don't see, which is the conditions under which animals live as they are transformed for human use.[160] The significance of exploitation being hidden from sight is evident in the guidelines, which instruct members not only to take action against a target, but also to reveal to the public the conditions from which animals are liberated. When members liberate animals from research laboratories, factory farms, and other places of exploitive confinement, and when they engage in economic sabotage, these are actions taken out of sense of obligation owed to the animals themselves.

Question Two: With reference to the regulatory semantic axis, are The Animal Liberation Front's members' attitudes toward law and illegal activity oriented toward neutral, wherein a moral imperative takes precedence over an unjust law, and furthermore, that the expected consequences of unlawful activity do not provide relief from performance, as would be the case for many of us?

Information can also be deduced here from relevant guidelines: (b) to inflict economic damage on those who profit from the misery and exploitation of animals; and (c) to reveal the horror and atrocities committed against animals behind locked doors by performing non-violent direct actions and liberations. Consistent with Fritsvold's observations of radical environmental groups such as The Earth Liberation Front, members of The Animal Liberation Front have a well-reasoned justificatory analysis. Animal exploitation is not a matter of individual cruelty but rather our anthropocentric and hierarchal approach to the status of animals in relation to humans. Instrumental use of animals is deeply embedded in our economic relations. Animal exploitation is facilitated by unjust laws, which not only allow for abuse but also protect against disclosure, the assumption being that consumers might change their consumption patterns if the information was made available.

A persistent theme conveyed by activists in the documentary is that law reform in these circumstances is not possible. Mann, for example, tells of his failed efforts at activities such as writing letters to legislators[161] or trying to attract the attention of regulators.[162] Nothing ever changes. He also explains how as consumers, we could all become animal liberators by no longer purchasing animal products, or products manufactured using methods that exploit animals.[163] Given the inadequacy of legal reform, direct action and the market are the only viable options. Melanie Arnold argues that consistent with the history of prior social movements, challenging laws that stand in the way of social change requires direct action.[164] Kevin Jonas[165] and Ron Coronado[166] both refer to the economic value of animal exploitation as such a significant aspect of our economy that law will always protect the profits of exploiters over the interests of animals. When the majority of humans have an interest in maintaining the status quo, social change will only come about through active resistance in the form of direct action.

Members of The Animal Liberation Front also consistently and emphatically affirm their sense of obligation to take action, notwithstanding the very real adverse consequences of engaging in unlawful activity. Mann explains that what keeps him up at night is not fear of prison but fear of not doing anything to help animals living in intolerable conditions.[167] He makes an interesting observation when he says that he doesn't think of himself or other members as special in any way. They just want to avoid the cruelty of animal exploitation, just like anyone else.[168] They are not, however, just like anyone else. The majority of people do not have a regulatory orientation of neutral. For most people, if their moral imperative conflicts with law, law will take precedence. John Curtin expressed this sense of obligation in explaining how The Animal Liberation Front is organized. The Animal Liberation Front is not an organization you can call if you see animal pain and suffering. The Animal Liberation Front is something you do yourself.[169]

Question Three: What are The Animal Liberation Front's members' understandings of violence, in terms of prescriptive limits placed on the nature and extent of violent behavior as part of the rules of resistance?

The relevant guideline for this question is: (d) to take all necessary precautions against hurting any animal, human and non-human. As discussed above, members of The Animal Liberation Front do not characterize economic sabotage as violence. I use the term in order to maintain consistent terminology, not to assess their arguments on this issue. The necessary implication from this guideline, and from the term economic sabotage, is that causing property damage and economic loss is not only permissible, but also obligated. As Coronado notes, the objective is to interfere with the economic functioning of industries and organizations that profit from animal exploitation.[170] While members of The Animal Liberation Front are passionate about their cause, they are not seeking vengeance on behalf of animals against individuals or corporations. As a matter of common sense, they do their best to avoid encountering the targets of their direct action. Confrontation, physical injury, and arrest would be counterproductive to their objective.

Coronado and Arnold, both of whom were imprisoned for arson committed in the course of economic sabotage, explain the precautions taken by members of The Animal Liberation Front to ensure that no animal, human or non-human, is placed at risk. In Arnold's case, the direct action was preceded by two months of comprehensive surveillance, both outside and within the facility, to ensure it would be empty at the time of the fire. Their detailed planning included using fuses that would ignite while they were still on site instead of at a safe distance, so as to leave no chance that someone would enter the facility in the interval.[171] Coronado estimates that for every direct action planned and carried out, five or six are discarded because the risks cannot be sufficiently minimized.[172] The guideline to ensure no human or non-human animal is harmed will always take precedence, even if it means having to abandon plans to liberate animals in suffering, or to cause economic interference with a facility that profits from animal exploitation. As Nancy Phipps argued, no one in The Animal Liberation Front has ever caused harm to a human or non-human animal.[173]

Question Four: Are The Animal Liberation Front's members' normative understandings of violence consistent with the shared normative understandings of the relevant community?

The guideline to take all necessary precautions applies here as well, working again in reverse order by looking first to the requirements for shared normative understanding established by The Animal Liberation Front. A person who does not take all necessary precautions against harming human or animal life cannot claim membership in The Animal Liberation Front. Assuming that the relevant normative community consists of members and supporters, a potential member's normative understanding of violence will be consistent with the shared normative understandings of the community. All of the participants in the documentary provided consistent accounts of the limits of economic sabotage with reference to the guidelines. Actions that damage property are permissible, with no upper limit placed on damages, but no one may cause harm to a human or non-human animal in the name of The Animal Liberation Front.

In the previous section, I referred in passing to the possibility of intra-group conflict. Recall that The Animal Liberation Front is organized as autonomous cells, although communication between cells occurs, and certain people are recognized as leaders within an ostensibly leaderless organization. Otherwise, the community would have no opportunity to reach consensus on how to interpret the guidelines. Agreement as to who constitutes a permissible target, for example, has changed over the years. Initially direct action was limited to primary targets, such as corporate locations, but now secondary targets are permitted, including direct action at the homes of the people employed by these corporations if they have personally engaged in abusing animals. While The Animal Liberation Front does not have sanctions, interpretations can be enforced, for example, by denying financial assistance to those charged with criminal offenses.

Nonetheless, the possibility exists that people will engage in an act of economic sabotage that violates guidelines, and then proceed to claim the results as the work of The Animal Liberation Front. One example involves an arson bombing of a pub in England. The pub was considered a secondary target because two people identified as profiting significantly from the live export industry were known to frequent the pub. The attack occurred at night when the pub was closed, but the landlord and his family lived upstairs and were asleep at the time. While they were not harmed, many people in The Animal Liberation Front thought this action violated the guidelines. After much debate, the agreement reached was that pubs with owners who have no interest in the affairs of their customers are not legitimate secondary targets. The defendants were initially denied financial support, although this decision was later reversed.

As Mann notes, both the debate and resulting compromise were divisive and painful. The process is necessary, however, to maintain the distinction between The Animal Liberation Front and other organizations. Groups such as The Justice Department and The Animal Rights Militia condone physical attacks against individual abusers.[174] As noted above in discussing The Earth Liberation Front, on the requirement of reciprocity, certain inferences can be made based on group membership and supporters. Apart from this, the relevant normative community is a matter that can only be decided by participants themselves.

Shared normative orientation

The objective in this section is to identify whether the attributes of alternity characters and the normative understandings of eco/animal activists examined in the case study demonstrate a shared normative orientation toward neutral good, as well as a shared normative understanding of the rules of resistance with respect to violence. Recall that the narrative/*nomos* obligational self is conceived as a nexus for mutually constitutive discourse of law and popular culture, and thus a means to answer with greater specificity the question of how popular culture might function as legal authority. With commonality evident across the four normative orientation questions, I can extrapolate support for the explanatory force, admittedly and necessarily partial, of the narrative/*nomos* obligational self.

With reference to the first question regarding the normative semantic axis, both Zeb as an alternity character and members of The Earth Liberation Front and The Animal Liberation Front are all oriented toward good. They have a sense of obligation to achieve justice for others and are not motived merely by self-interest in their own welfare or that of their family and friends. With reference to the second question regarding the regulatory semantic axis, all are oriented toward neutral, with the one caveat noted above that in the story time of a critical dystopia, the option to pursue lawful means of reform is no longer available. The relevant attribute, however, that distinguishes both alternity characters and radical eco/animal activists from everyone else is their commitment to act. Many of us may agree, when direct action turns our attention to the issues, that humans' instrumental use of nature and non-human animals in many cases crosses a line, even if we disagree as to where that line should be drawn. For most of us, however, we can avoid the consequences of acting on our beliefs on the basis that to do so would mean engaging in unlawful activity.

Recall the discussion of reified understandings of law in Chapter 3, wherein I argued that belief in law as an exogenous force allows us to avoid responsibility for our normative choices. When faced with normative heterogeneity, we can avoid the discomfort and disappointment of failing to live up to our expectations of ourselves by externalizing our normative failures onto what we conceive as the exclusive legal authority of state law. For those oriented toward neutral good, obligation never ends. For members of The Earth Liberation Front and The Animal Liberation Front, the very real threat of prosecution and imprisonment does not provide relief from performance. In a sense, for them the dystopia is already here. From their perspective, social and economic relations, reinforced by legal relations, authorize and incentivize global exploitation of nature and non-human animals. For radical animal activists, the burden of obligation includes as well the moral remainder, being the knowledge that successful direct action involves tactics, strategy, and choice; you cannot save them all.[175] The hope for utopia for radical eco/animal activists is their own sense of obligation.

With reference to the third question and the rules of resistance and the limits of violence, under Zeb's leadership, MaddAddam's bioform resistance targeted infrastructure only. The rules were proportional to the objective, which was to draw everyone's attention to how nature had been decimated, and their own lives rendered miserable, by the concentration of science, technology, and capital in the global corporations. Members of the MaddAddam resistance group did not engage in direct physical attacks on the CorpSeCorps. Zeb as an individual advocated a violent, confrontational approach in his conversations with Adam, but not in his leadership capacity of MaddAddam.

The rules of resistance are similar for members of The Earth Liberation Front and The Animal Liberation Front. Both groups have published guidelines that set out requirements to meet in order to claim that a direct action is carried out in the name of the organization. I noted that members of these groups do not consider direct action resulting in property damage as violent acts, although I retain the word here for the sake of consistency. The nature and extent of violent behavior permitted is limited to property damage or other actions intended to interfere with profits generated by exploiting non-human animals or nature. All necessary precautions must be taken to avoid harming life, in the case of The Earth Liberation Front, and human and non-human animals, in the case of The Animal Liberation Front.

As for the fourth question regarding shared normative understandings, the reciprocity requirement calls for some degree of consensus in the relevant normative community regarding the permissible limits of direct action. Moral imperatives and the rules of resistance can only be raised as legal claims when shared by members of the relevant normative community. Reciprocity is readily established among members of each group and their supporters, although as noted, intra-group disagreement does exist. A more difficult question is whether the relevant normative community in each case should be defined broadly by reference to the objective, or more narrowly by reference to shared tactics. The distinction between mainstream and radical environmental and animal advocacy groups is that the former pursue political advocacy and law reform while the latter are, as Fritsvold so aptly characterizes, intentional law breakers. Since law is an obligation accepted, while power is a requirement imposed, then apart from disagreement on the margins, arguably the groups should not expect to be held accountable to each other for contradictory attitudes. Once we move beyond inferences based on specific group membership and supporters, reciprocity is arguably a question that can only be answered by participants themselves.

As is evident from this discussion, a shared pattern of normative understanding exists among Zeb as an alternity character in Atwood's *MaddAddam* trilogy and in the beliefs and committed behaviors of eco/animal activist members of The Earth Liberation Front and The Animal Liberation Front. Recall that my argument is not one of cause and effect, as well as my caution that the case study is intended as proof of concept, not proof of result. Nonetheless, the case study demonstrates, for those who accept the premises, the efficacy of the concept of the narrative/*nomos* obligational self for exploring with specificity how legal subjectivity can be the nexus of law and popular culture as mutually constitutive discourse.

As with any hypothesis of law, the concept of narrative/*nomos* obligational selves is not a truth claim.[176] Nonetheless, if we accept McAdams's account of imagoes and identity formation, then the circulation of legal meaning among alternity characters and narrative/*nomos* obligational selves (which I have never claimed constitute the whole of our identities) is a plausible response to the question of how we might conceive of the legal authority of popular culture. In this case, the normative aspects of alternity characters would inform the imagoes we create as idealizations of how we understand the normative aspects of our identities as activists engaged in resistance. Simply stated, identity is obligation. I cannot tell myself the ongoing story of the person I am without referring to what

I am obliged to do, and whether I have lived up to the standards of my normative aspirations. For those for whom obligation never ends, the emancipatory potential of the narrative/*nomos* obligational self is the ability, if they so choose, to characterize the heavy burden of moral imperative as law.

Notes

1 Robert M. Cover, '*Nomos* and Narrative' (1983) 97 *Harvard Law Review* 4, 49.
2 Roderick A. Macdonald, 'Here, There and Everywhere: Theorizing Legal Pluralism; Theorizing Jacques Vanderlinden' in Nicholas Kasirer (ed), *Étudier Et Enseigner Le Droit: Hier, Aujourd'hui Et Demain – Études Offertes À Jacques Vanderlinden* (Éditions Yvon Blais 2006) 393.
3 Cover (1983).
4 Thomas Moylan, *Scraps of the Untainted Sky: Scienc Fiction, Uptopia, Dystopia* (Westview Press 2000) 194
5 See, for example: *The East* (Zal Batmanglij 2013)
6 Desmond Manderson, 'Mikhail Bakhtin and the Field of Law and Literature' (2012) 8 *Law, Culture, and the Humanities* 1.
7 As McAdams notes, we make our identity through many different psychological senses, although narrative is perhaps the most compelling of these. See: Dan P. McAdams, 'Narrative Identity' in Seth J. Schwartz, Koen Luyckx, and Vivian L. Vignoles (eds), *Handbook of Identity Theory and Research* (Springer 2011) 103.
8 Macdonald (2006) 408.
9 Roderick A. Macdonald, 'Critical Legal Pluralism as a Construction of Normativity and the Emergence of Law' in Andrée Lajoie, Roderick A. Macdonald, Richard Janda, and Guy Rocher (eds), *Théories Et Émergence Du Droit: Pluralisme, Surdétermination, Effectivité* (Éditions Thémis 1998) 22.
10 Mieke Bal, *Narratology: Introduction to the Theory of Narrative* (Third Edition, University of Toronto Press 2009) 113.
11 Bal (2009) 119.
12 Bal (2009) 8.
13 Bal (2009) 127. For the value of polarity's oscillation over the disruptive reconciliation of opposition, see: Desmond Manderson, 'Modernism, Polarity, and the Rule of Law' (2013) 24 *Yale Journal of Law & the Humanities* 475.
14 TV Tropes, 'Character Alignment' <http://tvtropes.org/pmwiki/pmwiki.php/Main/CharacterAlignment> accessed October 11, 2015.
15 'The Alignment System' <http://easydamus.com/alignment.html> accessed October 15, 2015.
16 TV Tropes, 'Character Alignment' <http://tvtropes.org/pmwiki/pmwiki.php/Main/CharacterAlignment> accessed October 11, 2015.
17 Macdonald (2006) 408.
18 Note that when I refer to narrative analysis of law in this sense, I am not referring to what might be termed "legal storytelling," that is to say, an alternative discourse wherein marginalized people and groups recount their experiences with and perceptions of state law. For an examination of legal storytelling as outsider jurisprudence, see: Martha-Marie Kleinhans, 'Rewriting Outsider Narratives: A Renaissance of Revolutionary Subjectivities' (2007) 2 *Charleston Law Review* 185.
19 Jerome Bruner, *Actual Minds, Possible Worlds* (Harvard University Press 1987); Jerome Bruner, 'The Narrative Construction of Reality' (1991) 18 *Critical Inquiry* 1.
20 Anthony G. Amsterdam and Jerome Bruner, *Minding the Law* (Harvard University Press 2002).
21 Jerome Bruner, *Making Stories: Law, Literature, Life* (Harvard University Press 2002).

22 Peter Brooks, *Troubling Confessions: Speaking Guilt in Law and Literature* (University of Chicago Press 2000); Peter Brooks, 'Narrative Transactions – Does the Law Need a Narratology?' (2006) 18 *Yale Journal Law & Human* 1.
23 Richard K. Sherwin, *When Law Goes Pop: The Vanishing Line Between Law and Popular Culture* (University of Chicago Press 2002). See also: Jessica M. Silbey, 'What We Do When We Do Law and Popular Culture' (2012) 27 *Law & Social Inquiry*.
24 Verstraten, for example, argues that Bal's approach to narratology, while founded on structuralist concepts of narrative, is at least partially poststructuralist. See: Peter Verstraten, *Film Narratology* (Stefan Van der Lecq tr, University of Toronto Press 2009).
25 Verstraten (2009) 6.
26 Arguably, this simply redirects the lack of interpretive certainty into a different line of inquiry, from the legitimacy of interpretive analysis to the validity of questions asked.
27 Bal (2009) 11.
28 Bal (2009) 152.
29 Bal (2009) 5.
30 Austin Sarat and Jonathan Simon, 'Beyond Legal Realism?: Cultural Analysis, Cultural Studies, and the Situation of Legal Scholarship' (2001) 13 *Yale Journal of Law and the Humanities* 3, 9.
31 Mieke Bal, 'Working with Concepts' (2009) 13 *European Journal of English Studies* 13, 16.
32 Bal (2009) 7.
33 Bal (2009) xix.
34 Manderson (2012).
35 Bal (2009) 113.
36 Bal (2009) 119.
37 Bal (2009) 147.
38 Bal is referring here to Bakhtin and Derrida. See: Bal (2009).
39 Manderson (2013).
40 Bal (2009) 12.
41 Bal (2009) 13.
42 Desmond Manderson, 'Modernism and the Critique of Law and Literature' (2011) 35 *Australian Feminist Law Journal* 107, 109.
43 For an understanding of the potential of infinite diversity in infinite combination, see: the Star Trek Wiki Memory Alpha, 'Vulcan (Star Trek)' (*Memory Alpha, the Star Trek Wiki*) <http://en.memory-alpha.wikia.com/wiki/IDIC> accessed June 24, 2015.
44 James Phelan, *Experiencing Fiction: Judgments, Progressions, and the Rhetorical Theory of Narrative* (Ohio State University Press 2007).
45 Bal (2009) 225.
46 The story level of analysis concerns how the content of the fabula is conveyed in a particular manner. See: Bal (2009) 75.
47 See, for example: Edward Abbey, *The Monkey Wrench Gang* (Lippincott 1975); D. Liss, *The Ethical Assassin* (Ballantine Books 2007); *The East* (2013).
48 H. Porter Abbott, *The Cambridge Introduction to Narrative* (Cambridge University Press 2008) 153.
49 Manderson (2011) 111.
50 Bal (2009) 226.
51 Bal (2009) 113.
52 Bal (2009) 127.
53 Bal (2009) 129.
54 TV Tropes, 'TV Tropes' <http://tvtropes.org> accessed October 15, 2015.
55 Uri Margolin, 'Character' in David Herman (ed), *The Cambridge Companion to Narrative* (Cambridge University Press 2007).
56 Elin K. Jacob, 'Ontologies and the Semantic Web' (2008) 51 *Communications of the ACM* 58, 21.

57 As Auray notes, the term "folksonomy" is generally attributed to Thomas van der Wal. See: Nicolas Auray, 'Folksonomy: The New Way to Serendipity' (2007) 65 *Communications et Strategies* 1, 4.

58 Thomas Vander Wal, 'Folksonomy' (February 2, 2007) <http://www.vanderwal.net/folksonomy.html> accessed October 15, 2015.

59 The editors of TV Tropes refer to the contribution and editing processes, as well as "wiki magic." See: TV Tropes, 'Wiki Magic' <http://tvtropes.org/pmwiki/pmwiki.php/Main/WikiMagic> accessed October 15, 2015.

60 See, for example: Thomas Gruber, 'Ontology of Folksonomy: A Mash-Up of Apples and Oranges' (2007) 3 *International Journal on Semantic Web & Information Systems* 1; Jie Tang, Ho-fung Leung, Qiong Luo, Dewei Chen, and Jibin Gong, 'Towards Ontology Learning from Folksonomies' (International Joint Conference on Artificial Intelligence, Pasadena, California, United States, July 11–17, 2009); Malte Kiesel and Gunnar Aastrand Grimnes, 'DBTropes – A Linked Data Wrapper Approach Incorporating Community Feedback' (EKAW 2010 – Knowledge Engineering and Knowledge Management by the Masses, Lisbon, Portugal, October 11–15, 2010); Malte Kiesel and Florian Mittag, 'Personalization in Skipforward, an Ontology-Based Distributed Annotation System' (Semantic Personalized Information Management: Retrieval and Recommendation (SPIM 2011), in conjunction with International Semantic Web Conference (ISWC 2011), Bonn, German, October 23–27, 2011); Clayton Mellina and Stacey Svetlichnaya, 'Trope Propagation in the Cultural Space' *Stanford CS224W: Social and Information Network Analysis*, Autumn 2011, Class Projects <http://snap.stanford.edu/class/cs224w-2011/proj/staceys_Finalwriteup_v1.pdf> accessed September 9, 2013; Linda K. Börzsei, 'Literary Criticism in New Media: A Critical Analysis of the Website Television Tropes and Idioms and the Place of Literature in Digital Culture' (2012) <http://works.bepress.com/linda_borzsei/1/> accessed May 27, 2014; Emily Brehob, 'Online Academics: The Wiki TV Tropes as a Community of Pseudo-Academic Producers' (Honors [Bachelor's], University of Michigan 2013).

61 TV Tropes, 'Administrivia: The Great Character Alignment Debate' <http://tvtropes.org/pmwiki/pmwiki.php/Administrivia/TheGreatCharacterAlignmentDebate> accessed October 15, 2015.

62 'Seekers of the Bat' <http://seekersofthebat.com/wp-content/uploads/TWbMo.jpg> accessed October 15, 2015.

63 Moylan (2000). Moylan has been criticized as taking an excessively prescriptive approach. See, for example: Rob Latham, 'A Tendentious Tendency in SF Criticism' (2002) 29 *Science Fiction Studies* 100. His discussion, however, of the definitive qualities of critical dystopia do not engage this type of concern.

64 See, for example: Jerome Bruner, 'Life as Narrative' (1987) 54 *Social Research* 11, 15.

65 See, for example: Dan P. McAdams, 'The Redemptive Self: Generativity and the Stories Americans Live By' (2006) 3 *Research in Human Development* 81.

66 I am mindful of Macdonald's insistence that a theory of critical legal pluralism does not purport to describe an external verifiable and objective truth. See: Roderick A. Macdonald, 'Pluralistic Human Rights? Universal Human Wrongs?' in René Provost and Colleen Sheppard (eds), *Dialogues on Human Rights and Legal Pluralism* (Springer Science & Business Media 2013) 35.

67 Bal (2009) 11.

68 Bal (2009) 113.

69 Bal (2009) 229.

70 Bal (2009) 131.

71 Bal (2009) 131.

72 Bal (2009) 132.

73 Bal (2009) 146.

74 Bal (2009) 146.

75 Thomas Nagel, *The View from Nowhere* (Oxford University Press 1989).

76 Verstraten (2009) 121.
77 Manfred Jahn, 'Focalization' in David Herman (ed), *The Cambridge Companion to Narrative* (Cambridge University Press 2007) 94.
78 Bal (2009) 176.
79 Bal (2009) 153.
80 Bal (2009) 145.
81 Bal (2009) 145.
82 Bal (2009) 149.
83 Bal (2009) 149.
84 Bal (2009) 157.
85 Abbott (2008) 74.
86 William Ian Miller, 'Clint Eastwood and Equity: Popular Cultue's Theory of Revenge' in Austin Sarat and Thomas R. Kearns (eds), *Law in the Domains of Culture* (University of Michigan 1998) 172.
87 Bal (2009) 149.
88 Bal (2009) 156.
89 Bal (2009) 157.
90 Bal (2009) 152.
91 Bal (2009) 153.
92 Bal (2009) 11.
93 Margaret Atwood, *Oryx and Crake* (McClelland & Stewart 2003).
94 Margaret Atwood, *The Year of the Flood* (McClelland & Stewart 2009).
95 Margaret Atwood, 'MaddAddam' (2013) <http://www.contentreserve.com/TitleInfo.asp?ID={7B7053BB-B675–4E6C-A25C-84843445CF23}&Format=410> accessed July 10, 2015.
96 Recall the discussion in Chapter Two regarding how to define popular culture. When I refer to Atwood's trilogy as works of popular culture, I do not mean to deny their contributions as literature. Atwood was short-listed for the Man Booker Prize (2003), the Giller Prize (2003), the Governor General's Award for Fiction (2003), and the Orange Prize (2004) for *Oryx and Crake*, and the Orion Book Award (2014) for *MaddAddam*. I have, however, adopted a broad definition of popular culture for this project.
97 Moylan (2000) 186.
98 Moylan (2000) 193.
99 Moylan (2000) 195.
100 Moylan (2000) 74.
101 Moylan (2000) 193.
102 Moylan (2000) 194.
103 Macdonald (2006) 406.
104 Cover (1983); Robert M. Cover, 'The Folktales of Justice: Tales of Jurisdiction' (1984) 14 *Capital University Law Review* 179, 181.
105 Moylan (2000) 50.
106 TV Tropes, 'Bio-Punk' <http://tvtropes.org/pmwiki/pmwiki.php/Main/BioPunk>.
107 TV Tropes, 'Bio-Punk' <http://tvtropes.org/pmwiki/pmwiki.php/Main/BioPunk>.
108 Atwood (2009) 251.
109 Atwood (2009) 332.
110 Atwood (2009) 331.
111 Atwood (2009) 190.
112 Atwood (2009) 256.
113 Atwood (2009) 252.
114 Atwood (2009) 108.
115 Atwood (2009) 256.
116 Atwood (2009) 332.
117 Atwood (2009) 270.

118 Atwood (2009) 254.
119 Atwood (2009) 332.
120 Atwood (2009) 268.
121 Atwood (2009) 275.
122 Erik D. Fritsvold, 'Under the Law: Legal Consciousness and Radical Environmental Activism' (2009) 34 *Law & Social Inquiry* 799, 818.
123 *Behind the Mask* (Shannon Keith 2006).
124 Steven Best and Anthony J. Nocella (eds), *Igniting a Revolution: Voices in Defense of the Earth* (AK Press 2006) 16.
125 Steven Best and Anthony J. Nocella, *Terrorists or Freedom Fighters?: Reflections on the Liberation of Animals* (Lantern Books 2004) 7; Best and Nocella (2006) 49.
126 Best and Nocella (2004) 11.
127 Best and Nocella (2006) 59.
128 Best and Nocella (2006) 49; Best and Nocella (2004) 11.
129 Best and Nocella (2004) 23; Best and Nocella (2006) 49.
130 Best and Nocella (2004) 23.
131 Best and Nocella (2006) 57.
132 For a comprehensive collection of essays by activists and academics, see: Best and Nocella (2004); Best and Nocella (2006).
133 The Animal Liberation Front, 'ALF REPORT: ALF Raid Genesis Labs Communique' (January 5, 2001) <http://www.all-creatures.org/aip/nl-5jan2001-alf.html> accessed October 12, 2015.
134 Best and Nocella (2004) 8.
135 Best and Nocella (2006).
136 Best and Nocella (2006) 50; Best and Nocella (2004) 25.
137 Best and Nocella (2006) 17. For a fictional account of an animal activist who takes moral imperatives to their logical conclusion, see: Liss (2007).
138 In the United States, activists who have committed criminal acts of property damage have been prosecuted under terrorism legislation specifically enacted to apply to environmental and animal activism. See, for example: John Hadley, 'Animal Rights Extremism and the Terrorism Question' (2009) 40 *Journal of Social Philosophy* 363; Will Potter, *Green is the New Red: An Insider's Account of a Social Movement Under Siege* (City Lights Books 2013).
139 Emmanuel Melissaris, *Ubiquitous Law: Legal Theory and the Space for Legal Pluralism* (Ashgate Publishing Company 2009) 7.
140 Best and Nocella (2004) 13.
141 For an account of modes of thought that do not create strict demarcations among humans, animals, and elements of nature, see: Paul Nadasdy, 'The Gift in the Animal: The Ontology of Hunting and Human-Animal Sociality' (2007) 34 *American Ethnologist* 25.
142 This would, however, be an ideal topic for further investigation, and the open-source nature of the analytical framework is amenable to psychological and related research.
143 Fritsvold (2009) 803.
144 For example, a digital humanities approach would be an ideal methodology for analyzing relevant source materials.
145 *Behind the Mask* (2006).
146 Fritsvold (2009) 881.
147 Fritsvold (2009) 809.
148 Fritsvold (2009).
149 Fritsvold (2009) 806.
150 Fritsvold (2009) 819.
151 Fritsvold (2009) 818, citing Michael McCann and Tracey March, 'Law and Everyday Forms of Resistance: A Socio-political Assessment' (1996) 15 *Studies in Law, Politics, and Society* 207, 230.

152 Fritsvold (2009) 818.
153 Fritsvold (2009) 819.
154 Fritsvold (2009) 820.
155 Fritsvold (2009) 806.
156 Fritsvold (2009) 819.
157 *Behind the Mask* (2006).
158 *Whale Wars* (Animal Planet 2008).
159 *Behind the Mask* (2006) 00:12:24.
160 *Behind the Mask* (2006) 00:12:24.
161 *Behind the Mask* (2006) 00:13:24.
162 *Behind the Mask* (2006) 00:14:23.
163 *Behind the Mask* (2006) 01:05:00.
164 *Behind the Mask* (2006) 01:05:00.
165 *Behind the Mask* (2006) 00:50:26.
166 *Behind the Mask* (2006) 00:29:40.
167 *Behind the Mask* (2006) 00:13:03.
168 *Behind the Mask* (2006) 00:11:16.
169 *Behind the Mask* (2006) 00:09:54.
170 *Behind the Mask* (2006) 00:27:55.
171 *Behind the Mask* (2006) 00:31:08.
172 *Behind the Mask* (2006) 00:31:53.
173 *Behind the Mask* (2006) 00:21:14.
174 K. Mann, *From Dusk 'til Dawn: An Insider's View of the Growth of the Animal Liberation Movement* (Puppy Pincher Press 2009) 453.
175 In *Behind the Mask*, Michelle Rokke, an undercover field investigator for PETA, describes how obtaining sufficient evidence can take months, during which time she has to participate in the activities that PETA is seeking to shut down. See: *Behind the Mask* (2006).
176 I am mindful of Macdonald's insistence that a theory of critical legal pluralism does not purport to describe an external verifiable and objective truth. See: Macdonald (2013) 35.

6 Conclusion

Who is being emancipated?

In Chapter 1, I explained the origins of this project as a question of the relationship between narrative and *nomos*, and more specifically, about whether popular culture might function as legal authority, unmediated by translation into state law. The nature of this relationship has been articulated and defended from a number of different perspectives, all insightful and comprehensive on their own terms. Yet by this same measure, none were sufficient on their own terms to provide a specific answer to the question asked. A legal pluralist approach corrects for the singularity that appears when cultural analysis of law focuses exclusively on state law. In turn, a cultural analysis of law corrects for the isolation that appears when legal pluralism conceives of law as autonomous and distinct from culture. To correct for both singularity and isolation, I propose a hypothesis of law and popular culture as mutually constitutive discourse.

Exploring this hypothesis requires an analytical framework. Legal pluralism can provide the theoretical foundation, provided I can locate a discursive theory of plural law that incorporates a narrative function and a means to understand law as alternity. An ideal approach will emphasize legal subjects' capacity for knowledge and meaning, and resist a pluralist tendency to focus on the correct and/or possible outcomes of normative heterogeneity. A re-imagined narrative/*nomos* will understand law as more verb than noun. I assess two discursive approaches, Macdonald's critical legal pluralism and Melissaris's ubiquitous law, which I refer to as definitional contextualism. These are in many ways complementary theories, particularly in their focus on the jurisgenerative capacity of legal subjects. The fundamental difference is on the definition of law, required by Melissaris and rejected by Macdonald.

Assessing these factors, critical legal pluralism provides an ideal theoretical foundation, although elaboration is required on the role of narrative. Macdonald's discussion on this point is explicit but not extensive. In the course of hypothesizing the jurisgenerative capacity of legal subjects, he refers to law as a function of personal narration and interaction. Narrative is primarily explained as a means by which we convey legal knowledge, but reference is made, albeit not in the main text, to narrative as a means for constituting identity. While my reading of Macdonald is admittedly creative here, I expand upon this reference to further develop the analytical framework. Incorporating cognitive and psychological theories of narrative identity formation, I hypothesize the jurisgenerative legal subject as a narrative/*nomos* obligational self.

Critical legal pluralism locates the nexus for law in the jurisgenerative capacity of the legal subject, who is responsible for creating and responding to proffered claims of legality. With reference to narrative identity formation, I locate the nexus of popular culture and law as mutually constitutive discourse in the self-narrations of our obligational selves. In narrating our identities, we draw upon collective cultural narratives and common narrative characters. We incorporate the attributes of these characters into the stories of our lives as imagoes, that is to say, idealized representations of different and at times conflicting aspects of our selves. When we encounter normative heterogeneity in our everyday lives, we will aspire to act in a manner consistent with our inherently normative identity, understood always as non-essential, non-unitary, and normatively heterogeneous.

Having developed the necessary analytical framework that results in the narrative/*nomos* obligational self, I provide a case study as proof of concept of the explanatory power of this approach. While necessarily representative rather than comprehensive, the illustrative examples of bio-punk critical dystopia narrative and eco/animal activism are nonetheless sufficient to establish shared patterns of normative understandings. The case study also demonstrates the efficacy of the open-source analytical framework, being neither discipline-specific nor confined to any particular methodology and thus amenable to adoption by others. This will facilitate, for those who are interested, a rigorous interrogation of my hypothesis.

In the case study, I identified shared narrative/normative understandings in the attributes of what I refer to as alternity characters in bio-punk critical dystopia, and the beliefs and behaviors of eco/animal activists. Analyzing the alternity character Zeb in Atwood's *MaddAddam* trilogy, and the accounts of belief and behavior provided by members of The Earth Liberation Front and The Animal Liberation Front, I demonstrated a shared normative orientation. I refer to this normative orientation as neutral good, a semantic pairing adapted from character alignments used in tabletop role-playing games. Alternity characters and activists oriented toward good on the normative semantic axis feel themselves obliged to achieve justice not simply out of self-interest, but also in the interest of all those concerned. Alternity characters and activists oriented toward neutral on the regulatory semantic axis feel themselves obliged to pursue moral imperatives in the face of unjust laws, regardless of the adverse consequences of unlawful behavior. I also demonstrated shared rules of resistance regarding the use of violence. Property damage and other types of economic harm are permitted, but harm of any kind to another living being is strictly prohibited.

With commonality in both normative orientation and the rules of resistance, I extrapolated support for the explanatory force, admittedly and necessarily partial, of the narrative/*nomos* obligational self. Against a potential objection that narratives merely reveal normative commitments already made, I argue here that mutually constitutive discourse is neither causal nor linear. The normative aspects of alternity characters inform the imagoes we create as idealizations of how we understand participation in eco/animal activism that violates state law. Identity is obligation, in that as I tell the story of the person I am, I necessarily refer to what I am obliged to do and consider whether I am living up to the standards of my normative aspirations. The emancipatory potential of the narrative/*nomos* obligational self is the ability if we so choose to characterize moral imperative as law.

Examining the beliefs and behaviors of members of The Animal Liberation Front raises an interesting question about the limits of our legal imaginations, and the potential for re-imagining law with reference to a narrative/*nomos* obligational self. Through their beliefs and behaviors, which include liberating animals and acts of economic sabotage, members of The Animal Liberation Front reconfigure normative discourse. They reject anthropocentric assumptions that humans are distinct from and hierarchically superior to animals, and engage in committed direct action to instantiate these beliefs. If animal activists were to conceive of their moral imperatives as legal claims, should their re-imagined narrative/*nomos* have a place for animals?

The issue is not whether the legal subjectivity of a narrative/*nomos* obligational self should be extended to include animals. Rather, if we re-imagine law as the jurisgenerative capacity of human legal subjects, what are the implications with respect to the legal status of animals? Humans create law for their own purpose, which results in an anthropocentric distinction between humans as legal subjects and animals as legal objects. As legal persons, the interests of humans count. If anthropocentric legality ended with this self-reference, the implications of re-imagining law need not be considered. Animals, however, have already been incorporated into human law as objects of property, and unlike humans, their interest do not count.[1]

Legal categories are prescriptive, not descriptive, and humans do not treat animals harshly because they are classified as property. We classify animals as property so that we may treat them harshly with legal impunity.[2] For many advocates, the solution is to accord legal personhood to animals.[3] That we use the label personhood to describe legal subjectivity is an indication of the nature of the challenge. Law reform is proceeding slowly but steadily, with animals now having a liminal status, no longer treated solely as property but not treated as persons. The *German Civil Code* defines animals through absence: animals are not things, but the rules that apply to things apply to animals unless stated otherwise.[4] Proposed changes to the *Québec Civil Code* define them as sentient beings, but again, the rules that apply to property apply to animals unless stated otherwise.[5] Animals are not absent, but neither are they present in the tripartite division of persons, property, and obligations.

A transition in legal status from property to legal person is necessary in the short term, and if nothing else, excising anthropocentrism from law will improve the lives of billions of animals.[6] Personhood, however, is not a long-term solution to legal relations between humans and animals. As Wolfe argues, the difficulty with liberal humanism as an organizing principle of law is its reliance on pluralism. We extend a sphere of consideration, such as legal personhood, to a previously marginalized group, such as animals. In the process, however, we affirm the normative subjectivity of a knowing human subject upon which the concept of personhood is based.[7] Our legal relations with animals begin with instrumental use, as we incorporate them into law on our terms. We then respond to criticisms that instrumental use is exploitative and proceed once again to incorporate animals into law on our own terms, albeit this time with the best of intentions.

I am not suggesting changes to political or legal advocacy. The situation of animals is so dire and so pervasive that a pragmatic approach is their only option. But I do wonder if re-imaging law with reference to a narrative/*nomos* obligational self can accommodate a posthumanist jurisprudence as an alternative to liberal humanism. Briefly stated, a posthumanist jurisprudence is distinct from a non-anthropocentric approach. A liberal humanist jurisprudence might reject anthropocentric assumptions, such as hierarchal relations between humans and animals, but retain humanist assumptions when considering the interests of animals. This is most self-evident in the legal protection accorded to companion animals, such as it is, and corresponding lack of protection for all others.[8] A posthumanist jurisprudence guards against anthropomorphic legal projection by attending to the relationship between human modes of thought and corresponding understandings of subjectivity.[9]

The understanding of subjectivity that informs the narrative/*nomos* obligational self is indeed irredeemably humanist, in that animals are unlikely to watch Netflix. Posthumanism as argued by Wolfe, however, does not reject the human but rather invites greater specificity in describing the human as a species co-evolving with other life forms. Modes of human experience are the means by which our species brings forth a world, alongside other species with other modes of experience who bring forth their worlds.[10] That a narrative/*nomos* obligational self, as a human mode of experience, is inapplicable as a legal subjectivity for non-human species is irrelevant. The objective after all is not to repeat the process of pluralism whereby animals are accorded legal personhood. We could never devise a sufficiently transversal category of legal subject capable of accounting for the specific subjectivity of all life forms, human and non-human. Nor should we attempt the opposite, which would be to devise innumerable specific legal subjectivities for every life form.

Arguably, we should acknowledge that legal relations between humans and animals will always be a legal fiction. We may imagine that we are recognizing animals as legal subjects, but in the absence of their agreement, we are actually symbolizing a human consensus of how to govern ourselves in relation to animals. The relevance of a posthumanist jurisprudence for animals is not how we might bring animals into legal relations with humans, but how we might conceive of our normative obligations toward animals. This does not mean that in the absence of shared subjectivity no vector for commonality exists. Wolfe, for example, argues for an ethics of compassion, based on what Derrida identifies as a passivity, or finitude, shared by all human and non-human animals.[11]

The posthumanist potential of the narrative/*nomos* obligational self is the willingness of human legal subjects to include, in their constructive capacity, normative considerations that are relevant to animals on their own terms. The challenge of a posthumanist jurisprudence is whether we can imagine obligation from a perspective other than our own. Recall that for both Macdonald and Melissaris, jurisgenerative capacity emancipates us from legal relations conceived as an imposition of authority from addressors to addressees. As narrative/*nomos* obligational selves, how do we conceive of our legal relations with animals? Animals have not reciprocated our claims, whether as objects of property or more recently as legal subjects. In this circumstance of normative heterogeneity, what are we obliged to do?

Notes

1 Maneesha Deckha, 'Initiating a Non-Anthropocentric Jurisprudence: The Rule of Law and Animal Vulnerability under a Property Paradigm' (2013) 50 *Alberta Law Review* 783.
2 Wendy A. Adams, 'Human Subjects and Animal Objects: Animals as Other in Law' (2009) 3 *Journal of Animal Law & Ethics* 29.
3 For an alternative perspective, see: Sue Donaldson and Will Kymlicka, *Zoopolis: A Political Theory of Animal Rights* (Oxford University Press 2011). Rather than addressing capacity or moral status, Donaldson and Kymlicka focus on relational obligations based on a political theory of group-differentiated citizenship.
4 "Animals are not things. They are protected by special statutes. They are governed by the provisions that apply to things, with the necessary modifications, except insofar as otherwise provided." See: Civil Code in the version promulgated on January 2, 2002 (Federal Law Gazette [Bundesgesetzblatt] I page 42, 2909; 2003 I page 738), last amended by Article 4 para. 5 of the Act of October 1, 2013 (Federal Law Gazette I page 3719), Article 90a.
5 "Animals are not things. They are sentient beings and have biological needs. In addition to the provisions of special Acts which protect animals, the provisions of this Code concerning property nonetheless apply to animals." See: Bill 54, 'An Act to Improve the Legal Situation of Animals,' *Québec National Assembly* (2015), Part I, Art. 1.
6 Posthumanism challenges anthropocentric modes of thought and the resulting legal systems based on a strict demarcation between humans and animals. Not all modes of thought involve anthropocentric ontologies. See, for example: Paul Nadasdy, 'The Gift in the Animal: The Ontology of Hunting and Human-Animal Sociality' (2007) 34 *American Ethnologist* 25.
7 Cary Wolfe, 'Human, All Too Human:"Animal Studies" and the Humanities' (2009) 124 *PMLA* 564, 568.
8 For an explanation of the difference between these two approaches in the context of a recent Canadian decision, see: Deckha (2013).
9 Cary Wolfe, *What is Post-Humanism?* (University of Minnesota Press 2009) 115.
10 Wolfe (2009) xxii.
11 Wolfe (2009) 139.

References

Abbey E., *The Monkey Wrench Gang* (Lippincott 1975)

Abbott H. P., *The Cambridge Introduction to Narrative* (Cambridge University Press 2008)

Adams W. A., 'Human Subjects and Animal Objects: Animals as Other in Law' (2009) 3 *Journal of Animal Law & Ethics* 29

———, '"I Made a Promise to a Lady": Critical Legal Pluralism as Improvised Law in *Buffy the Vampire Slayer*' (2006) 6 *Critical Studies in Improvisation* <https://journal.lib.uoguelph.ca/index.php/csieci/article/viewArticle/1083>

'The Alignment System' <http://easydamus.com/alignment.html> accessed October 15, 2015

Amsterdam A. G. and Bruner J., *Minding the Law* (Harvard University Press 2002)

Arthurs H., *Without the Law: Administrative Justice and Legal Pluralism in Mid 19th-Century England* (University of Toronto Press 1985)

Atwood M., *Oryx and Crake* (McClelland & Stewart 2003)

———, *The Year of the Flood* (McClelland & Stewart 2009)

———, 'MaddAddam' (2013) <http://www.contentreserve.com/TitleInfo.asp?ID=%7B7B7053BB-B675–4E6C-A25C-84843445CF23%7D&Format=410> accessed July 10, 2015

Auray N., 'Folksonomy: The New Way to Serendipity' (2007) 65 *Communications et Strategies* 1

Bakhtin M. M., *The Dialogic Imagination: Four Essays* (University of Texas Press 2010)

Bal M., *Travelling Concepts in the Humanities: A Rough Guide* (University of Toronto Press 2002)

———, *Narratology: Introduction to the Theory of Narrative* (Third Edition, University of Toronto Press 2009)

———, 'Working with Concepts' (2009) 13 *European Journal of English Studies* 13

Behind the Mask (Shannon Keith 2006)

Best S. and Nocella A. J., *Terrorists or Freedom Fighters?: Reflections on the Liberation of Animals* (Lantern Books 2004)

——— (eds), *Igniting a Revolution: Voices in Defense of the Earth* (AK Press 2006)

Bill 54, 'An Act to Improve the Legal Situation of Animals,' Québec National Assembly (2015)

Börzsei L. K., 'Literary Criticism in New Media: A Critical Analysis of the Website Television Tropes and Idioms and the Place of Literature in Digital Culture' (2012) <http://works.bepress.com/linda_borzsei/1/> accessed May 27, 2014

Bourdieu P., *Distinction: A Social Critique of the Judgment of Taste* (Nice R. tr, Reprint Edition, Harvard University Press 1984)

Brehob E., *Online Academics: The Wiki TV Tropes as a Community of Pseudo-Academic Producers* (Honors [Bachelor's], University of Michigan 2013)

Brooks P., *Troubling Confessions: Speaking Guilt in Law and Literature* (University of Chicago Press 2000)

———, 'Narrative Transactions – Does the Law Need a Narratology?' (2006) 18 *Yale Journal of Law & Human* 1

Bruner J., *On Knowing: Essays for the Left Hand*, vol 67 (Harvard University Press 1979)

———, *Actual Minds, Possible Worlds* (Harvard University Press 1987)

———, 'Life as Narrative' (1987) 54 *Social Research* 11

———, *Acts of Meaning* (Harvard University Press 1990)

———, 'The Narrative Construction of Reality' (1991) 18 *Critical Inquiry* 1

———, 'A Narrative Model of Self-Construction' (1997) 818 *Annals of the New York Academy of Sciences* 145

———, 'Self-Making and World-Making' in Brockmeier J. and Carbaugh D. (eds), *Narrative and Identity: Studies in Autobiography, Self, and Culture* (John Benjamins 2001)

———, *Making Stories: Law, Literature, Life* (Harvard University Press 2002)

———, 'Life as Narrative' (2004) 71 *Social Research: An International Quarterly* 691

Canada Go, *Report on the Royal Commission of Aboriginal Peoples* (1996)

A Civil Action (Steven Zaillian 1998)

Civil Code in the Version Promulgated on January 2, 2002 (Federal Law Gazette [Bundesgesetzblatt] I page 42, 2909; 2003 I page 738), last amended by Article 4 para. 5 of the Act of October 1, 2013 (Federal Law Gazette I page 3719)

Collis C. and Bainbridge J., 'Introduction – Popular Cultures and the Law' (2005) 19 *Continuum: Journal of Media & Cultural Studies* 159

Coombe R. J., 'Objects of Property and Subjects of Politics: Intellectual Property Laws and Democratic Dialogue' (1990) 69 *Texas Law Review* 1853

———, 'Critical Cultural Legal Studies' (1998) 10 *Yale Journal of Law & the Humanities* 463

———, 'Contingent Articulations: A Critical Cultural Studies of Law' in Sarat A. and Kearns T. R. (eds), *Law in the Domains of Culture* (University of Michigan Press 2000)

———, 'Is There a Cultural Studies of Law?' in Miller T. (ed), *A Companion to Cultural Studies* (Blackwell Reference Online Edition, Blackwell Publishing 2005) <http://www.blackwellreference.com/subscriber/tocnode.html?id=g9781405141758_chunk_g97814051417584%3E> accessed April 12, 2016

Cover R. M., '*Nomos* and Narrative' (1983) 97 *Harvard Law Review* 4

———, 'The Folktales of Justice: Tales of Jurisdiction' (1984) 14 *Capital University Law Review* 179

———, 'Violence and the Word' (1986) 95 *The Yale Law Journal* 1601

Davies M., 'The Ethos of Pluralism' (2005) 27 *Sydney Law Review* 87

Deckha M., 'Initiating a Non-Anthropocentric Jurisprudence: The Rule of Law and Animal Vulnerability Under a Property Paradigm' (2013) 50 *Alberta Law Review* 784

Derrida J., 'Force de Loi: le fondement mystique de l'autorité' (1989) 11 *Cardozo Law Review* 920

de Sousa Santos B., 'Three Metaphors for a New Conception of Law: The Frontier, the Baroque, and the South' (1995) 29 *Law and Society Review* 569

———, *Toward a New Legal Common Sense: Law, Science and Politics in the Paradigmatic Transition (After the Law)* (Routledge 1995)

Donaldson S. and Kymlicka W., *Zoopolis: A Political Theory of Animal Rights* (Oxford University Press 2011)

Donlan S. P. and Bronaugh R., 'Ubiquitous Law: Legal Theory and the Space for Legal Pluralism (2009)' (2012) 25 *Canadian Journal of Law & Jurisprudence* 177

Dyzenhaus D., *Hard Cases in Wicked Legal Systems: Pathologies of Legality* (Oxford University Press 2010)

The East (Zal Batmanglij 2013)

Engel D., 'How Does Law Matter in the Constitution of Legal Consciousness' in Bryant G. G. and Sarat A. (eds), *How Does Law Matter* (Northwestern University Press 1998)

Ewick P. and Silbey S. S., *The Common Place of Law: Stories from Everyday Life* (University of Chicago Press 1998)

Felman S., 'To Open the Question' (1977) 55/56 *Yale French Studies* 5

Fludernik M., 'Identity/Alterity' in Herman D. (ed), *The Cambridge Companion to Narrative* (Cambridge University Press 2007)

Fritsvold E. D., 'Under the Law: Legal Consciousness and Radical Environmental Activism' (2009) 34 *Law & Social Inquiry* 799

Front TAL, 'ALF REPORT: ALF Raid Genesis Labs Communique' (January 5, 2001) <http://www.all-creatures.org/aip/nl-5jan2001-alf.html> accessed October 12, 2015

Fuller L. L., *The Morality of Law* (Yale University Press 1969)

Geertz C., *Local Knowledge: Further Essays in Interpretive Anthropology* (Basic Books 1983)

Gies L., 'Law as Popular Culture: Cross-Disciplinary Encounters' (2005) 19 *Continuum: Journal of Media & Cultural Studies* 165

Goodman D. J., 'Approaches to Law and Popular Culture' (2006) 31 *Law & Social Inquiry* 757

Goodwin P., 'Ethical Problems in Translation: Why We Might Need Steiner After All' (2010) 16 *The Translator* 19

Gruber T., 'Ontology of Folksonomy: A Mash-Up of Apples and Oranges' (2007) 3 *International Journal on Semantic Web & Information Systems* 1

Hadley J., 'Animal Rights Extremism and the Terrorism Question' (2009) 40 *Journal of Social Philosophy* 363

Hermans H. J., 'Voicing the Self: From Information Processing to Dialogical Interchange' (1996) 119 *Psychological Bulletin* 31

Holquist M., *Dialogism: Bakhtin and His World (New Accents)* (Second Edition, Routledge 2002)

Hursthouse R., *On Virtue Ethics* (Oxford University Press 1999)

Jacob E. K., 'Ontologies and the Semantic Web' (2008) 51 *Communications of the ACM* 58

Jahn M., 'Focalization' in Herman D. (ed), *The Cambridge Companion to Narrative* (Cambridge University Press 2007)

James E. L., *Fifty Shades Trilogy Bundle: Fifty Shades of Grey; Fifty Shades Darker; Fifty Shades Freed* (Random House LLC 2012)

Kahn P. W., *The Cultural Study of Law: Reconstructing Legal Scholarship* (University of Chicago Press 2000)

Kamir O., 'Why "Law and Film" and What Does It Actually Mean? A Perspective' (2005) 19 *Continuum: Journal of Media & Cultural Studies* 255

Kasirer N., 'Larger Than Life' (1995) 10 *Canadian Journal of Law and Society* 185

——— (ed), *La solitude en droit privé* (Éditions Thémis 2002)

———, 'Legal education as métissage' (2003) 78 *Tulane Law Review* 481

Khoday A., 'Prime-Time Saviors: *The West Wing* and the Cultivation of a Unilateral American Responsibility to Protect' (2009) 19 *Southern California Interdisciplinary Law Journal* 1

Kiesel M. and Grimnes G.A., 'DBTropes – A Linked Data Wrapper Approach Incorporating Community Feedback' (EKAW 2010 – Knowledge Engineering and Knowledge Management by the Masses, Lisbon, Portugal, October 11–15, 2010)

Kiesel M. and Mittag F., 'Personalization in Skipforward, an Ontology-Based Distributed Annotation System' (Semantic Personalized Information Management: Retrieval and Recommendation [SPIM 2011], in Conjunction with International Semantic Web Conference [ISWC 2011], Bonn, German, October 23–27, 2011)

Kill Bill: Vol. 1 (Quentin Tarantino 2003)

King Jr M.L., 'Letter from Birmingham Jail' (1992–1993) 26 *UC Davis Law Review* 835

Kleinhans M.-M., 'Plural Corporate Persons: Displacing Subjects and (Re)forming Identities' (2006) 57 *Northern Ireland Legal Quarterly* 634

———, 'Rewriting Outsider Narratives: A Renaissance of Revolutionary Subjectivities' (2007) 2 *Charleston Law Review* 185

Kleinhans M.-M. and Macdonald R.A., 'What Is a Critical Legal Pluralism?' (1997) 12 *Canadian Journal of Law and* Society 25

Knox S.L. and Davies C., 'The Force of Meaning' (2013) 27 *Cultural Studies* 1

Kogut B. and Metiu A., 'Open-Source Software Development and Distributed Innovation' (2001) 17 *Oxford Review of Economic Policy* 248

Korsgaard C.M. and O'Neill O., *The Sources of Normativity* (Cambridge University Press 1996)

Kovala U., 'Cultural Studies and Cultural Text Analysis' (2002) 4 *CLC Web: Comparative Literature and Culture* 2

Latham R., 'A Tendentious Tendency in SF Criticism' (2002) 29 *Science Fiction Studies* 100

Lee S. and Ditko S., 'The Amazing Spider Man' (1962) 15 *Marvel Comics: Amazing Fantasy*

Liss D., *The Ethical Assassin* (Ballantine Books 2007)

Lobel O., 'The Paradox of Extralegal Activism: Critical Legal Consciousness and Transformative Politics' (2007) 120 *Harvard Law Review* 937

Macdonald R.A., 'Critical Legal Pluralism as a Construction of Normativity and the Emergence of Law' in Lajoie A., Macdonald R. Janda R. and Rocher G. (eds), *Théories Et Émergence Du Droit: Pluralisme, Surdétermination, Effectivité* (Éditions Thémis 1998)

———, 'Metaphors of Multiplicity: Civil Society, Regimes, and Legal Pluralism' (1998) 15 *Arizona Journal of International and Comparative Law* 69

———, *Lessons of Everyday Law* (Published for the Law Commission of Canada and the School of Policy Studies, Queen's University by McGill-Queen's University Press 2002)

———, 'Here, There and Everywhere: Theorizing Legal Pluralism; Theorizing Jacques Vanderlinden' in Kasirer N. (ed), *Étudier Et Enseigner Le Droit: Hier, Aujourd'hui Et Demain – Études Offertes À Jacques Vanderlinden* (Éditions Yvon Blais 2006)

———, 'Three Metaphors of Norm Migration in International Context' (2008) 34 *Brooklyn Journal of International Law* 603

———, 'Custom Made – For a Non-Chirographic Critical Legal Pluralism' (2011) 26 *Canadian Journal of Law and Society* 301

———, 'Pluralistic Human Rights? Universal Human Wrongs?' in Provost R. and Sheppard C. (eds), *Dialogues on Human Rights and Legal Pluralism* (Springer Science & Business Media 2013)

Macdonald R.A. and McMorrow T., 'Wedding a Critical Legal Pluralism to the Laws of Close Personal Adult Relationships' (2007) 1 *European Journal of Legal Studies* 1

Macdonald R.A. and Sandomierski D., 'Against Nomopolies' (2006) 57 *Northern Ireland Legal Quarterly* 610

MacIntyre A., *After Virtue* (University of Notre Dame Press 1981)

MacKinnon C.A., *Feminism Unmodified: Discourses on Life and Law* (Harvard University Press 1987)

———, 'Of Mice and Men: A Feminist Fragment on Animal Rights' in Sunstein C.R. and Nussbaum M.C. (eds), *Animal Rights: Current Debates and New Directions* (Oxford University Press 2004)

Malinowski B., *Crime and Custom in Savage Society* (Harcourt Brace 1926)

Manderson D., 'Beyond the Provincial: Space, Aethetics, and Modernist Legal Theory' (1995) 20 *Melbourne University Law Review* 1048

———, 'From Hunger to Love: Myths of the Source, Interpretation, and Constitution of Law in Children's Literature' (2003) 15 *Law and Literature* 87

———, 'Modernism and the Critique of Law and Literature' (2011) 35 *Australian Feminist Law Journal* 107

———, 'Trust Us Justice: *24*, Popular Culture, and the Law' in Sarat A. (ed), *Imagining Legality: Where Law Meets Popular Culture* (The University of Alabama Press 2011)

———, 'Mikhail Bakhtin and the Field of Law and Literature' (2012) 8 *Law, Culture, and the Humanities* 1

———, 'Judgment in Law and the Humanities' (2013) 1 *Revista Forumul Judecatorilor* 43

———, 'Memory and Echo: Pop Cult, Hi Tech and the Irony of Tradition' (2013) 27 *Cultural Studies* 11

———, 'Modernism, Polarity, and the Rule of Law' (2013) 24 *Yale Journal of Law & the Humanities* 475

Mann K., *From Dusk 'til Dawn: An Insider's View of the Growth of the Animal Liberation Movement* (Puppy Pincher Press 2009)

Margolin U., 'Character' in Herman D. (ed), *The Cambridge Companion to Narrative* (Cambridge University Press 2007)

Markus H. and Nurius P., 'Possible Selves' (1986) 41 *American Psychologist* 954

McAdams D.P., 'The Development of a Narrative Identity' in David M. Buss and Nancy Cantor (eds), *Personality Psychology: Recent Trends and Emerging Directions* (Springer 1989)

———, *The Stories We Live By: Personal Myths and the Making of the Self* (Guilford Press 1993)

———, 'Personality, Modernity, and the Storied Self: A Contemporary Framework for Studying Persons' (1996) 7 *Psychological Inquiry* 295

———, 'The Psychology of Life Stories' (2001) 5 *Review of General Psychology* 100

———, 'The Redemptive Self: Generativity and the Stories Americans Live By' (2006) 3 *Research in Human Development* 81

———, 'Personal Narratives and the Life Story' in John O.P., Robins R.W. and Pervin L.A. (eds), *Handbook of Personality: Theory and Research* (Third Edition, Guilford Press 2008)

———, 'Self and Identity Across the Lifespan' in Lerner R.M., Lamb M.E., and Freund A.M. (eds), *The Handbook of Life-Span Development: Social and Emotional Development*, vol 2 (John Wiley & Sons 2010)

———, 'Narrative Identity' in Schwartz S.J., Luyckx K., and Vignoles V.L. (eds), *Handbook of Identity Theory and Research* (Springer 2011)

McCann M. and March T., 'Law and Everyday Forms of Resistance: A Socio-Political Assessment' (1996) 15 *Studies in Law, Politics, and Society* 207

McKee D., 'Review Essay: Emmanual Melissaris' Ubiquitous Law: Legal Theory and the Space for Legal Pluralism' (2010) 11 *German Law Journal* 573

Melissaris E., 'The More the Merrier? A New Take on Legal Pluralism' (2004) 13 *Social & Legal Studies* 57

———, 'Chronology of the Legal, The' (2005) 50 *McGill Law Journal* 839

———, 'The Limits of Institutionalised Legal Discourse' (2005) 18 *Ratio Juris* 464

———, 'Perspective, Critique, and Pluralism in Legal Theory' (2006) 57 *North Ireland Legal Quarterly* 597

———, *Ubiquitous Law: Legal Theory and the Space for Legal Pluralism* (Ashgate Publishing Company 2009)

———, 'From Legal Pluralism to Public Justification' (2013) 6 *Erasmus Law Review* 173

Mellina C. and Svetlichnaya S., 'Trope Propagation in the Cultural Space' Stanford CS224W: Social and Information Network Analysis, Autumn 2011, Class Projects <http://snap.stanford.edu/class/cs224w-2011/proj/staceys_Finalwriteup_v1.pdf> accessed September 9, 2013

Memory Alpha tSTW, 'Vulcan (Star Trek)' (*Memory Alpha, the Star Trek Wiki*) <http://en.memory-alpha.wikia.com/wiki/IDIC> accessed June 24, 2015

Mezey N., 'Law as Culture' (2001) 13 *Yale Journal of Law and the Humanities* 35

Miller W. I., 'Clint Eastwood and Equity: Popular Cultue's Theory of Revenge' in Sarat A. and Kearns T. R. (eds), *Law in the Domains of Culture* (University of Michigan 1998)

Moylan T., *Scraps of the Untainted Sky: Science Fiction, Uptopia, Dystopia* (Westview Press 2000)

Muñiz-Fraticelli V. M., *The Structure of Pluralism* (Oxford University Press 2014)

Nadasdy P., 'The Gift in the Animal: The Ontology of Hunting and Human-Animal Sociality' (2007) 34 *American Ethnologist* 25

Nagel T., *The View from Nowhere* (Oxford University Press 1989)

Orwell G., *Nineteen Eight-Four* (Random House 1992)

Phelan J., *Experiencing Fiction: Judgments, Progressions, and the Rhetorical Theory of Narrative* (Ohio State University Press 2007)

Phillips N., Lawrence T. B., and Hardy C., 'Discourse and Institutions' (2004) 29 *Academy of Management Review* 635

Picasso P., 'There Are Painters Who Transform the Sun Into a Yellow Spot, But There Are Others Who, Thanks to Their Art and Intelligence, Transform a Yellow Spot Into the Sun' in Simpson J. B. (ed), *Simpson's Contemporary Quotations* (Houghton Mifflin Company 1988)

Potter W., *Green Is the New Red: An Insider's Account of a Social Movement Under Siege* (City Lights Books 2013)

Ricoeur P., *Time and Narrative. Volume I* (University of Chicago Press 1984)

Sandomierski D., 'Pursuing Virtue: Human Potential, Citizenship, and a Research Agenda for Legal Education ' in Janda R., Jukier R., and Jutras D. (eds), *The Unbounded Level of the Mind: Rod Macdonald's Legal Imagination* (McGill-Queen's University Press 2015)

Sarat A. and Simon J., 'Beyond Legal Realism?: Cultural Analysis, Cultural Studies, and the Situation of Legal Scholarship' (2001) 13 *Yale Journal of Law and the Humanities* 3

Sarat A., 'Redirecting Legal Scholarship in Law Schools' (2000) 12 *Yale Journal of Law & the Humanities* 129

Scarry E., 'The Made-up and the Made-real' (1992) 5 *The Yale Journal of Criticism* 239

Schlag P., 'Fish v. Zapp: The Case of the Relatively Autonomous Self' (1987) 76 *Georgetown Law Journal* 37

———, 'Le Hors de Texte, C'est Moi: The Politics of Form and the Domestication of Deconstruction' (1990) 11 *Cardozo Law Review* 1631

———, 'The Problem of the Subject' (1990) 69 *Texas Law Review* 1627

Sharp R.A., 'Interrogation at the Borders: George Steiner and the Trope of Translation' (1989) 21 *New Literary History* 133

Sherwin R.K., *When Law Goes Pop: The Vanishing Line Between Law and Popular Culture* (University of Chicago Press 2002)

The Shield (Shawn Ryan 2002–2008)

Silbey J., 'What We Do When We Do Law and Popular Culture' (2002) 27 *Law & Social Inquiry* 139

———, 'Truth Tales and Trial Films' (2007) 40 *Loyola of Los Angeles Law Review* 551

Silbey S.S., 'After Legal Consciousness' (2005) 1 *Annual Review of Law and Social Science* 323

Solum L.B., 'Virtue Jurisprudence A Virtue-Centred Theory of Judging' (2003) 34 *Metaphilosophy* 178

———, 'Virtue Jurisprudence: An Aretaic Theory of Law (Working Paper)' (2004) Unpublished Paper 105

———, 'Virtue Jurisprudence: Towards an Aretaic Theory of Law' in Huppes-Cluysenaer L and Coelho, N.M.M.S. (eds), *Aristotle and the Philosophy of Law: Theory, Practice and Justice* (Springer 2013)

'Seekers of the Bat' <http://seekersofthebat.com/wp-content/uploads/TWbMo.jpg> accessed October 15, 2015

Spider-Man (Sam Raimi 2002)

Steiner G., *After Babel: Aspects of Language and Translation* (Oxford University Press 1975)

Storey J, *Cultural Theory and Popular Culture: An Introduction* (Fifth Edition, Pearson Education Limited 2009)

The Sweet Hereafter (Atom Egoyan 1997)

Tamanaha B.Z., 'The Folly of the "Social Scientific" Concept of Legal Pluralism' (1993) 20 *Journal of Law and Society* 192

———, 'A Non-Essentialist Version of Legal Pluralism' (2000) 27 *Journal of Law and Society* 296

———, 'Understanding Legal Pluralism: Past to Present, Local to Global' (2007) 29 *Sydney Law Review* 375

Tang, J., Leung H., Luo Q., Chen D., and Jibin Gong J., 'Towards Ontology Learning from Folksonomies' (International Joint Conference on Artificial Intelligence, Pasadena, California, United States, July 11–17, 2009)

Taylor C., *Sources of the Self: The Making of the Modern Identity* (Harvard University Press 1989)

Teubner G., 'Two Faces of Janus: Rethinking Legal Pluralism, The' (1992) 13 *Cardozo Law Review* 1443

Tropes T., 'Administrivia: The Great Character Alignment Debate' <http://tvtropes.org/pmwiki/pmwiki.php/Administrivia/TheGreatCharacterAlignmentDebate> accessed October 15, 2015

———, 'Bio-punk' <http://tvtropes.org/pmwiki/pmwiki.php/Main/BioPunk> accessed October 11, 2015

———, 'Character Alignment' <http://tvtropes.org/pmwiki/pmwiki.php/Main/CharacterAlignment> accessed October 11, 2015

———, 'TV Tropes' <http://tvtropes.org> accessed October 15, 2015

———, 'Vigilante Man' <http://tvtropes.org/pmwiki/pmwiki.php/Main/VigilanteMan> accessed June 22, 2015

———, 'Wiki Magic' <http://tvtropes.org/pmwiki/pmwiki.php/Main/WikiMagic> accessed October 15, 2015

Turner V. W., *From Ritual to Theatre: The Human Seriousness of Play* (Performing Arts Journal Publications 1982)

Twining W., 'Normative and Legal Pluralism: A Global Perspective' (2009) 20 *Duke Journal of Comparative & International Law* 473

Unbreakable (M. Night Shyamain 2000)

Unforgiven (Clint Eastwood 1992)

Union Pac. Ry. Co. v. Cappier 66 Kan 649

Vander Wal T., 'Folksonomy' February 2, 2007 <http://www.vanderwal.net/folksonomy.html> accessed October 15, 2015

Verstraten P., *Film Narratology* (Lecq SVd tr, University of Toronto Press 2009)

Webber J., 'Legal Pluralism and Human Agency' (2006) 44 *Osgoode Hall Law Journal* 167

West R., 'Literature, Culture, and Law at Duke University' in Sarat A., Frank C. O., and Anderson M. D. (eds), *Teaching Law and Literature* (Modern Language Association of America 2011)

Whale Wars (Animal Planet 2008–)

White H. V., *Tropics of Discourse: Essays in Cultural Criticism*, vol 70 (Johns Hopkins University Press 1978)

Wolfe C., 'Human, All Too Human:"Animal Studies" and the Humanities' (2009) 124 *PMLA* 564

———, *What Is Post-Humanism?* (University of Minnesota Press 2009)

Index

For Product Safety Concerns and Information please contact our EU representative GPSR@taylorandfrancis.com
Taylor & Francis Verlag GmbH, Kaufingerstraße 24, 80331 München, Germany

www.ingramcontent.com/pod-product-compliance
Ingram Content Group UK Ltd.
Pitfield, Milton Keynes, MK11 3LW, UK
UKHW021303190926
475701UK00009B/619

* 9 7 8 0 3 6 7 5 9 6 3 9 2 *